the **100** best vacations

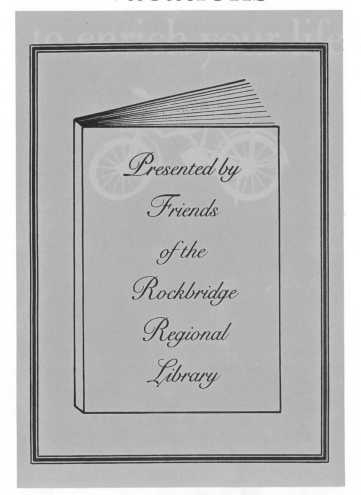

Presented by

Friends

of the

Rockbridge

Regional

Library

OTHER BOOKS BY PAM GROUT

Recycle This Book:
And 72 1/2 Even Better Ways to Save "Yo Momma" Earth

Art and Soul:
156 Ways to Free Your Creative Spirit

Living Big:
Embrace Your Passion and Leap into an Extraordinary Life

Kansas Curiosities:
Quirky Characters, Roadside Oddities & Other Offbeat Stuff

Colorado Curiosities:
Quirky Characters, Roadside Oddities & Other Offbeat Stuff

Girlfriend Getaways:
You Go, Girl! and I'll Go, Too

You Know You're in Kansas When: 101 Quintessential Places, People,
Events, Customs, Lingo, and Eats of the Sunflower State

Jumpstart Your Metabolism: How to Lose Weight
by Changing the Way You Breathe

God Doesn't Have Bad Hair Days

the **100** best vacations to enrich your life

PAM GROUT

NATIONAL GEOGRAPHIC

WASHINGTON, D.C.

Published by the National Geographic Society
1145 17th Street, N.W., Washington, DC 20036-4688

ISBN-10: 1-4262-0095-1
ISBN-13: 978-1-4262-0095-3

Library of Congress Cataloging-in-Publication Data available upon request.

The information in this book has been carefully checked and to the best of our knowledge is accurate. However, details are subject to change, and the National Geographic Society cannot be responsible for such changes, or for errors or omissions. Assessments of sites, hotels, and restaurants are based on the author's subjective opinions, which do not necessarily reflect the publisher's opinion. The publisher cannot be responsible for any consequences arising from the use of this book.

Founded in 1888, the National Geographic Society is one of the largest nonprofit scientific and educational organizations in the world. It reaches more than 285 million people worldwide each month through its official journal, NATIONAL GEOGRAPHIC, and its four other magazines; the National Geographic Channel; television documentaries; radio programs; films; books; videos and DVDs; maps; and interactive media. National Geographic has funded more than 8,000 scientific research projects and supports an education program combating geographic illiteracy.

For more information, please call 1-800-NGS LINE (647-5463) or write to the following address: National Geographic Society, 1145 17th Street N.W.,Washington, D.C. 20036-4688 U.S.A.

Visit us online at: www.nationalgeographic.com/books.

Interior design by Melissa Farris.

Printed in the U.S.A.

contents

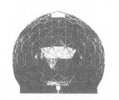

This book, like all my books, is for Taz.

introduction

"And what happened then...?
Well...in Who-ville they say
That the Grinch's small heart
Grew three sizes that day!"
—Dr. Seuss, *How the Grinch Stole Christmas*

This is a book of what I call "before and after" vacations. Any one of the hundred vacations listed here has the potential to seriously change your life. With the possible exception of the "Make Yourself Over" that's listed in the wellness escapes chapter, you probably won't look much different to the naked eye. But you'll be different, guaranteed. Your heart will be bigger, your purpose will be clearer, the petty things that used to seem so overwhelming will shrink and eventually disappear. You'll be puzzled: "Whatever compelled me to worry about that silly thing in the first place?"

The book is divided into four chapters. There are vacations to stretch your creativity, your heart, and your mind, plus vacations to challenge and treat your physical self.

If you can, resist the urge to pack your cell phone, your BlackBerry, or any kind of to-do list. At first, that might seem impossible—*leave my cell phone behind, who are you kidding?* Within a day or two, however, you'll settle into a rhythm and realize that all those "normal" things, those "work" things that you spend so much time obsessing over, *just don't matter*. So get ready to slow down. Make new friends. Scratch a dog behind the ears. Build a sand castle. Smile a lot.

And, best of all, remember what it is you really want out of life. To contribute, to create, and to grow. —Pam Grout

CHAPTER

1

arts & crafts getaways

Shiver awake now at the doing of your dream . . .
—Bob Savino, author and poet

By day, you're a doctor. Or a teacher. Or a stay-at-home mom. Maybe you file income tax forms for a living or drive a taxi. But in the still of the night, in those last few moments before drifting off, there's a dream that keeps peeking around the corner of your consciousness. Maybe it's a poem tapping on your heart, or a screenplay that won't leave you alone, but there's a dream you keep pushing aside with some comment like "Nah! I could never sing or dance like that" or "I could never make a film."

Now is the time to quit pushing that dream aside.

In this chapter, you'll find 24 arts-and-crafts getaways. They're vacations that will give you uninterrupted time to pursue that childhood dream, whether it's playing the guitar or designing your own home.

It doesn't matter if the song you write is never heard on the radio. Who cares if it doesn't make the Top 40? Somebody out there needs to hear it. Maybe it's the 92-year-old shut-in who lives next door who giggles every time she overhears you sing "I Wish I Were an Oscar Mayer Weiner" in the shower. Isn't that enough?

In these workshops that range from learning the cha-cha to firing pots in an ancient Japanese kiln, you'll get the chance to share who you really are, to say "This is who I am, and this is what I stand for."

All of us have so much to express. We have so many thoughts rolling around in our heads, so many boiling, seething dreams and plans. But instead of expressing them, instead of saying, "Here's what I think," we buy a Hallmark card and let somebody else say it for us.

Very early on, we turn over the reins to someone or something outside ourselves. The coach tells us whether or not we're good enough to be on the basketball team. The music teacher decides if we have the talent to sing in the choir. Our teachers give us grades that are supposed to indicate if we're smart enough to make the honor roll, bright enough to get into college. Our art teachers give us the rules we're expected to follow: Grass is green, skies are blue, and flowers do not have faces.

Robert Fulghum's now famous essay "All I Really Need to Know I Learned in Kindergarten" was made into a stage play. In one of the first scenes, the kindergarten teacher asks her fresh young students how many of them are dancers?

"I am! I am!" they all shout exuberantly.

"And how many of you are singers?" she continues.

Again, all of them wave their hands wildly.

"Painters?"

Unanimous hand-waving.

"Writers?

More unanimous hand-waving.

In fourth grade, another teacher asks the same questions of the same students. Now, only a third of the students are dancers, singers, painters, or writers.

By high school, the number who are willing to claim artistic talent is down to a paltry handful. Where did the confidence and enthusiasm go?

Some well-meaning parent or teacher probably told them they were not really painters. Some aptitude test with a fancy title gave an official score that said they had better give up that misguided ambition to be a writer. Try accounting instead. Some guidance counselor broke the news that only a chosen few have artistic talent.

But when we were told the same things, *why did we listen?*

At times, it seems like a daunting task, adding your voice to the chorus. You wonder: "What do I have to add to the world's great body of art?" "Who am I to join the likes of Bette Midler, Mikhail Baryshnikov, and Peter Ustinov?"

Perhaps the better question is: Who are you *not* to? What right do you have to refuse the voice that whispers to you every morning, every afternoon, and every night as you retire spent and exhausted from denying again and again the hand of the Great Collaborator.

"But hasn't everything already been said?" Of course not. Until we hear or see or read *your* version of this fierce and joyful world, there is still more to be said. Each of us looks upon the sunset with a slightly different eye.

All of us long for a rich, participatory life. We all have the same recurrent longing to break down our defenses, to be able to give and receive our gifts. When we compose a piece of music or shape a lump of clay into something we find interesting, we finally wriggle out of the straitjacket and come away shouting, "Yes, yes, yes!"

Alexander Papaderos, who started a monastery and peace center on the island of Crete, carries a piece of a broken mirror in his wallet. When he was a small boy, he found the broken mirror next to a motorcycle that someone had wrecked and then abandoned along a road near his small village. He spent hours trying to put the mirror back together. Unfortunately, some of the pieces were missing, so he had little choice but to give up—but not before plucking out the biggest piece, which he rubbed against a rock until it was smooth and round. Papaderos spent much of his childhood playing with that piece of mirror. He discovered that when he held it just right, he could shine the sun's light into the dark, lighting up unknown cracks and crevices.

That's what this chapter is all about. Your piece of the mirror is just a fragment. Nobody knows for sure how big and vast "the whole" really is. But if you take your small piece and hold it just right, you can shine light into the world's dark places.

The choice is yours. You can use your mirror to shine light. Or you can keep it in your wallet. But the mirror will never be whole without you.

make a windsor chair at a folk school

BRASSTOWN, NORTH CAROLINA

It ain't "virtual," and you can't just watch.
It is hands-on and all senses engaged.
—Jan Davidson, director of the John C. Campbell Folk School

1 On the side of one of the barns at the John C. Campbell Folk School is the school's motto: "I sing behind the plow." It's fitting because it demonstrates the school's real goal—not to teach canning or blacksmithing or quilting but to celebrate life, to sing with the joy of a job well done.

Not that you won't leave with a finished something-or-other (after all, there are more than 800 classes each year in a wide array of crafts), but that's not why participants come. They come to find a bigger vision of who they are.

Says Jan Davidson, the banjo-strumming director of the octogenarian school that's a good two-and-a-half hours from the nearest airport: "We're a crafts school, but we're not object oriented. It might seem like a clash of terms, but that's the core of the difference between us and other places that teach crafts. Our concern is primarily that people have a sense of discovery of themselves—and that they do it in the company of other people."

So, while you won't find a course called "Discover Yourself" in the school's bulging catalog, you will find a school that aims to engage both the hands and the heart. This lofty goal goes way back to 1925 when the school was launched by a pair of progressive women from New England.

Olive Dame Campbell, whose work collecting the ballads of the mountain people inspired the 2000 movie *Songcatcher* (see sidebar), traveled the Appalachians in a horse-drawn wagon-home with her husband, John C. Campbell, a New England educator and social reformer. Together, they studied mountain life—she gathered the songs, he studied the agriculture—and made it their mission to improve the lives of the humble rural people they grew to love.

After John died in 1919, Olive joined with colleague Marguerite Butler and the tiny community of Brasstown that said, Heck, yes, we'll help you start a school. Locals donated land, labor, and hard-earned cash.

Modeled after Danish folk schools (Olive and Marguerite spent the summer of 1922 visiting these "schools for life"), the John C. Campbell Folk School has always had one mission: to use the performing arts, agriculture, and crafts of Appalachia to develop students' inner growth as creative, thoughtful individuals and their social development as tolerant, caring members of a community. Only now, instead of "outsiders" educating the local mountain people, the locals are educating the outsiders who literally come from around the world. Instructors teach them to build furniture, make banjos, throw pots, and piece together quilts—and the list goes on. There are classes in dyeing, enameling, making kaleidoscopes, knitting, working leather, playing the dulcimer, you name it.

Offered year-round, the weeklong courses, which run Sunday through Saturday morning, include three family-style meals per day (complete with the school's signature homemade bread), early morning group walks through the woods, and a daily pre-breakfast songfest that invites everyone (even those with nary a note in

---

AT THE MOVIES

Although the movie *Songcatcher* tells the story of a university doctor named Lily Penleric who comes to Appalachia to wheedle, befriend, and pester the local people into sharing their ancient Scots-Irish ballads, it was loosely based on Olive Campbell, one of two New England women who started the folk school on the westernmost edge of North Carolina.

Before director Maggie Greenwald wrote the movie, she spent two weeks in North Carolina going through Olive's letters and ballad collections. Greenwald had already read Olive's 1917 book, *English Folks Songs from the Southern Appalachians,* which she wrote after compiling the ballads she heard while traveling around Appalachia with her husband, John. Back in 1908 and 1909, when the Campbells were visiting the front porches and barns of Appalachian families, Olive noted the local ballads that had changed little in the four or five generations since European settlers carried music into the mountains.

A documentary with the real story of Olive Campbell and the folk school she started is being produced by North Carolina Public Television.

---

their repertoire) to join together in harmony. MorningSong, as it's called, is an important part of the communal experience.

Classes are small (no more than 12 in a class), hands-on, and noncompetitive. Grades? What are those? Credits? Never heard of 'em. It's not unusual to find returning students who have already taken 10 or 20 different classes at the school. Some regulars have taken as many as 100.

Nestled on 380 beautiful mountain acres, the folk school's 27 buildings have been designated a historic district on the National Register of Historic Places. Among the buildings are a history center, a craft shop (featuring the juried work of more than 300 regional artists), fully equipped crafts studios, a sawmill, a blacksmith shop, an organic vegetable garden, and the Keith House community building, a handcrafted structure with handwrought door latches, woven-seat oak chairs, and iron wall sconces.

On Fridays, there's a student exhibition, a free acoustic music concert (people from nearby communities show up and everyone sits on hay bales), and the sad task of saying goodbye to new and old friends.

The school also offers 14 weekend sessions throughout the year. Tuition ranges from $250 for weekend classes to $442 for weeklong sessions, and the combined lodging and meal rates run $140 on weekends to $480 for the week. Those who prefer to camp in a tent or RV pay a per-site fee of $30 (weekends) to $165 (weeklong).

HOW TO GET IN TOUCH
John C. Campbell Folk School, 1 Folk School Road, Brasstown, NC 28902, 7 miles east of Murphy, 800-365-5724 or 828-837-2775, www.folkschool.org.

whip up goat cheese & arugula ravioli

NAPA VALLEY & OTHER FOODIE HAUNTS ACROSS THE COUNTRY

I've done motorcycle racing, hang gliding, . . . just found
a bullfighting school. Cooking is not as suicidal—except when
we get to the hot chili recipe.
—Larry Kaplan, participant in several cooking classes

2 Remember when people vacationed to get out of the kitchen? Not anymore. Thanks in part to Food Network, which since 1993 has been entertaining viewers with its celebrity chefs, cooking vacations are one of the hottest new travel trends. Shaw Guides, publisher of *The Guide to Cooking Schools,* says the number of travel-and-cook listings has more than doubled since Emeril Lagasse began urging us to "kick it up a notch."

And it's not just serious foodies imbibing in the new trend. Participants in cooking culinary vacations include everyone from professional chefs to newbies trying to figure out which end of the knife to use, not to mention a lot of folks who simply enjoy the soul-satisfying experience of creating a meal together.

With the options so diverse and so abundant (after all, whole books are written on opportunities for cooking school vacations), we've decided to list a mere three to whet your appetite. Choices are available in many exotic locations, but also consider finding a cooking school near home. That way, you'll be getting pointers on locally grown produce and cuisine that you can readily put to use in your own kitchen.

Adventures in Thai Cooking. For an exotic adventure to a foreign land—without the expense of international travel or even the bother of getting a passport—try

Adventures in Thai Cooking in Oakland, California. Award-winning cookbook author Kasma Loha-unchit, who was been teaching cooking classes since 1985, offers intensive five-day courses in Thai cuisine. Loha-unchit grew up in Thailand and learned to cook at her mother's side, and she has written two books about her native country's subtle spicing: *Dancing Shrimp: Favorite Thai Recipes for Seafood* and *It Rains Fishes: Legends, Traditions and the Joys of Thai Cooking*.

Unlike some cooking schools, with their six-burner stoves and antiseptic institutionalized kitchens, Loha-unchit's class is held right inside the cozy kitchen of her own home. She weaves stories about her life and Thai culture into the casual, homespun classes as well.

Tuition includes five all-day workshops, preparation of seven to ten dishes a day, meals throughout the day, and food field trips to such places as Oakland's Chinatown. The five-day workshops are held in July and August and cost $550. Although accommodations are not included, Loha-unchit sends a list of nearby B&Bs and motels upon registration and makes daily pickups from the local BART subway station for guests staying outside of Oakland.

Kasma Loha-unchit, P.O. Box 21165, Oakland, CA 94620, 510-655-8900, www.thaifoodandtravel.com.

BBQ University. Barbecue guru Steven Raichlen guides guests through a crash course on grilling, smoking, and barbecuing. Among other things, the savvy author of *The Barbecue Bible* will introduce you to dry-rub ribs from Memphis, "Smoke-la-homa" brisket from Oklahoma, and Wisconsin-style bratwurst. You'll also learn how to grill unconventional items from soup (grilled corn chowder) to nuts (coco loco brûlée), plus all the major food groups—barbecue food groups, that is: smoke-roasted prime rib, Memphis-style baby backs, beer-can game hens, cedar-planked salmon, and more.

The campus for BBQ U is the Culinary Arts Center at The Greenbrier, a historic resort in White Sulphur Springs, West Virginia. The Greenbrier has been offering cooking classes since 1977, way before there was a Food Network. Of course, The Greenbrier has been doing most everything in the hospitality field since before there was any network TV. Welcoming guests since 1778 and taking its present form in 1910, the 6,500-acre estate nestled in the beautiful Allegheny Mountains has been a World War II hospital, employer to Sam Snead, who served as The Greenbrier's golf pro off and on from 1936 until his death in

2002, and host to 26 presidents as well as royalty such as the Prince of Wales (in 1919) and celebrities like Bob Hope. The hotel even has a secret underground bunker from the Cold War era that was designed to house members of Congress in case of nuclear attack.

The Greenbrier was the country's first resort to offer cooking schools. BBQ U, which has logged four popular seasons on PBS television, is held several times a year (May, June, and August in 2007) and the cost to attend the three-day event is $2,349 per person. This price includes accommodations, welcome reception and dinner, and daily lunch tastings. In addition to BBQ U, the Culinary Arts Center offers such classes as "The Perfect Picnic," "Brilliant Brunch for a Bunch," and "Hors d'Oeuvres to Impress." The Greenbrier also has a falconry academy, an off-road driving school, and an afternoon tea with concert that has been held since 1931.

Greenbrier Culinary Arts Center, 300 W. Main Street, White Sulphur Springs, WV 24986, 800-228-5049, www.greenbrier.com.

Hugh Carpenter's Camp Napa. At this weeklong gourmet camp, you'll get an insider's tour of the Napa Valley's elite small wineries. The daily hands-on cooking classes are held at such unique places as Cakebread Cellars (any celebrity chef worth his or her apron strings has cooked in Jack and Dolores Cakebread's wonderful kitchen) and the 19th-century estate property of Georges de Latour, founder of Beaulieu Estates. You'll make such scrumptious delicacies as tuna carpaccio with capers, chilies, and ginger; Tex-Mex wontons with New Age guacamole; Brutus Caesar salad; and coconut curry soup explosion.

The week starts with a dinner party welcome at the home of your tour guide, Hugh Carpenter, author of 14 cookbooks. Along with his wife, photographer Teri Sandison, Carpenter serves pizzas from his outdoor wood-burning oven, chilled prawns, pan-fried dumplings, smoked baby back pork ribs, chilled soup with lobster, homemade ice cream, and, of course, Napa Valley wines.

Also included in the weeklong workshop are five cooking classes, a croquet tournament, a bocce tournament, and special tours that in the past have included such private estates as actor Fred MacMurray's 19th-century ranch (it's now owned by the Gallo family and not open to the public) and the home (recently featured in *Architectural Digest)* of Fred and Mary Constant, owners of Constant Wines, producers of what the *Wine Spectator* calls "can't-be-missed Cabernets."

Afternoons at Camp Napa are free so participants can partake in Napa's luxurious spas, artists' studios, and balloon rides over the vineyards. The seven-day camp includes lunches, receptions, dinner, tours, and cooking classes for $2,100. Sessions are held in July, September, and October.

Carpenter also offers cooking camp in San Miguel. This cobblestoned, artsy village snuggles in central Mexico's high desert country. It's a three-hour drive north of Mexico City; or you can fly into León, only 90 minutes away. Carpenter's crew will provide additional travel and hotel information. Sessions at Camp San Miguel, held in August, November, and February, are $1,920.

Camp Napa Culinary, 1214 Hagen Road, Napa, CA 94558, or P.O. Box 114, Oakville, CA 94562, 888-999-4844 or 707-944-9112, www.hughcarpenter.com.

MORE COOKING SCHOOLS TO WHET YOUR APPETITE

La Villa Bonita School of Mexican Cuisine. Chef Ana Isabel Garcia Morena teaches the art of Mexican cuisine based on traditional recipes handed down in her family for generations. Cuernavaca, Morelos, Mexico, 800-505-3084, www.lavillabonita.com.

New Orleans Cooking School Experience. Learn to cook New Orleans classics in an antebellum setting from esteemed New Orleans chefs. New Orleans Cooking School Experience, 2275 Bayou Road, New Orleans, LA 70119, 866-500-6623 or 504-945-9104, www.neworleanscookingexperience.com.

Wine Country Cooking School. Cooking classes on an estate winery showcase the relationship between regional food and wine. Wine Country Cooking School, 1339 Lakeshore Road, Niagara-on-the-Lake, ON Canada, 905-468-8304, www.winecountrycooking.com.

blacksmith (or sculpt or weave) by the ocean

DEER ISLE, MAINE

Every time I attend Haystack, my life stretches, changes,
and finds new dimensions.
—Alice Simpson, student at Haystack

3 A word to the wise: If you're new to Haystack, forget the short courses and opt for one of the two- or three-week workshops. You'll need that much time because you're bound to spend the first day or two of your stay just gawking at the scenery, soaking in the salty air, and reveling in the clean, coastal light that overlooks Merchants Row, an archipelago of 30 or so islands.

Perched on an ocean cliff overlooking Maine's Jericho Bay, Haystack's more than 40 wooded acres are drop-dead gorgeous. Even the facility itself is capable of taking your breath away. The cluster of 36 simple, cedar-shingled buildings that cling like lichen to the pink granite outcrops won its architect, Edward Larrabee Barnes, a special 25 Year Award from the American Institute of Architecture in 1994.

Haystack's dramatic location on the sleepy little island is a classic case of making lemonade from lemons. When Haystack began in 1950 as a place to explore creativity, it was located at the foot of Haystack Mountain near Augusta, Maine. People came for weaving and pottery classes. There was a benefactor. Life was good. But in 1961, construction of Me. 3 threatened the artists' idyllic existence, so founder Fran Merritt and his cronies moved to Deer Isle, a remote location that, as far as they were concerned, would never tempt a highway planner.

What it does lure are more than 80 folks per week who come to blow glass, throw pots, weave baskets, fold paper, hammer metal, and turn wood. Ages range from 18 to 98, and experience levels run the gamut from rank beginners to emerging success

BETWEEN A ROCK AND A HARD PLACE

If you go to Stonington, the only real town on Deer Isle, you'll probably stumble across a statue dedicated to the island's stonecutters. In fact, the little town used to be called Green's Landing, but in 1897 the citizens decided to change its name to honor the granite boom that revitalized the economy. Indeed, Deer Isle's granite was used to build New York's Rockefeller Center, the New York County Courthouse, and the John F. Kennedy Gravesite in Arlington National Cemetery. It was also used to build the Manhattan and George Washington Bridges in New York City.

Steel and concrete, of course, put the kibosh on Stonington's granite boom, but by then, the city leaders decided to go ahead and keep the name.

---

stories. But even many of the already established craftspeople who flock to the place often choose to jump ship and learn a craft in which they, too, are beginners.

Haystack's faculty—internationally renowned craftspeople, some of whom are studio artists, and university and college art school professors working in more than 40 different combinations of media—varies from year to year, so naturally its workshops do, too. But you can bet there will always be offerings in blacksmithing, clay, fibers, glass, graphics, metals, and wood.

The main hive of activity is the crafts studios that branch off from wooden walkways connecting the precariously perched buildings. In the high summer season, these studios are open 24/7, yet even though they exude an aura of energy and intense concentration, someone described Haystack as a completely angst-free environment. The school also runs programs in the spring and fall for locals and residents of Maine.

Although Haystack has no art gallery on campus, it does have a craft auction at the end of each session. Classes are held May through October, and tuition for the two- to three-week workshops is between $675 and $900. Room and board costs between $280 for a day student and $2,160 for a three-week single room. Apply by April 15 for priority consideration.

HOW TO GET IN TOUCH
Haystack Mountain School of Crafts, P.O. Box 518, Deer Isle, ME 04627, 207-348-2306, www.haystack-mtn.org.

learn the trapeze
with wavy gravy

LAYTONVILLE, CALIFORNIA

Camp Winnarainbow is the best place on Earth to learn things.
Even if you screw up, there will still be people cheering like you
are an Olympic gold medalist.
—Jasper Jackson-Gleisch, former student at Camp Winnarainbow

4 Walking a tightrope or flying on a trapeze might not spring to mind as the art or craft you most want to master. But the side effects of Wavy Gravy's Camp Winnarainbow—things like snorting, uncontrollable laughter, and compassion—make this circus-skills camp taught by the old Grateful Dead circus clown a must-stop on the arts-and-crafts circuit. Surely you haven't forgotten that childhood dream of running away and joining the circus?

Every day at the 700-acre Black Oak Ranch, located in northern California's rural Mendocino County, campers perform in two talent shows. They sleep side by side under a magnificent stand of oaks in a circle of tepees fluttering with rainbow-colored banners and spend afternoons swimming, zooming down a 350-foot waterslide into Lake Veronica (so-named for the sultry siren of the silver screen Veronica Lake), and playing bingo on a raft named George (after actor George Raft).

All meals, sumptuously prepared from the camp's organic garden, are considered dress-up affairs—but don't pack your tux. The camp's on-site costume barn provides everything you could possibly need, from beanies with propellers to false teeth embedded with stars and squiggles to miscellaneous gorilla parts.

If this sounds a little like kid's camp, slather on the sunscreen and listen up. For 12 weeks every summer, Camp Winnarainbow *is* a kid's camp. Thanks to royalties from Jerry Garcia's namesake Ben and Jerry's ice cream flavor and grants from the Grateful Dead's Rex Foundation, camp scholarships are

SEVEN DEGREES OF WAVY GRAVY

"You, too, can be sucked up in the tornado of talent."
—Wavy Gravy

You might have played the trivia game Six Degrees of Kevin Bacon. The idea is that any actor can be linked via film roles to actor Kevin Bacon. Although the college students who came up with the game back in 1994 picked Bacon for their demonstration of the "it's a small world" phenomenon because his name rhymed with the stage play *Six Degrees of Separation,* they might have made the game quicker by using Wavy Gravy. Here are just a few of the stellar somebodies the court jester of counterculture is related to:

- **Lenny Bruce:** Before Lenny became a stand-up comedian in his own right, he served as road manager for Wavy Gravy.
- **Harrison Ford:** Wavy, who taught improv to contract players at Columbia Pictures, counts Harrison as one of his former students.
- **The Grateful Dead:** Not only did the band donate the camp's awesome sound system (it allows Wavy Gravy to blast the children out of bed each morning with Jimi Hendrix's version of "The Star-Spangled Banner"), but Mickey Hart, the band's drummer, often shows up at Camp Winnarainbow to teach the fine art of tom-tom making.
- **B. B. King:** When he was born, Wavy's parents named him Hugh Romney. But, while doing a comedy show for B. B. King in 1969, it was the King of Blues himself who bequeathed Wavy the nickname he still uses today.
- **Tom Wolfe:** Wavy provided the name for Wolfe's first novel, *The Electric Kool-Aid Acid Test,* about the psychedelic sixties. While traveling with Ken Kesey's Merry Pranksters, Wavy started calling LSD "electric kool-aid," and Wolfe, who was also traveling with the Pranksters, figured it was the perfect name for his book.
- **Everyone at Woodstock:** It was Wavy who got up on the Woodstock stage in 1969 and famously announced: "What we have in mind is breakfast in bed for 400,000."

provided to homeless kids from the San Francisco Bay Area, as well as to Native American kids from a South Dakota reservation.

But in June, the week before Camp Winnarainbow kicks off its official summer schedule, Wavy Gravy—the fast-quipping 1960s icon who emceed all three Woodstock rock concerts—begins the season with a circus and performing arts camp for grown-ups. Among the offerings are classes in stilt walking, unicycling, trapeze, clowning, miming, acting, and improvisational theater. According to the former Grateful Dead clown, "Adult camp is exactly like kids camp, only we don't make you brush your teeth."

Every morning at 8, Wavy circles the tepees with a conch shell wake-up call. After breakfast and an inspiring Wavy-read passage from, say, Walt Whitman or the *Tao Te Ching* or even his own 1992 autobiography, *Something Nice for a Change*, it's off to practice improv or maybe psychotic Shakespeare or contact juggling.

The six-day adult camp takes place in mid-June and costs $550 for the week or $100 per day. Kids can attend from one to nine weeks for $750 to $6,138.

HOW TO GET IN TOUCH

Camp Winnarainbow, 1301 Henry Street, Berkeley, CA 94709, 510-525-4304 (September–May) or P.O. Box 1359, Laytonville, CA 95454, 707-984-6507 (June–August), www.campwinnarainbow.org.

revive your novel at a famous writing school

IOWA CITY, IOWA

What are the best things and worst things in your life and when are you going to get around to whispering them or shouting them?
—Ray Bradbury,
1967 graduate of the Writers' Workshop, University of Iowa

5 The Iowa Summer Writing Festival is not a social event. Oh sure, there are a couple shared meals and a reception on Monday night, but the only friend the attendees of the renowned writing workshop hope to make is their muse.

It's nice (although intimidating at times) meeting the stellar writers who lead the one-week and weekend workshops, but they're not necessarily the main draw for the summer's 1,500 attendees. Instead, people come to the University of Iowa so they can come face to face with their own strong, heroic voices.

The Iowa Summer Writing Festival is an offshoot of the famous Writers' Workshop, the country's first creative writing degree program and the model for MFA (master of fine arts) writing programs everywhere.

Just hanging out at the university can make you feel literary. Between the famous campus; the nearby Prairie Lights, a fantastic independent bookstore that regularly features on National Public Radio; and the Iowa Avenue Literary Walk, lined by bronze relief panels of the workshop's many Pulitzer prize winners, it's impossible not to lure a muse or two. Flannery O'Connor, John Irving, Tennessee Williams, and Kurt Vonnegut are just a few of the folks who famously honed their literary voices on the picturesque campus that hugs the Iowa River.

The Summer Writing Festival offers more than 130 noncredit workshops over the season, on fiction, nonfiction, poetry, essays, and more. In fact, the biggest challenge is narrowing down the many options. Some of the alluring topics have been:

- Writing a Novel When You Don't Know How
- "It Was a Dark and Stormy Night": Novel Beginnings
- Writing for the Heck of It
- The Art of the Anecdote
- This Too Is Life: Memoirs on Illness and Health
- Writing about Sex
- Push Comes to Shove: Write a New Play a Week

Whether you've got the 13th draft of a short story or one semi-legible verse scribbled on the back of last week's dry cleaner receipt, you're welcome to attend the workshops. The only requirement is an interest in the written word. The weeklong sessions in June and July meet from 2 to 5-ish, Monday through Friday. You'll also get a 20- to 30-minute conference with your workshop leader, which most students find is worth the price of the workshop in itself. Weekend workshop times vary, but generally begin Saturday morning and end by 4:00 Sunday afternoon.

Oh, and if your muse simply refuses to show up, it *is* possible to fraternize with other human beings. Writers gather for breakfast each morning in the Iowa House's River Room. There's a daily lecture series on writers and the writing life called the Elevenses (because it meets at 11 a.m.), featuring a different topic and workshop leader each day. There's also a Wednesday evening open mike and nightly readings at the Prairie Lights Bookstore. And while you're on Dubuque Street, the tree-lined pedestrian mall where the esteemed bookstore is located, check out its record stores, funky clothing shops, cafés, and art galleries.

The cost of the workshop is $475 ($225 per weekend course). Housing options range from an on-campus hotel (the Iowa House at $69 per night) to chain hotels scattered around town, many of which offer special rates to festival participants.

HOW TO GET IN TOUCH
Iowa Summer Writing Festival, C215 Seashore Hall, University of Iowa, Iowa City, IA 52242, 319-335-4160, www.continuetolearn.uiowa.edu/iswfest.

TAKE THAT, PAPA!

Ernest Hemingway wasn't a fan of writing instruction. But it should be pointed out that this great writer had the benefit of one-on-one tutorials with Gertrude Stein, Ford Maddox Ford, and others who helped set him on the right path. Even the most promising writers can use sound advice every now and again. Here are four other writers' workshops worth mentioning:

Aspen Summer Words Writing Retreat and Literary Festival. Sometimes called the "Sundance Film Festival of literary publishing," this three-decade-old tradition brings first-rate writers to a town that has been among the writer friendliest since Hunter Thompson showed up close to a half century ago. Two- to four-day retreats range from $150 to $375. *Aspen Writer's Foundation, 110 E. Hallam Street, Suite 116, Aspen, CO 81611, 970-925-3122, http://aspenwriters.org.*

Community of Writers at Squaw Valley. Since 1969, the writing community of Squaw Valley near Lake Tahoe has mounted summer workshops in fiction, non-fiction, screenwriting, playwriting, poetry, and nature writing. Admissions are based on submitted manuscripts. The six-day workshops are $700 to $750, dinners included. Houses and condominiums rent to conference attendees for an additional fee. *Squaw Valley Community of Writers, P.O. Box 1416, Nevada City, CA 95959 (winter) or P.O. Box 2352, Olympic Valley, CA 96146 (summer), 530-470-8440, www.squawvalleywriters.org.*

Key West Literary Seminar. Going strong for 25 years, this popular January gathering features panel discussions and reading and writing workshops. As the organizers like to say, "It provides a perfect blend of serious literary discussion and festive Key West parties." The seminar and workshop, each lasting four days, are $450 individually or $850 for both. *Key West Literary Seminar, 718 Love Lane, Key West, FL 33040 (December–April) or 16 Prayer Ridge Road, Fairview, NC 28730 (May–November), 888-293-9291, www.keywestliteraryseminar.org.*

Maui Writers Conference and Retreat. Less highbrow than some of the workshops, this program's beautiful setting on Maui's southern coast attracts fans of genre writing, not to mention lots of agents and editors willing to sign up writer wannabes. They even have a manuscript marketplace. Held at the Wailea Marriott in late August or early September, you can combine a week of writer's retreat, where you'll have lots of time to write and work with an author, with the actual writer's conference that follows. The conference, held over Labor Day weekend, is $495, and the five-day retreat is $1,095. *Maui Writers Conference, P.O. Box 1118, Kihei, HI 96753, 888-974-8373 or 808-879-0061, http://mauiwriters.com.*

make a film in the city that never sleeps

NEW YORK, NEW YORK

If I had decided to attend a four-year film school, I would have spent two years talking about the greats like Bergman and Fellini. I believe in learning 'hands-on' and getting straight to the point.
—Kristen Coury, film director

6 Orson Welles once said, "If you give me three days, I can show you the ABCs of film." The New York Film Academy (NYFA) graciously gives you a week. In the academy's six-day movie camps, abbreviated versions of its yearlong program, you will write, direct, shoot, and edit a film. Granted, your four-minute movie probably won't win any Oscars, but it will be screened before a studio audience (your fellow movie campers), and it will give you the basic tools needed for film storytelling and production.

Be forewarned: Many graduates of the weeklong course get hopelessly hooked and end up abandoning perfectly good careers for NYFA's four-, six-, and eight-week courses.

Like the longer courses, the weeklong camp provides practical hands-on experience. The philosophy of the school, which has taught everyone from Stephen Spielberg's son to Peter Bogdanovich's daughter, is you learn best by doing. Not that you won't get feedback and encouragement (instructors include award-winning filmmakers and professors from the nation's elite film schools), but the NYFA believes strongly that trial and error is the best way to master new skills.

From day one, you will be behind the camera, setting up lights, creating 3-D models, perhaps performing a scene. The pace of the course is feverish. For six harried days, you will eat,

STAR SEARCH

Okay, so you've got your movie. You need a star. A good place to look (besides William Morris which may not be ready to field your calls just yet) is New York's Mandarin Oriental, the hip five-star hotel where many of the hottest stars hang out.

Located on the 35th through 54th floors of the Time-Warner Building overlooking Central Park, this stunning hotel has a 14,500-square-foot, Asian-inspired spa where many stars take "Time Rituals." Here you'll find amethyst steam baths, stone Jacuzzis with built-in chaise-lounges, a Spa Suite with a built-in fireplace, a 75-foot lap pool with one heck of a view of the New York skyline, an Oriental-style tea lounge, and Chinese, Ayurvedic, Balinese and Thai healing therapies. Although the spa's bamboo flooring, color therapy lighting, gold leaf millwork and Japanese rice paper treatments are meant to create serenity and a respite from New York City streets, it could never hurt to slip a star a script or a tape of your new film. 80 Columbus Circle at 60th Street, New York, New York 10023, 212-805-8800, www.mandarinoriental.com.

---

drink, and breathe the movie business. Besides operating your own camera, you will crew on the films of your fellow classmates as well.

The New York Film Academy opened its doors in 1992 with the idea that education in filmmaking should be accessible to everyone. The first classes were held in Robert DeNiro's Tribeca Film Center, a commercial office building dedicated to housing film, television, and entertainment companies. Since then, they've moved into larger facilities in Union Square and SoHo. NYFA has also opened film academies at Universal Studios in Los Angeles and in London's historic Bloomsbury neighborhood. The one-week programs are also held several times each year at venues such as Disney-MGM Studios in Orlando, Harvard and Princeton Universities, Paris, and Florence.

Tuition for the weeklong program is $1,500. Room and board is not included.

HOW TO GET IN TOUCH
New York Film Academy, 100 E. 17th Street, New York, NY 10003, 212-674-4300, www.nyfa.com.

BROOKGREEN GARDENS

sculpt at a public sculpture garden

PAWLEYS ISLAND, SOUTH CAROLINA

We study anatomy and drapery by actually looking at real sculpture.
Sure beats referring to photos in a book.
—Garland Weeks, sculpting instructor

7 If you're interested in sculpture, particularly American sculpture, there's no better place to visit than Pawleys Island, South Carolina. You've probably never heard of this laid-back little island, connected to the mainland by two bridges, but as far as the island's approximately 150 year-round residents are concerned, that's all for the best. They don't call themselves "arrogantly shabby" for nothing. Being right next to the more than 9,000-acre Brookgreen Gardens, however, the first public sculpture garden in America, the largest outdoor collection of figurative sculpture, and a national historic landmark since 1992, it's getting downright difficult to remain obscure.

Not only does Brookgreen Gardens have the most significant collection of American sculpture in its Huntington Sculpture Garden (more than 1,000 works, 500 of which are spread out over 50 beautifully landscaped acres), but prominent sculptors from around the country are brought in to lead workshops, classes, and on-site internships. Which means you, budding sculptor that you are, can rent a quaint beachside vacation home and be within a clam's throw of Brookgreen's Campbell Center for American Sculpture, where classes are held.

Your sculpting options include mold making, human anatomy, sculpting the portrait, casting, and carving in plaster. If you're a total novice, sign up for Sandy Scott's workshop, where you'll learn how to make your own armatures and sculpt a bird.

Back in early 1930, when Archer and Anna Hyatt Huntington, the wealthy Northerners who started Brookgreen, began buying up the low-country seashore between the Waccamaw River and the Atlantic, their aim was to preserve the native flora and fauna. Then they realized that the former rice and indigo plantations they were snatching up would make the perfect outdoor setting to display Anna's sculptures.

Anna Huntington, a pioneering sculptor and one of America's most prolific artists, has 95 pieces displayed in the Brookgreen Sculpture Garden, including "Fighting Stallions," one of the largest sculptures ever to be cast in aluminum, and her masterpiece, "Joan of Arc." Besides her work, the Brookgreen collection also includes "The Puritan" by Augustus Saint-Gaudens, "The Fisher Boy" by Hiram Powers, and "Resting Stag" by Elie Nadelman. There are also two indoor collections.

Brookgreen doubles as the Lowcountry History and Wildlife Preserve, with plants and animals in their native forest and swamp settings. The preserve, an accredited zoo, offers nature- and history-themed pontoon boat trips around Brookgreen, the freshwater creeks, and the carefully managed rice paddies. Scattered throughout the public gardens, its many nature trails, and adjacent marshland are 2,000 plant species, many of which are identified, such as the longleaf pine and Spanish moss–draped live oak, with vistas of the river and adjacent marshland.

Five-day workshops, held throughout the year, range from $450 to $750, plus materials and fees for modeling, where applicable.

HOW TO GET IN TOUCH
Brookgreen Gardens, P.O. Box 3368, Pawleys Island, SC 29585, on U.S. 17 South at 1931 Brookgreen Dr. between Murrells Inlet and Pawleys Island, 800-849-1931 or 843-235-6000, www.brookgreen.org.

master the clarinet at a famous music camp

INTERLOCHEN, MICHIGAN

My whole life, I've wanted to come play at Interlochen.
Now I can kick the bucket.
—Fred Luety, camper at Interlochen

8 Even though your trumpet case is gathering dust in the front closet, you've never quite given up that dream you had of playing first chair in band. Well, guess what? It's never too late.

Interlochen, a famous music camp and school for kids, hosts a five-day band camp in June for the over-18 set, too. For adults, it offers a twice-yearly composers institute, a six-day chamber music institute in August, and an instrument-making workshop in June where you'll spend five days learning about the origins and history of musical instruments from around the world, the nature of materials, and their resonant qualities and methods of manipulation. In August, they even host the New Horizons Music Camp, an organization that reconnects adults who used to be musically active with music-making. And, as a bona fide grown-up, you won't be required to wear the dark blue pants and baby-blue button-down shirt that younger Interlochen students are required to wear.

Just visiting Interlochen's 1,200-acre North Woods campus is stimulating. It's situated in a magnificent stand of tall pines between two glacial lakes—the "lochen" that Interlochen is

IN GOOD COMPANY

Here are just a few of Interlochen's most well-known graduates and what they studied:

- singer Josh Groban (theatre arts)
- actress Felicity Huffman (drama)
- actress Linda Hunt (drama)
- singer Norah Jones (jazz piano)
- actor Dermot Mulroney (cello)
- newscaster Mike Wallace (radio production)

WHILE YOU'RE IN THE NEIGHBORHOOD

No big surprise that skiing, sledding, and skating are popular sports in northern Michigan. But a gold star to anyone who can name another popular north Michigan sport beginning with an S. If you guessed scuba diving, go straight to the front of the class.

Because thousands of ships have sunk in the Great Lakes, wreck diving is many Michiganders' sport of choice. In Lake Michigan's Manitou Passage alone, there are estimated to be at least 130 downed vessels. Many of them are still buried under the sand. Take the *Three Brothers*, for example. For years, this 160-foot steamer that disappeared off South Manitou Island in 1911 eluded treasure hunters. Finally in 1996, when sands and currents shifted, the ship was discovered in a mere 12 feet of water.

Local dive shops rent gear and organize guided diving trips, including a popular one to the Manitou Passage State Underwater Preserve, 282 square miles of blue water surrounded by the Sleeping Bear Dunes National Lakeshore.

Of course, if you'd rather not bother with the scuba gear, the *Francisco Morazon,* a steel freighter that sank in 1960, sticks right out of the water in the Manitou Passage.

"inter" are Green Lake and Duck Lake, or Wahbekaness and Wahbekanetta in the language of the Ottawa who once lived in the area. The campus is southwest of Traverse City near the famed Leelanau Peninsula, home of Sleeping Bear Dunes National Lakeshore, a 35-mile strip of Lake Michigan coastline featuring immense sand dunes on which to climb and play.

Even if you aren't brave enough to get out your cello, the Interlochen concert calendar boasts more than 600 events per year, putting it ahead of even New York City's Carnegie Hall. Choose between orchestra, band, choral, and chamber music concerts, instrumental or vocal recitals, pop music shows, and everything in between.

John Philip Sousa and Van Cliburn are just a couple of the distinguished guests who have performed in Interlochen's hallowed concert halls, which include the outdoor Interlochen Bowl, Kresge Auditorium, a massive roofed concert hall that's open on the sides, and Corson Auditorium, a winter-friendly enclosed venue.

In 1927, the camp was founded as the National High School Orchestra Camp, and when Sousa was a guest conductor for the band between 1930 and 1931, the name was changed to the National Music Camp. In 1977, Interlochen Center for the Arts was adopted as the umbrella title for all the various organizations, and finally in 1990, the camp was again renamed the Interlochen Arts Camp to acknowledge the fact that this prestigious boarding school offers training in theater, dance, visual arts, creative writing, and motion-picture making—though it will forever shine gloriously as the music school that it is.

Prices for the adult camp ("Interlochen for Life," as it's called in the brochures) range from around $250 for the three-day guitar festival (or $89 per day) to $549 for the five-day composers institute. Lodging is available at the McWhorter residence hall and meal plans can be arranged.

HOW TO GET IN TOUCH

Interlochen Center for the Arts, 4000 Highway M-137, P.O. Box 199, Interlochen, MI 49643, 800-681-5912 (admissions) or 231-276-7200, www.interlochen.org.

learn to knit with the wind in your hair

ABOARD THE *ISAAC H. EVANS*

Yes, we knitters are a lawless bunch! We wield our needles recklessly, throwing caution and reason to the four winds.
—Wendy Johnson, knitting guru

9 It was inevitable. When Julia Roberts took up knitting, every cruise line, B&B, and knit shop began offering knitting retreats. They're given clever names like "knit-inns" or "knitwits unite," and they're as plentiful as stitches in a Fair Isle sweater.

On the *Isaac H. Evans,* a historic 1886 windjammer that offers twice-yearly knitting cruises, you'll get in lots of UKT (uninterrupted knitting time) and FT (face time) with a knitting expert. You'll even get a pattern for a nautical sweater named for the very vessel on which you'll be sailing. For a preview, Capt. Brenda Walker, who owns the ship and has been known to wield a mean pair of knitting needles herself, is wearing the sweater on the home page of the *Evans*'s website.

Besides the sweater, Beth Collins, the knitting instructor from Unique One Sweater and Yarn in Camden, Maine, also passes out patterns for Gansey socks, cabled scarves, and warm hats—all important items for the sometimes breezy cruises in Maine's Penobscot Bay. The 30-year knitting veteran can also assist in picking out yarns and needles.

"Knitting retreats, whether on a boat or at a country inn, are just a good excuse to travel with people who share your interests," Collins says. "I've found knitters to be a very adventurous group. They like to travel, see new things. The old stereotype of grandmothers sitting around by themselves knitting in front of the TV is just not true. Knitting is a very social event."

The *Isaac H. Evans* was built in 1886 to carry oysters. It was lovingly refitted in 1973 to offer cruises and in 1991 earned a spot on the National Register of Historic Places. The knitting cruises last three and four days and include homemade breads,

THE KNITTY GRITTY

Here are a couple other knitting retreats worth mentioning:

Princess Cruises. Stitch Diva Studios, described as offering "knitting and crochet patterns for hipsters," has teamed with Princess Cruises to such exotic crochet and knitting cruises as "Knit and Stitch through the Glaciers" aboard the *Dawn Princess* in September and "Pirates of the Caribbean" on the *Sun Princess* in April. Both feature 24 hours of knitting classes, knitting events, and trunk shows by the instructors. The ten-day cruises range from $1,130 to $2,245, and the knitting classes add $300. The cruises can be booked through Princess's website, www.princess.com, or through local travel agencies.

Rip Van Winkle Knitting Retreats. Countrywool, a retail outlet in Hudson, New York, sponsors weekend knitting retreats in the Catskill Mountains several times a year. Claudia Krisniski, owner of Countrywool, teaches everything from how to make a Nordic sweater to how to shear an angora bunny. The retreats are $150. The Catskill retreats are hosted by the Winter Clove Inn, which offer three meals a day with your room rental. In late March, Countrywool also presents a knitting workshop in Gloucester, Massachusetts, at the Cape Ann Motor Inn ($200, meals not included), and it will also customize a spinning class for guilds and groups of up to 30 guests for $2,000 at the Winter Clove. *Countrywool, 59 Spring Road, Hudson, NY 12534, 518-828-4554, www.countrywool.com.*

---

soups, desserts, and other scrumptious foods prepared on a 1904 woodstove, a lobster bake on a deserted island, hot rocks (for warming your berth at night), and complimentary chocolates. And if you want to supplement your knitting with sailing instructions, Captain Walker invites guests to take their hand at the helm, raise and lower the sail, swab decks, or peel carrots.

The *Evans* has 11 cabins with 22 berths, and the knitting cruise costs $540 to $650.

HOW TO GET IN TOUCH

Schooner *Isaac H. Evans*, P.O. Box 791, Rockland, ME 04841, 877-238-1325, www.midcoast.com/~evans/.

shake your booty at a dance workshop

PROVO, UTAH

*I could have spread my wings and done a thousand
things I've never done before.*
—Eliza Doolittle, *My Fair Lady*

10 If, like Eliza Doolittle, you could dance all night and still beg for more, consider enrolling in one of Brigham Young University's Dance Camps. For more than 25 years, BYU has been offering summer dance instruction in ballroom, ballet, tap, and other popular dance forms. The price for a five-day workshop is less than you'd pay for an eight-week Arthur Murray class that only meets Thursday nights. And in your free time, you can explore Salt Lake City and the beautiful Wasatch Mountains.

WHILE YOU'RE THERE

BYU's Harold B. Lee Library, ranked fourth by the *Princeton Review* on its Great College Library list, has more than six million items in its collections, contains 98 miles of shelving, and can seat 4,600 people.

The Adult Ballroom Dancing Camp, directed by Lee and Linda Wakefield, 18-time winners of the British Formation Championships, includes up to seven hours of daily dance instruction, a midweek banquet, and a closing awards ceremony and showcase where you show off what you've learned. If you're paying attention, you will have learned international jive, American-style tango, the cha-cha, the rumba, the waltz, and the West Coast swing.

Tuition for the dance camps ranges from $189 for the three-day tap camp to $390 for the five-day ballroom camp. Packages for food and housing can be arranged on campus for $71 for the three-day camp to $175 for the five-day package.

BYU Dance Camps, c/o BYU Conferences and Workshops, 47 Harman Continuing Education Building, Provo, UT 84602, 801-422-4851, www.ce.byu. edu/cw/cwdance.

ONE-TWO CHA-CHA-CHA

The following is a pair of other notable dance vacations:

River Dance. REO Rafting Resort, near Vancouver, British Columbia, offers a weeklong Irish Dance Camp. Each day, participants enjoy four hours of dance training (Michelle Kilby from the Sionnaine Irish Dance Academy does the honors) on a stage literally backed up to the Nahatlatch River. When you're not hoofing it, you can be white-water rafting, rock climbing, rappelling, or partaking in ropes courses and Pilates workouts. There's even an outdoor slumber party in the rafts. At the end of the week, the "River Dancers" put on a show complete with fiddlers and other musicians playing Irish jigs. This camp costs $530, meals and tent cabin included, and is usually held in July. *REO Adventure Resort, 845 Spence Way, Anmore, BC V3H 5H4, Canada, 800-736-7238, www. reorafting.com.*

Demi-Plié. If ballet is more your cup of tea, consider Sun King Dance in Richmond, Virginia, which provides intensive instruction in ballet at its Adult Dance Camp. As director Heidi Pankoff says: "Dance has been the greatest joy in my life, sharing it has been the second. Our mission is to support and assist those who continue to dance throughout their lives." Classes in ballet technique, men's technique, pointe, pirouettes, and variations will fill your morning. After lunch, you'll indulge in pas de deux, stretching, jazz, modern, kinesiology, character, and lectures. The program culminates with a videotaped student performance. The weeklong camp, offered in June and twice in August, is held at four spacious studios at the Richmond Ballet facilities in downtown Richmond. Tuition is $595 and includes lunch each day. Special rates at the Crowne Plaza Hotel adjacent to the studios are available for camp participants. *Sun King Dance, 3126 W. Cary Street, #172, Richmond, VA 23221, 804-484-6092, www.adultdancecamps.com.*

build yourself a house in the berkshire hills

WASHINGTON, MASSACHUSETTS

I wanted to show my kids that a dream can come true. . . . Also, I was getting a divorce and pounding nails got the frustration out.
—Jennifer Lee, participant in a Heartwood School workshop

11 According to Will and Michele Beemer, owners of the Heartwood School, building your own home can feed your soul, empower your hands, train your eye, and allow you to live more honestly with the planet. Plus, savings in the old pocketbook doesn't hurt either. The Beemers estimate that people who build their own homes pay a mere 40 percent of what they'd pay for a commercially built house. Even those who don't actually pound the nails but act as their own contractor can save as much as 20 percent.

"Who wants to settle for somebody else's prestamped plans?" Michele asks. "Building your own home makes it more affordable and more interesting."

Heartwood, which opened in 1978 and offers classes from summer through fall, is one of a handful of schools in the United States that teach laypeople (plus the odd architect or contractor) the skills they need to build their own homes. Although Heartwood's mainstay is the two-week homebuilding course, they also offer shorter seminars on such topics as timber framing, cabinetmaking, scribing, compound joining, and the fundamentals of woodworking. A current favorite is "Carpentry for Women," which encourages self-sufficiency in home repair and remodeling. Classes average ten people, so there's lots of opportunity for personal attention.

More than 3,000 people have completed the Heartwood homebuilding program or shorter seminars. Students have ranged in age from 12 to 72, divided equally among men and women, and have traveled from as far away as Scotland, Hawaii, and Japan to take a course. The majority have little

IF YOU BUILD IT, THEY WILL COME

Critics—notably professional contractors—have scoffed that it's impossible to teach a novice to build a house in two or three weeks. But Heartwood, and the other schools listed below, have proved them wrong. "America is based on pilgrims coming over here and knocking together log cabins," says Patrice Hennin, founder of the Shelter Institute. "Everyone, deep down in his heart, knows he can build a house. It's not as if we're sending rockets to the moon here; we're just building houses."

Arcosanti. This experimental town in the high desert of Arizona offers workshops in building throughout the year that focus on eliminating urban sprawl and lessening our impact on Mother Earth. A one-week workshop, including meals and dorm- or apartment-style accommodations, is $475 and includes seminars explaining the concept of "arcology" (architecture with an eye toward ecology), tours around the alternative urban site, and a silt-casting workshop. Collective work projects and in-depth studies of the departments at Arcosanti begin in the second week and cost an extra $250. Actual hands-on intensive work takes place in the final two weeks of the four-week workshop, which runs $1,125. *Arcosanti, HC74, Box 4136, Mayer, AZ 86333, 928-632-7135, www.arcosanti.org.*

Shelter Institute. Near Bath, Maine, students learn to design, build, plumb, wire, and finish their own homes. A five-day timber-framing class costs $775 per person or $1,250 for a couple, and the two-week, all-inclusive design-and-build class runs $1,225, or $1,800 per couple. *Shelter Institute, 873 Route 1, Woolwich, ME 04579, 207-442-7938, www.shelterinstitute.com.*

Solar Living Institute. Since 1998, this 12-acre demonstration center has offered hands-on workshops on renewable energy, ecological design, sustainable living practices, and alternative construction materials such as straw bales, corncobs, and bamboo. Prices range from $95 for a one-day workshop to $700 for a week-long intensive program offered year-round. *Solar Living Institute, P.O. Box 836, 13771 S. Highway 101, Hopland, CA 95449, 707-744-2017, www.solarliving.org.*

or no construction experience. Just so you know, once you have the know-how doesn't mean you'll have a house right away … it takes anywere from two to five years to build your new residence, depending on the time and help you have.

The rustic Heartwood Schoolhouse is located on ten acres in the Berkshire Hills of western Massachusetts. Built by the staff and students in 1978 to 1979, the schoolhouse contains Heartwood's office, a classroom, a greenhouse, a woodworking shop with all the equipment you'll need, a 500-plus-book library devoted to housebuilding, and the dining area where delicious home-cooked lunches are served up.

Students pay $1,150 each, or $2,100 per couple, for a two-week course that includes morning lectures and afternoons doing hands-on work—for example, to review a morning's lesson on framing, students might lay rafters in a nearby house. The one-week seminars run $600, or $1,100 per couple. Upon enrollment, the school can supply a list of accommodations in the area, ranging from rustic campgrounds to cozy B&Bs.

HOW TO GET IN TOUCH

Heartwood School for the Homebuilding Crafts, Johnson Hill Road, Washington, MA 01223, 413-623-6677, www.heartwoodschool.com.

go weaving at an appalachian craft school

PENLAND, NORTH CAROLINA

I WILL FIGHT THE MAN! As we all should . . .
and perhaps get in a two-weeker [at Penland] once again.
—Chris Taylor, an artist who takes classes at Penland

12 Penland School of Crafts is not the kind of place where you can just wake up one morning and decide to take a class there the next week. If you haven't submitted your application for spring, summer, or fall classes by the end of February, it's likely you won't win one of the coveted spots. In fact, so many folks try to enroll in the hundred-plus classes offered by the venerable school each year that they've been forced to institute a lottery. You send in your application for the one-, two-, two-and-a-half-, or eight-week pottery, glassblowing, metalworking, weaving, dyeing, or woodworking classes and cross your fingers.

The good news is that if you *do* get in, you are guaranteed an amazing experience. Neophyte weavers, for example, work alongside folks who make their living at weaving. Best of all, you'll be part of the Penland community, which is so tight that enthusiasts have started their own unofficial website (http://penlandforum.org) to stay in touch, organize rides back to Penland (nearly all participants' perpetual goal), and share work and photos.

Located in an idyllic valley in the Blue Ridge of western North Carolina, Penland encompasses 400 acres, only

START YOUR OWN PENLAND LIBRARY

Besides having its own series of illustrated master-class books (*The Penland Book of Jewelry, Ceramics, Woodworking*, etc.), Penland has inspired many others, including the inspiring history *The Story of the Penland Weavers* by Bonnie Willis Ford, manuals on such rare techniques as vegetable dyeing, and *Gift of the Hills*, a biography of school founder Lucy Morgan by LeGette Blythe.

15 percent of which are developed. It has 14 teaching studios and more than 40 historic and contemporary buildings.

Penland has been around in one form or another since 1923, when Lucy Morgan, a teacher at the Appalachian Industrial School, got the notion to teach handweaving to the local mountain women who desperately needed income. She provided looms, materials, and instruction, even securing a government grant to build a tiny cabin and then a larger hall where the weavers could work together. In Old Ridgeway Hall, one of the first buildings on the property, the women wove downstairs while their kids roller-skated upstairs.

Lucy bought an old Model T truck and drove from Appalachian resorts to county fairs to church meetings displaying and selling the goods created by her weavers, by that time known as the Penland Weavers. She even talked her way into the 1933 Chicago World's Fair, selling her fellow weavers' wares from a homemade log cabin booth.

By 1929, Penland had added pottery to its repertoire, then pewter and other media. Today there are ten media taught by faculty (usually working artists) from around the world. Classes are a mix of demonstrations, lectures, individual studio work, and field trips. Stays at Penland also allow visits to nearby studios, volleyball games, dances, and swimming in the Toe River. Popular events include the annual Easter egg hunt (chickens don't lose any sleep over this unique event—all the eggs, each unique, are created by students), the big Penland arts auction, and fireworks on the Fourth of July.

One of Penland's most unique features is the daily movement classes that, according to Penland philosophy, keep the artistic spirit loose and free and eliminate tension, which no one wants showing up in their work. These classes might include yoga, tai chi, volleyball, or hikes to Bailey's Peak.

Students stay in dorms and old log cabins, none of which have phones, TVs, or air-conditioning. Three meals are served each day. The one-, two-, and two-and-a-half-week classes in summer run $397 to $877 ($566 to $1,250 for glassblowing), with rooms and meals ranging from $337 to $818 for dorms that house three to ten students and $1,058 to $2,569 for a single room with private bath. The eight-week fall and spring sessions cost $3,024 ($3,947 for the glassblowing workshop); room and meal plans cost between $2,551 for dorm rooms and $3,185 for a single with private bath. For those who prefer to stay off campus, summer workshop meals can be arranged for $211 to $512 for all meals or $72 to $175 for just lunches; in the fall and spring, it's $1,287 for three meals a day or $540 for lunches only. Also, be advised that there is a materials fee for most workshops.

HOW TO GET IN TOUCH
Penland School of Crafts, 67 Doras Trail, P.O. Box 37, Penland, NC 28765, 828-765-2359, www.penland.org.

make a flower knot basket or cast a line

LAYTON, NEW JERSEY

I don't like to say I have given my life to art.
I prefer to say art has given me my life.
—Frank Stella, American artist

13 She's dying to take a class in Japanese basket weaving; he just wants to fish. Peters Valley could provide the compromise they're looking for. Not only is Peters Valley an internationally recognized arts-and-crafts school, attracting top-notch instructors in ceramics, textiles, fine metal, photography, and blacksmithing, but it's also located smack dab in the middle of the largest national recreation area on the East Coast. So while she's constructing a flower knot basket from sedori cane, he can cast his lure in the 40 miles of the Delaware River that run through the Delaware Water Gap National Recreation Area where the school is located.

There are other artist-in-residence programs offered by the National Park Service—at 29 of its parks, from the two one-week residencies at Wyoming's Devils Tower National Monument to the six residencies for photographers, filmmakers, sculptors, composers, and visual artists at Everglades National Park—but Peters Valley is the only one that hosts fledgling artists, more than 1,200 each year.

Located at the north entrance of the 67,000-acre park, Peters Valley operates out of some three dozen 18th-century buildings (16 of them are on the National Register of Historic Places, and one dates back as far as 1790) that center around an 1838 Dutch Reformed church. Once a thriving community known as Hens Foot Corner (also at one time or another, the Corner and Bevans), the buildings were condemned in the 1950s when the federal government decided to build a dam and recreation area.

Politics being what they are, the dam never got built (the Delaware River is still the largest undammed river in the United States) and the picturesque buildings sat

KILN BILL

The anagama kiln, a unique wood-burning kiln, at Peters Valley Craft Center is larger than most people's living rooms. Measuring 63 feet long and 8 feet wide, it's one of the country's biggest anagama kilns. *Anagama* is Japanese for "cave kiln," and this monster at Peters Valley is modeled after the medieval kilns that originated in Shigaraki, Japan. Anagama firing is known for its natural ash glazes and the excitement of the long firing. Firings can be anywhere from three to eight days, and somebody has to throw wood in the anagama kiln every ten minutes or so for up to six days to maintain the final optimal temperature of roughly 2400°F.

Shiro Otani, a famous potter from Shigaraki (he has been designated a "living treasure" in Japan, the highest honor bestowed on a Japanese artist), gives workshops at Peters Valley. The center also offers the Open Studio, where folks can throw or build anything from delicate teacups to large-scale sculptural works for firing in the huge kiln.

---

vacant until 1969 when Rosamond DeGelleke, wife of the park's superintendent, enlisted a group of area crafts people to teach mountain handicrafts. The old buildings then took on a new life as dorms, studios, and galleries.

Although Peters Valley, like other arts-and-crafts schools, offers some weeklong classes, their specialty is shorter two- and three-day crafts classes. "Because we're located so close to New York," says director Jimmy Clark, "we've found students want to get in, get out, and master a particular skill. Take the woodworkers, for example. They don't want to come and build a whole cabinet. They just want to learn a particular type of joinery."

"We found that one size doesn't fit all." Clark adds.

Even the five-day courses are unconventional. While most craft schools run from Sunday or Monday through Friday, Peters Valley offers five-day workshops that start on Fridays and end the following Tuesday. The center also offers classes in each of its eight specialties for beginners who have never taken a class before.

Peters Valley can sleep only 30 to 40 students, but is happy to set you up at one of the park campgrounds or at nearby B&Bs. Three square meals are served each day in the dining room. At one time, Peters Valley was known as the vegetarian crafts school (there was even a book, *The Artists Table: Recipes from the Peters Valley Kitchen,* touting its famous recipes), but it has since added meat.

As far as the Delaware Water Gap goes, this steep and wooded valley straddling New Jersey and Pennsylvania is dramatic and beauitful, offering everything from camping, hiking, and biking to boating, canoeing, and fishing. For classic hilltop views, you have no choice but to climb—follow the white-blazed Appalachian Trail from Lenape Lake parking area in the town of Delaware Water Gap, for instance, to reach the crest of 1,463-foot Mount Minsi; or tackle the rocky 1.5-mile round-trip Red Dot Trail, from the I-80 rest area east of the Kittatinny Point visitor center, to reach the spectacular 1,545-foot sumit of Mount Tammany in New Jersey. Other gap highlights include Sunfish Pond in New Jersey, a glacially carved basin that's a popular swimming hole; Dingmans Falls on the Pennsylvania side, where a series of boardwalks takes you through ravines of rhododendron and ancient hemlocks to waterfalls; and the Pocono Environmental Education Center, housed in a former honeymoon hotel.

Classes at Peters Valley run mid-May through mid-September and culminate with a huge arts-and-crafts fair of 150 juried craftspeople selling their work. Tuition ranges from $250 for a two-day class to $450 for a five-day workshop. Accommodations are from $40 a night for a shared dorm room (a reservation is required for linen rental at $10 per workshop stay) to $110 per night single for a motel-style room that includes linens, towels, and a private bath. Meal plans range from $41 for the two-day workshops to $122 for the five-day classes.

HOW TO GET IN TOUCH

Peters Valley Craft Center, 19 Kuhn Road, Layton, NJ 07851, 973-948-5200, www.pvcrafts.org. **Delaware Water Gap National Recreation Area,** HQ River Road off Route 209, Bushkill, PA 18324, 570-828-2253 (summer) or 570-426-2451 (off-season), www.nps.gov/dewa.

fine-tune your photo skills

AT PICTURESQUE LOCALES IN THE U.S. & AROUND THE GLOBE

Don't go for the easy story.
Find something that challenges you, that scares you.
—Lois Raimondo, photographer

14 You'll leap out of bed before the sun rises, tromp through prickly brush, battle bugs, straddle fences, and carry about 20 pounds of gear. If you're serious about photography, you're guaranteed to have the time of your life.

Photography and vacations have gone together since 1900 when George Eastman first introduced the Brownie camera. Costing a mere one dollar (plus 15 cents for film), the simple box with the easy-to-load film rolls opened the mysterious world of photography to everyday people, who immediately began trotting around the globe documenting their travels.

Today, thousands of photography workshops are available for honing your travel-documenting skills. Whether you want pointers on the best angle for capturing a red-breasted sapsucker, advice on how to shoot a sunset over the Grand Canyon, or simple tips for getting your teenager to say "Cheese," a photography vacation is the way to go.

Needless to say, photography vacations are staged in places with dramatic scenery and light. The views alone should be enough to convince you. However, here are four more reasons to sign up for a photography vacation.

1. *Good company.* It takes time to set up a good shot, and nothing is more annoying than a traveling companion in a rush: "Okay, honey, we've seen that. Let's get out of here." There's something to be said for hanging out with other shutterbugs.
2. *Total immersion.* From the treasured light of dawn until well after darkroom dark, you get the chance to look at life through the lens of your camera.
3. *New technical skills.* No matter how many frames you've shot and

processed, there is always something new to learn. Photo vacations are guaranteed to open your eyes to new ways of seeing.

4. *Expanding networks.* Photo workshops expand a photographer's world. Staying in touch with classmates can lead to ongoing conversations, feedback, and coaching years down the road. You might even "get discovered." One student photographer did so well that he impressed a well-connected photojournalist who hooked him up with a couple magazines and agencies. Before the weeklong class was up, he was told, "You have appointments in New York—next week."

Although there are hundreds of photography workshops out there (*Peterson's Photographic*, *Modern Photography*, *Popular Photography*, and other photo magazines all publish directories), here are three of the best:

The Maine Photographic Workshops. This prestigious school in Rockport, Maine, offers more than 250 one- and two-week workshops in fine art, nature and wildlife, advertising, portrait, architectural, and corporate photography; digital imaging; photojournalism; darkroom techniques; antique processes; and personal vision. You'll study with some of the world's most accomplished photographers and filmmakers. Prices range from $175 for a three-day career and portfolio weekend to $1,495 for the one-week multimedia storytelling course. For the longer workshops, rooms and three meals run from $915 for a private single on campus ($1,230 for a double) or $805 for a single in a motel nearby ($1,130 for a double). You can also reserve an economy single room with shared bathroom at a private residence in Rockport Village for $655. For a three-day class, rates are half price. Workshops are also held in such far-flung places as Venice; Rio de Janeiro; Paris; Prague and Budapest; and Kampala, Uganda, with other locations planned for the future.

The Workshops, 2 Central Street, P.O. Box 200, Rockport, ME 04856, 877-577-7700 or 207-236-8581, www.theworkshops.com.

National Geographic On-Assignment Photography Workshops. Limited to 25 participants, these popular sessions for both amateur and serious photographers teach techniques used to capture the images used in National

Geographic's books and magazines. The all-inclusive seven-day trips include daily critique sessions, assignments, location shoots, and lots of technical information on cropping, sizing, manipulating, and archiving digital images. Led by the very photographers who grace the pages of the magazine (for example, Joel Sartore, who has produced 21 articles for NATIONAL GEOGRAPHIC, leads one of the Santa Fe workshops), you'll get the opportunity to go on daily photo shoots. A seven-day workshop in Santa Fe, New Mexico, including hotels, meals, and instruction, is $2,950. The one in San Miguel de Allende, Mexico, is $2,615 in February and $2,950 in November. Workshops are also held in Italy.

National Geographic Expeditions, 1145 17th Street NW, Washington, DC 20036, 888-966-8687, www.nationalgeographicexpeditions.com.

VII Photo Workshops. In 2001, seven of the world's top photojournalists started a photo agency to efficiently document an unflinching record of the injustices created and experienced by world events. This team of award-winning reporters is now trotting around the country doing weekend workshops and offering trips for amateur and serious photographers. For example, in November 2006, Gary Knight and Alexandra Boulat took 20 participants to Israel for a seven-day course that produced a photo essay of the historic city of Jerusalem. Later that month, Knight took yet another group of 20 to Cambodia. Prices and events vary greatly; the Cambodia trip, which included accommodations at the Foreign Correspondents Club, was $2,800, and the Jerusalem trip, without accommodations, was $1,550. Check the website for upcoming workshops.

VII New York, 236 W. 27th Street, Suite 1300, New York, NY 10001, 212-337-3130, or **VII Los Angeles,** 920 Abbot Kinney Boulevard, Venice, CA 90291, 310-452-3600, www.viiphoto.com.

throw pots on a colorado ranch

SNOWMASS, COLORADO

To create is human.
—motto of Anderson Ranch

15 Besides its awe-inspiring Rocky Mountain elevation (the student handbook offers suggestions on how to acclimate to life at 8,200 feet), Anderson Ranch is different from other arts-and-crafts centers because it was started by a master artist who is internationally recognized for his contributions to contemporary ceramics. Paul Soldner, who has exhibited from London to Kyoto and created many innovations that potters from Peoria to Pensacola regularly use, helped to found Anderson Ranch Arts Center in 1966 after locals in Aspen, Colorado, asked him to teach them a thing or two about clay.

When developers of nearby Snowmass Resort offered the prospective art school a choice of abandoned buildings, Soldner and his cronies opted for Anderson Ranch, an old sheep ranch, because, as Soldner said, "It had more character." The artists cleared out the barns for studios, set up a gallery, and inaugurated informal workshops. "It was meant to be a full-time alternative to graduate school: just as intense, but without academic degrees," Soldner explains.

In the beginning, students lived and worked with their mentors, making and selling artwork to defray the costs. Although Soldner, who served as the artist colony's first artistic director, turned over the administrative reins in the mid-1970s, he still returns each summer to teach one of the clay workshops. And he still leads students out to dig clay from nearby hillsides (and to pick dandelions for a batch of dandelion wine that next year's students can enjoy).

Soldner is joined by the nation's most renowned craftspeople—prize winners, career craftsmen, academics in the field—who flock to Anderson Ranch each summer to teach weekend, one-, two-, and three-week classes in ceramics, woodworking and furniture design, art history, photography, printmaking, digital imagery, sculpture, and painting.

BEAM ME UP, ASPEN!

Anderson Ranch is only 10 miles from Aspen, a mecca not only for Hollywood's vacationing glitterati but also for arts and culture. In other words, you can spend your days making photography and your evenings soaking up world-class performing arts.

Aspen is home to the Aspen Music Festival, the Aspen Institute, the Aspen Santa Fe Ballet, the Aspen Center for Physics, Theatre Aspen, the Aspen Art Museum, the Aspen Filmfest, Jazz Aspen Snowmass, and on and on. But one of the most unlikely Aspen cultural events is the Ultimate Taxi.

Operated by Jon Barnes, a former ski bum, the remodeled Checker cab has strobes, a fog machine, disco lights, a dry ice machine, stage lights, neon, and a multidisk CD/DVD system. Driving with his elbows, he croons Pink Floyd and other classic rock while a laser light show, enhanced by diffraction glasses and fog, wows his guests. Barnes has also taught himself to do magic tricks (while stopped at a stoplight, of course) and to play the sax. And if that repetoire doesn't entertain passengers, Barnes offers a telescope (for spotting alien invasions) or digital drums and a keyboard on which riders can produce their own music. He has enough wattage in the 25-year-old cab to power your average Kansas town.

The one essential of being an ultimate taxi driver, says Barnes, is that "you have to have an insurance company that has never actually seen inside your car."

A 30-minute musical, magical ride around Aspen costs $150 and includes toys, photos, 3-D glasses, rainbow glasses, and a page on Barnes's website next to photos of some of his other passengers such as Jerry Seinfeld, Clint Eastwood, Pierce Brosnan, and Lee Iacocca, to name a few. Call him at 970-927-9239 or check out his website at www.ultimatetaxi.com.

The reputations of Anderson Ranch's teachers are so stellar that they attract other working professionals, who oftentimes make up a third of the classes alongside sheer novices. The opportunities for the beginners are obvious.

Each summer, Anderson Ranch offers more than 130 workshops, beginning soon after Memorial Day and running through the end of September. Yoga classes are offered twice a day on Tuesdays and Thursdays as well, and there are lots of great hikes in the area. Every Sunday and Tuesday night during the summer, the ranch hosts a community slide lecture by visiting faculty. An interesting adjunct is the Children's Program, offering a wide range of workshops that change each year with such names as "Oodles of Noodles: Clay Creations" and "Lions & Tigers & Bears: Mixed Media."

In the winter, when Snowmass and nearby Aspen are buzzing with skiers, Anderson Ranch buzzes with its own sport—artists who have landed a coveted spot in the ranch's popular residency program. Working artists from around the world vie for one- to six-months use of the ranch's wide selection of kilns, Apple G-5 computers, and Fischer Photography Center.

"In an art world where it's typical for people to carry their loneliness to museums and galleries, seeking fashion, social visibility and self-importance, Anderson Ranch represents a rare opportunity for authenticity, communion and growth," says Enrique Martinez Celaya, a painter, poet and 2005 visiting artist in printmaking.

Tuition for the summer workshops, including lab fees, starts at about $800 per week (children's and teen classes are cheaper), to which you add on-campus room and board costs of $540 for simple dorm rooms to $1,400 per week for a three-bedroom condo near the ranch, with several meal plan options.

HOW TO GET IN TOUCH

Anderson Ranch Arts Center, 5263 Owl Creek Road, P.O. Box 5598, Snowmass Village, CO 81615, 970-923-3181, http://andersonranch.org.

design your dream home

OAK PARK, ILLINOIS

A great architect is not made by way of a brain nearly so much as he is made by way of a cultivated, enriched heart.
—Frank Lloyd Wright

16 Frank Lloyd Wright built 362 houses. You have the chance to build one more at the Frank Lloyd Wright Preservation Trust's architecture fantasy camps. Not only will you learn basic drafting techniques and execute framable floor plans for this dream house of yours, but you'll do it in the very studio from which Wright and his innovations rocked the world. Wright worked from the two-level drafting room next to his Oak Park home for nearly 20 years. It's where he conceived his groundbreaking prairie style and where he germinated the concepts behind Fallingwater, Taliesin, and New York's Guggenheim Museum.

"It's impossible to be in the drafting room without feeling the energy," says Jan Kieckhefer, the trust's director of education, who calls herself the "den mother" for the fantasy camp and for the dozens of other workshops and special events planned by the Oak Park trust. "It's inspiring no matter what field you're in."

Indeed, the attendees of the trust's four-night fantasy camps hail from many fields: stay-at-home moms, retirees wanting to build their dream retirement home, doctors, you name it. The only field missing among the students is architects, but that's because the workshop is open to laypeople only. Volunteer architects, however, show up to assist with drafting techniques and to go over plans.

The camp grew out of a Youth Architecture Class that the trust has offered for 15 years. After the dad of one of the teenagers lusted after his son's class, Kieckhefer thought, "Hmmm." That "hmmm" turned out to be a brilliant stroke of genius. The camp, which can accept only 12 per session (two to each of the six drafting tables in Wright's studio), fills up quicker that you can say "Frank Lloyd Wright was a veritable genius of the 20th century."

"We get people who spent their childhood drawing floor plans, people who pore over magazines like *Architectural Digest* and *Metropolitan Home,* people who always wanted to design and build their own home," Kieckhefer says.

Plans that have come out of the camp vary from that of a woman who designed a nifty garden shed to one from a man who designed a grand gallery for his contemporary art collection.

The preservation trust also offers daily tours of Wright's Oak Park home, his studio, and the Frederick C. Robie House, the home that revolutionized architecture with its sweeping horizontal lines, dramatic overhangs, art-glass windows, and open floor plans. In addition, the trust organizes bike tours, hosts special events, and leads what it calls "Wright Way Tours," educational tours to California, Japan, upstate New York, and other locales where Wright's masterpieces are located.

The fee for Architecture Fantasy Camp is $600 for preservation trust members and $650 for nonmembers. The class is held in the third week of June or the last week of September.

HOW TO GET IN TOUCH

Frank Lloyd Wright Preservation Trust, 951 Chicago Avenue, Oak Park, IL 60302, 708-848-1976, www.wrightplus.com.

handmake a book

AT CAMPS & ARTIST COLONIES AROUND THE COUNTRY

I'm stubborn enough to want to tell a story just the way I want to tell it.
If I have to try and sell it to a book publisher, my voice gets lost.
—Bea Nettles, professional book artist

17 The book you're holding in your hands is mass-produced. It was printed on a giant press along with thousands and thousands of clones. The books you'll make at the Paper & Book Intensive (PBI), by contrast, are unique handmade books that nobody but you (and those you care to appoint) will ever see. Each one is an original piece of art.

In today's Internet-driven world, handmade books might seem passé. But in the past ten years, interest in the book arts—which, loosely speaking, includes handmade art books, bookbinding, papermaking, mail art, and calligraphy—has grown faster than the readership for *The Da Vinci Code*.

Nonprofits such as the Center for Book Arts (CBA) in New York City regularly stage exhibitions and host workshops (2006's hundred-plus lineup at the CBA ranged from how to make comic books to hand typesetting). At the same time, stores like Hollander's in Ann Arbor, Michigan, a 5,000-plus-square-foot retail shop, sell decorative papers and bookbinding tools, and little mom-and-pop outfits like Joyce Miller and Gary Frost's Iowa Book Works hawk book craft kits and classes in epic journaling.

Perhaps the best place to hone your book-arts talents is at the Paper & Book Intensive, an action-packed eight-day conference that travels in the spring and summer like a book-arts Chautauqua from venue to venue, state to state. In 2006, for example, PBI was staged at La Lumiere School in La Porte, Indiana. The year before, it was held in rustic log cabins at the Lowell Whiteman School in Steamboat Springs, Colorado, and before that at a YMCA camp near Portland at the end of the Oregon Trail.

Suffice it to say, PBI is pretty savvy when it comes to picking scenic and interesting venues. For example. the 2003 PBI was held at Camp Wapiti outside Tooele, Utah.

EAT YOUR WORDS

Every April 1, the International Edible Book Festival invites bibliophiles, book artists, and food lovers to create edible books. Each group or individual gathers among themselves to exhibit, photograph, and then consume the entries, with images being posted at www.books2eat.com for the world to see. The result? Absurdly creative concoctions made from phyllo, nori, pasta, peanut butter, and everything in between. Bea Nettles, for example, an Illinois book artist, made *The Toast of the Town* by binding six pieces of toast together. Two L.A. performance artists provided ingredients and dry ice for guests at a High/Low Tea to make their own individual scoops of ice cream in plastic bags. An artist from Toledo made the entire world atlas out of cookie dough. You have to see it to believe it.

With inspiring views of Lake Bonneville, the Oquirrh Mountains, and Settlement Canyon, participants could fish, ride horses, or mountain bike when they weren't making Japanese block prints or cooking, beating, and pressing leaves and grasses into sheets of paper. Before PBI took on its gypsy wanderings, it was held each year at a picturesque artist college in Michigan called Ox-Bow.

Daily classes at PBI are combined with lectures, discussions, and communal meals. During the first four-day session, participants take two classes—one in the morning and one in the afternoon. The second session features one all-day class. Choices include making paper from plants, intuitive imagemaking, making and sharpening knives, and reproducing one of the Nag Hammadi codices, a group of single-quire bindings from third- or fourth-century Egypt.

Tuition runs roughly $1,200 for the eight-day sabbatical and includes lodging, daily meals, workshops, and all equipment and supplies. The only thing you're responsible for is the creativity.

HOW TO GET IN TOUCH

Paper & Book Intensive, www.paperbookintensive.org. For questions, contact Steve Miller, University of Alabama School of Library and Information Studies, P.O. Box 870252, Tuscaloosa, AL 35487, 205-348-1525, e-mail: stevemiller@ bookarts.ua.edu.

build a wooden boat from scratch

BROOKLIN, MAINE

When I finish high school, I'll go home with a diploma.
When I finish up here, I'll go home with a boat.
—Chris Everett, participant in a boatbuilding workshop

18 If you don't have the time or freedom to apprentice yourself to one of the handful of American boatbuilders, consider a vacation to Brooklin, Maine. This little town on Penobscot Bay is known as the "boat building capital of the world." Even the K–8 Brooklin school system offers a boatbuilding program for students that ends in junior high with a finished boat. Ninety-five percent of Brooklin's 850 residents have either built their own boat or plan to someday.

The town also has a one-of-a-kind school that teaches would-be Popeyes how to build their own boats. Whether your fancy is a yacht, a canoe, a skiff, or a sloop, the WoodenBoat School teaches traditional boatmaking skills. Stay long enough and you'll even leave with your own boat. At the 60-acre campus that overlooks the Atlantic, you can also take courses in seamanship, marine carving, and other crafts related to boatbuilding.

Most of the boatbuilding and seamanship classes begin at 8 a.m. and run through 5 p.m. Lunch is brought in and served at the shops, at the Boathouse, or on board the teaching

MARITIME SUPERSTITIONS

Boats (which are always "she") should never be renamed (unless you perform an elaborate ceremony), never be painted blue (lest the ocean be jealous), and never be launched on a Friday (it's been considered bad luck for years). Also, a silver coin with the date of the boat's birth should be placed under the mast as a tribute to the winds.

ALSO FLOATS

A good place to study the revival of wooden boats is at Seattle's Center for Wooden Boats. Founded in 1976 by Dick Wagner, a longtime lover of wooden boats who can spin tales as windy as any sailor, the center owns 200 wooden boats, 75 of which are on display at any given time, with 25 available for rent. They also offer dozens of classes in such subjects as sailmaking, tying knots, and other topics relevant to wooden boats. The small fleet at the Seattle Center includes rowboats such as Whitebears and Davises, or you can let the wind do the work for you in one of the center's sailboats, such as a Concordia sloop, Beetle Cat, or Blanchard Junior. "There are plenty of museums with large boats—boats you can look at but not touch," Wagner says. "Ours are intended to be touched." Boats are available for daily rental and range from $10 to $45 an hour. *Center for Wooden Boats, 1010 Valley Street, Seattle, WA 98109, 206-382-2628, www.cwb.org.*

---

boats at noon. In the evening, students can visit local boatyards (there are nine in Brooklin), explore the quaint little town where E. B. White wrote *Charlotte's Web,* or ply the Maine coast in one of the school's fleet of wooden boats.

More than a hundred classes, from beginner to advanced, are offered each year. Classes at Brooklin run from June through September, but the famous school also offers boatbuilding classes at various maritime museums and similar facilities during the spring and fall. The curricula for the off-campus courses are identical to the classes at the main campus, except that students at the off-site locations must find their own accommodations.

For tuition of around $700 for a weeklong course ($1,100 for two people), students can study such subjects as boat repair, oar- and paddlemaking, or marine photography. For another $425 per week, you'll get housing and home-cooked meals at the rambling frame house that serves as the school's dormitory. Alternatively, you can park your RV or pitch a tent at their beautiful campground for a weekly charge of $100 per campsite (no electrical hookups or dumping stations are offered), or moor your boat for $100 a week.

HOW TO GET IN TOUCH
WoodenBoat School, 41 WoodenBoat Lane, P.O. Box 78, Brooklin, ME 04616, 207-359-4651, www.thewoodenboatdschool.com.

paint with o'keeffe's ghost

ABIQUIU, NEW MEXICO

> Ghost Ranch is a magical sanctuary where the veil between
> heaven and earth seems almost transparent.
> —Lesley Poling-Kempes, author of *Ghost Ranch*

19 Georgia O'Keeffe, who lived to the ripe old age of 99, said her only regret about dying was that she would never again be able to see the beautiful country of northern New Mexico. "Unless," she quipped, "the Indians are right and my spirit will walk here after I'm gone."

Whether or not O'Keeffe's spirit is still walking Ghost Ranch, the 21,000-acre spread that inspired her most famous paintings, depends on whom you talk to. She did request that her body be cremated and that her ashes be scattered from the top of her beloved Pedernal Mountain. In 1986, longtime friend Juan Hamilton hiked to the top of the mountain she immortalized in so many paintings (she used to say that God told her if she painted Pedernal enough times, he would give it to her) and let the famous painter's remains be carried off by the winds.

Georgia or not, the stark beauty of Ghost Ranch's high northern New Mexico desert still inspires painters, including professionals and wannabes who come to Ghost Ranch for painting workshops. The Presbyterian-owned conference center sponsors its own classes (a recent offering was "Bones and Blossoms: Drawing and Painting the Desert's Forms") and leases the facilities out to others such as Chris Zydel, an art therapist from Oakland, California, who hosts "Painting from the Wild Heart" retreats every year (see sidebar).

Not that painting is the only type of workshop available at Ghost Ranch. You can choose between classes in everything from photography to opera appreciation to paleontology. North America's oldest dinosaur was discovered at one of Ghost Ranch's many paleontological digs, and an IMAX movie on dinosaur digging was recently filmed there. The Ruth Hall Museum of Paleontology is one of the ranch's two museums, along with the Florence Hawley Ellis Museum of Anthropology.

The motto of the world-famous institution is "Let our world change your

WHAT'S IN A NAME?

The 21,000 acres that compose Ghost Ranch were part of a land grant to Pedro Martín Serrano from the king of Spain in 1766. At first it was called Piedra Lumbre ("shining rock"), but eventually it became known as El Rancho de los Brujos ("ranch of the witches") after ranchers hanged a gang of cattle rustlers who, according to locals, still haunted the place. Carol Stanley, a Boston-born musician who won the ranch in a 1927 poker game and built its casitas and bunkhouses, changed the Spanish name to the simpler Ghost Ranch.

Wealthy publisher Arthur Pack bought the ranch from Stanley, and before he gave the massive spread to the Presbyterian Church in 1955, Ghost Ranch was a dude ranch, attracting the likes of Charles and Anne Lindbergh, D. H. Lawrence, Ansel Adams, and other artists attracted to what historian Lesley Poling-Kempes called its "epic beauty."

Ghost Ranch is still a working ranch, complete with cattle and covered with bleached white animal bones. Before O'Keeffe moved to New Mexico permanently in 1949, she used to ship barrels of cattle skulls to her studio in New York. If you want to get a preview of the place, just rent the movie *City Slickers*.

world," and its mission is "to affect individual and social transformation through education." To that end, Ghost Ranch offers a wide variety of workshops in social justice and peacemaking, plus guided hikes and desert pilgrimages to sacred sites.

Housing at the ranch is rustic and modest. There are no phones or TVs (by design), and meals (three hearty, wholesome meals featuring local produce) are served cafeteria style, with guests expected to bus their own tables.

Ghost Ranch is located approximately two hours' drive from the Albuquerque airport, an hour north of Santa Fe. It offers dozens of workshops, seminars, adventures, and service opportunities for people of all ages. Since 1990, the Ghost Ranch has also run a campus in Santa Fe (800-821-5145).

Six-day workshops are priced between $240 and $370; housing and meal plans range from $425 to $1,275. For those who want to camp and cook for themselves, sites are available for $105 per week.

HOW TO GET IN TOUCH

Ghost Ranch Abiquiu, HC77, Box 11, Abiquiu, NM 87510, 877-804-4678 or 505-685-4333, www.ghostranch.org.

fiddle in a kansas campground

WINFIELD, KANSAS

Life has slings and arrows enough for us all.
Winfield is where we go to heal.
—Dan Bynum, longtime attendee of the Walnut Valley Festival

20 Not only is Winfield—the proper name is the Walnut Valley Festival, but everybody calls it Winfield—the national championship for just about every acoustic string instrument known (flatpick guitar, finger-style guitar, autoharp, mountain and hammered dulcimer, banjo, fiddle, and mandolin), but it's also probably the best place in the world to learn to play one. Held every September on the banks of the Walnut River, the festival draws 20,000 or so campers, most of them musicians. And since most of those musicians spend the better part of the 5 to 14 days (some stay as long as three weeks) jamming with other musicians, it's an incredible place to get lots of practice. Anybody's welcome to sit in.

At any given time, day or night (midnight is when the fun really begins), there are hundreds of camp circles with people singing and playing their instruments. Even if you're still trying to remember which of those six guitar strings is a C, you're heartily invited to pull up a hay bale, a bucket, or a stool and join in the fun. The bass player for Spontaneous Combustion, a Winfield favorite, claims he learned everything he knows about playing his instrument from watching other bass players at Winfield. Suffice it to say, music here is not a spectator sport.

Oh sure, there are formal workshops on, say, the finer points of hammered dulcimer playing, but lots of people do go to Winfield just to listen—after all, Winfield features five days and five stages of live acoustic music with such performers as the Dixie Chicks, Laurie Lewis, John McCutcheon, Tom Chapin, and hundreds of others. But why pass up this rare opportunity to jam with the likes of Alison Krauss (this Grammy Award winner won the fiddling competition in 1984) and Beppe Gambetta, who was quoted in a prominent guitar magazine as saying that his favorite place to play was at the makeshift Stage 5 at Winfield. (Stage 5 is not one of the official stages—it's basically an elevated wheat truck with a tie-dyed backdrop in the middle of the Pecan Grove campground where the campers themselves sign up for the 30-minute sets.)

The number-one goal for most campers, many of whom haven't missed a single year since the festival started in 1972, is to stay up as long as humanly possibly and soak up as much music as their tired, sunburned, bug-bitten bodies can tolerate. After the official shows shut down around midnight, coffee is brewed and most everyone, regardless of age or physical condition, begins to wander.

The music changes as you move from campsite to campsite. Irish ballads blend into renditions of Grateful Dead tunes. You might hear an old sea shanty played on a pennywhistle or see someone playing a string bass made out of car parts. In the distance, there's a bagpipe and somebody always brings a beat-up trumpet to play taps (funny at first, annoying by 4 a.m.). And there is always the crackling of campfires, the smell of wood smoke, and the laughter of friends.

Although the Walnut Valley campground (divided into the Pecan Grove and the Walnut Grove) has been described as an upscale refugee camp (there are thousands of tents, sleeping bags, pop-up campers, and even recycled parachutes hanging from trees), the individual campsites are often elaborate affairs with matching sofas and La-Z-Boys.

Encouraged by the annual campsite contest, festivalgoers decorate their temporary digs with intense planning, much of which would give Martha Stewart pause. It's not unusual to see castles, tropical paradises, "log cabins," and re-creations of Granny's back porch. One year's runner-up in the campsite contest featured dozens of pink flamingos, two ponds, all kinds of funny National Wildlife signs, and Christmas lights that must have put a cramp on the local electric grid.

The makeshift campsites often have names—for example, the "Blue Bayou" that has been known to have a pond with an alligator or a turtle in it or the "Chicken Train Camp" that often hosts chicken bingo, a clucking competition, and tie-dye Fridays where any camper can bring a T-shirt, a pair of underwear, or an old scarf for an application of dye. One campsite might throw a salsa competition,

WHILE YOU'RE IN KANSAS

It's a bit of a drive from Winfield (about 200 miles), but if you're coming to Kansas anyway, you'd be a fool to pass on a visit to Lucas, Kansas, a veritable mecca for grassroots art. Also called outsider art or primitive art—though some merely call it bizarre—grassroots art thrives in Kansas with more grassroots artists per capita than any other state.

Lucas (pop. 422), an anything-but-sleepy town in north-central Kansas, has five major grassroots art museums. It attracts scads of international visitors, mainly because those five museums provide raw testament to the indomitable will of the human being to create.

The Lucas legacy began in 1907 when S. P. Dinsmoor, a retired farmer, nurse, and Civil War veteran, began building the concrete **Garden of Eden** (305 E. Second Street, 785-525-6395, www.garden-of-eden-lucas-kansas.com). When all was said and done, Dinsmoor had used 113 tons of cement to sculpt grape arbors, American flags that swiveled on flagpoles, 40-foot trees, a life-size Adam and Eve, a devil whose eyes light up (he was the first in Lucas to have electricity), and a hundred other statues.

Also in Lucas is the **Florence Deeble's Rock Garden** (126 Fairview Street, 785-525-6118), where giant concrete postcards of Mount Rushmore made by a retired English and history teacher are on display in her home; the **Grassroots Arts Center** (213 S. Main Street, 785-525-6118, $6 adult admission, http://home.comcast.net/~ymirymir), a fascinating three-building museum with art made with everything from grapefruit peels and dried chewing gum to empty milk of magnesia bottles; and **Mri Pilar's Garden of Isis** (213 S. Main Street, 785-525-6118), a museum that features art made from recycled materials and "rebarb," a recycled Barbie doll or Barbie doll part.

If that's not enough wackiness, Lucas is also home base for the **World's Largest Collection of the World's Smallest Versions of the World's Largest Things Traveling Roadside Attraction and Museum** (www.worldslarge stthings.com), a reconstituted bus that tours the country. It contains exhibit space for an unusual collection of miniature replicas of all things deemed the "world's largest," including the world's largest ball of twine.

the infamous "Carp Camp" has a Friday parade complete with wacky hats, and another traditionally holds a costume contest (one year's winner was Dorothy from *The Wizard of Oz* with tattoos from head to toe).

People are such fanatics about Winfield that they've started bulletin boards, chat rooms, mailing lists, photo galleries, memoirs, and even a radio station.

If you can, come for Land Rush, a prefestival dash for the best camping spots. Many fans come as much as three weeks early to get numbers and wait for the 7 a.m. starting gun that signals the opening day of the fairgrounds where the festival is staged. Land Rush happens a week before the festival begins, and thousands come to stake out their favorite site along the river or under the same sycamore tree where they've been meeting friends for years.

Walnut Valley Festival is held the third weekend of September at the Cowley County fairgrounds. Tickets for the five-day festival are $80 in advance. Camping is $7 a day or $10 with electric hookups.

HOW TO GET IN TOUCH
Walnut Valley Festival, 918 Main Street, P.O. Box 245, Winfield, KS 67156, 620-221-3250, www.wvfest.com.

indulge your inner john wayne

SCOTTSDALE, ARIZONA

*I have never had so much fun, done so much work, and been
so tired in all my life. I'd do it all over again tomorrow.*
—John Hersey, student at Arizona Cowboy College

21 Arizona Cowboy College is not a dude ranch. There are no cutesy hay wagons or line-dancing lessons. You will get up at dawn. You will sleep on the ground. You will sweat. You will ache. You will continue to be sore for at least a week after. But in the process of doing these things, you will learn a dying art—an art that has more or less defined the American West for more than a hundred years. You will also learn some amazing things about yourself: that you're a lot stronger, more resilient, and more heroic than you ever dreamed possible.

The late Lloyd Bridwell, the fourth-generation cowboy who started the Cowboy College in 1989, said he never coached a student who didn't consider the six-day crash course in riding, roping, and rounding up one of the best experiences of his or her life.

Cowboys and cowgirls in training sleep under the stars, cook over campfires, and live like actual cowboys for a week. Add some bucking broncs and ornery heifers, and you've got one heck of a classic Western—with you as the star.

The first two days of Cowboy College are not the stuff epic Westerns are made of. You'll begin at the Lorill Equestrian Center getting to know your horse and your equipment. You'll learn to rope by lassoing a fiberglass cow on wheels. Other things you'll learn include how to shoe a horse, brand a cow, and castrate a bull. But once you've got those basic cowboy skills down, you'll be out on the high chaparral on an honest-to-goodness roundup, camped and working side by side with real cowboys. Nearby ranchers claim the help they get from the greenhorns at Cowboy College cuts their workload in half.

HOMEWORK ON THE RANGE

If Rocco Wachman, the head wrangler-instructor at Arizona Cowboy College, looks vaguely familiar, it could be because you've seen him on CMT's hit TV series *Cowboy U*, which takes "city slickers" through the paces of cowboy boot camp "where wimps are not welcome, phones are forbidden, and the outdoor shower is considered a luxury." According to the CMT website, it's the longest-running original series on the network. In six mud-and-manure-covered seasons, contestants have mastered horse survival skills, bull riding, and calf roping before a grueling trail ride and final rodeo challenge, with the winners walking off with a $25,000 prize.

In the evenings, you'll grill hamburgers and steaks over a barbecue pit, and Rocco Wachman, the head instructor who wouldn't be caught dead without his white Stetson, will get out his guitar and sing campfire songs.

The Bridwell Ranch is located in the Sonoran Desert just outside Scottsdale. The property backs up to Tonto National Forest with the McDowell Mountains rimming the edge. The desert landscape is dominated by all things prickly, including centuries-old saguaro cactuses, scratchy mesquite, and chollas, which some claim throw their spiny branches at unsuspecting passersby.

Classes are limited to eight students and are scheduled ten months out of the year to coincide with the spring and fall roundups. The $2,250 tuition includes all meals and rustic bunkhouse accommodations.

HOW TO GET IN TOUCH
Arizona Cowboy College, Lorill Equestrian Center, 30208 N. 152nd Street, Scottsdale, AZ 85262, 888-330-8070 or 480-471-3151, www.cowboycollege.com.

turn wood in the great smoky mountains

GATLINBURG, TENNESSEE

*The purpose of art is to lay bare the questions
which have been hidden by the answers.*
—James Baldwin, American author

22 Taking a weeklong workshop at Arrowmont is akin to taking an acting class with Meryl Streep or Jack Nicholson. The faculty at this world-renowned contemporary arts school is the best of the best in such media as ceramics, fibers, metals, jewelry, wood turning, and woodworking. "Look through any craft magazine—say *Ceramics Monthly* or *American Craft*—and you'll see our instructors, often on the cover," says Kim Newman, public relations coordinator for the institution that even gives undergraduate and graduate credit and continuing education units.

Don't let that intimidate you. Sure, the handiwork of Arrowmont's faculty can regularly be found in art galleries across the national and all over the world, but the classes, which are all welcoming, open, and nonjudgmental, attract everyone from what's-a-paintbrush? types to serious artists looking for a wisp of inspiration.

Located less than three minutes from the Gatlinburg entrance to Great Smoky Mountains National Park, Arrowmont offers weekend, one-week, and two-week classes in, well, you can just about name it. There are more than 150 annual offerings in media from painting and drawing to stoneware, ceramics, wood carving, and textile arts.

Arrowmont's 70-acre campus also has five art galleries, a bookstore, an incredibly well-stocked supply store (everything from sterling silver for metalmaking to bolts of silk fiber), and housing that ranges from dormitory-style rooms in a renovated red barn to rustic cottages furnished with antiques to newer accommodations with private baths.

WHILE YOU'RE IN THE NEIGHBORHOOD

The Smoky Mountain Field School, sponsored by Great Smoky Mountains National Park and the University of Tennessee, offers more than 75 outdoor classes throughout the year taught by biologists and naturalists. Steve Tilley of Smith College in Massachusetts, for example, comes to the field school every year to teach a class on finding salamanders. Known as the "Salamander Capital of the World," the national park has more than ten species of salamanders. Or take a class on edible and medicinal plants. Ila Hatter, the interpretative naturalist who teaches the class, even prepares a meal at the end of the day from plants collected during the forages. A typical menu might include kudzu pasta with poke pesto, Aztec pork stew with ground cherries, apple-elderberry-blueberry pie, elderflower sorbet, and either dandelion wine or mint-ginger punch. One-day classes are from $29 to $49, while two-day courses, bird-watching and fishing trips, and overnight hikes run between $95 and $155. A five-day, fall backpacking trip that treks through seasonal scenery on the Appalachian Trail costs $455. *Smoky Mountain Field School, University of Tennessee Conference Building, 600 Henley Street, Suite 105, Knoxville, TN 35713, 865-974-0150, www. outreach.utk.edu/smoky/.*

Arrowmont began life as a Settlement School in 1912. Sponsored by the Pi Beta Phi fraternity (the first fraternity for women in the United States), the innovative rural school brought education and health care to the little outpost in the Appalachians where schooling didn't exist. Teachers at the school couldn't help but notice the amazing artwork of the parents of many of their students and decided selling it might be a way to support the families' other needs. By 1945, the school, which helped formed the Southern Highland Craft Guild, a nine-state regional craft education and marketing organization, was offering summer arts-and-crafts workshops.

One thing led to another until Arrowmont morphed into a virtual hub for contemporary artists. The school offers artists' residencies (a highly sought-after program that gives five artists 11 months' time and studio space to develop a body of work), artist assistantships, art conferences, and even an outside arts education program for public schools. And Pi Beta Phi is still behind it all.

A weeklong workshop at Arrowmont starts on Sunday evening and continues with hands-on teaching Monday through Friday. Three meals a day are served, but instructors say they sometimes practically have to tear their students away from their work to eat. One-week courses are offered in the spring, summer, and fall (weekend classes also take place when the leaves turn), and you can also take the more intensive, in-depth two-week versions in summer. Classes are small (15 students to one teacher).

Arrowmont, although cozy and self-contained, is literally right off the main drag (Tenn. 441) of Gatlinburg, one of the country's busiest and gaudiest tourist traps, and there's time available for visiting Gatlinburg's Hard Rock Café, hiking in the national park, or taking the kids to Dollywood. But many students get so immersed in their projects—with the studios, resource center, and galleries open until midnight—that they never leave the hallowed woodside retreat.

An average workshop at Arrowmont with tuition, lab fees, and room and board costs between $700 and $1,350, depending on the season and whether you prefer dorm-style or private accommodations. Students staying off-campus have the option of individual meals or plans starting at $60 for weekends, $171 for a week, or $378 for the two-week summer workshops.

HOW TO GET IN TOUCH
Arrowmont School of Arts and Crafts, 556 Parkway, P.O. Box 567, Gatlinburg, TN 37738, 865-436-5860, www.arrowmont.org.

play guitar with the who's roger daltrey

LOS ANGELES, CALIFORNIA & NEW YORK, NEW YORK

I was as giddy as a kid on his first trip to Disneyland as I stood onstage with Roger Daltrey, belting out the background vocals to "I Can See for Miles."
—Michael Molenda, Rock 'n' Roll Fantasy Camp participant

23 Although Jay Leno joked that enrolling in drug rehab was a cheaper way to meet rock stars, Rock 'n' Roll Fantasy Camp, a five-day boot camp for learning the music biz, offers much more than the chance to rub elbows with the Who's Roger Daltrey and the Grateful Dead's Mickey Hart. Sure, you'll take the stage with those legends (as well as nosh with them over buffet lunches), but you'll also hone your electric guitar– or drum- or keyboard-playing skills, write a song (Daltrey himself might even perform it), learn the ins and outs of the record industry, and jam with your fellow bandmates. According to participants, some of whom have come back as many as four or five times, the camp is "life changing."

When David Fishof, manager and promoter for Ringo Starr, threw out the idea of rock 'n' roll camp back in 1997, he was practically booed off the stage. Won't fly, he was told. Folks with that kind of money wouldn't spend it to play "rock star." Undeterred, he decided to try it as a onetime gig. Then at the urging of fans and the artists themselves, he began offering the camps again in 2000. Rock 'n' Roll Fantasy Camp has consistently sold out, and Fishof is currently adding camps in London, Las Vegas, Sydney, and Tokyo.

The camp itinerary includes a day of auditions (camp counselors such as Bruce Kulick, lead guitarist from Kiss, and Markey Ramone from the Ramones form bands after hearing each of the campers' chops), three days of band practice at professional rehearsal studios (much classier and soundproof than mom's garage), and a one-night live concert playing with the musicians who sell millions of dollars' worth of albums. In Los Angeles, the final battle of the bands takes place at the House of Blues on Sunset Strip; in New York, it's B. B. King's Blues Club in Times Square. Both live concerts sell out.

Each of the camp's bands chooses a name for their band, learns two classic rock songs, and spends what-would-be-exhausting-if-it-wasn't-so-exhilarating 14-hour workdays practicing for their big debut. Also included in the package are seminars on such topics as buying a custom-made guitar and stage showmanship (you think Mick Jagger learned that walk on his own?) and three meals a day, including dinner/gossip sessions (ask about Mötley Crüe and the 99-cent burritos) with musicians, roadies, and other music insiders. Needless to say, the movie *This Is Spinal Tap* is usually shown.

Most participants are men in their 40s and 50s (it's popular as a 50th birthday present) eager to relive a slice of their youth, but anyone, regardless of sex, age, or whether they are better on lead guitar or air guitar, is welcome. Some participants save up for years and consider the camp a possible toe in the door. There's even room for backup vocalists, tambourine players, and stage manager wannabes. On that final night, each participant receives a gold record that says, "I jammed with the Allman Brothers [or Cheap Trick or Journey, etc.]." And, of course, you get to keep your backstage pass.

The only downfall: the price tag. Be prepared to spend upward of $8,500, groupies not included.

HOW TO GET IN TOUCH
Rock 'n' Roll Fantasy Camp, 61 W. 62nd Street, Suite 18-M, New York, NY 10023, 888-762-2263, www.rockandrollfantasycamp.com.

weave a navajo rug with a tribal elder

NAVAJO RESERVATION, NEW MEXICO

If you're a troubled person, sit down to your weaving and your bad feeling all goes away and the good one comes in.
—Sarah Natani, master rug weaver

24 Twice a year, Sarah Natani, a Diné elder who has been passing down Navajo weaving techniques for some 40 years, opens her hogan in Table Mesa, New Mexico, to people interested in exploring Navajo weaving. Although it's possible to catch Sarah's rug-weaving classes in arts-and-crafts schools around the country (the internationally known weaver is a regular at Sievers School of Fiber Arts on Washington Island, Wisconsin, for example, and has traveled to Italy and China to give demonstrations and lead workshops), the most authentic way to learn the sacred craft that has been passed down for centuries is to come to her weeklong workshop at the family ranch in Table Mesa. It's near Four Corners, about 12 miles south of Shiprock on the Navajo Reservation.

Natani learned to weave at her mother's knee when she was seven. By the time she was nine, she had sold her first rug. She used $3 of that first $15 sale to buy a weaving comb that she carefully branded with her initials and still has more than 50 years later. Today, one of her four-by-five-foot rugs sells for around $6,000.

MOVE OVER, RITZ DYE

The Diné or Navajo, who make use of the flora and fauna around them, use natural dyes made from such plants as alder bark, globe mallow, ground lichen, Indian paintbrush, juniper bark, scarlet bugler, sumac berries, and sweet yellow clover.

When Natani first began giving workshops to Anglos, she was criticized. "Why would you want to teach them our ways?" many in her tribe wondered. But she knew

FRUIT OF THE LOOM

One of the legends Sarah Natani is guaranteed to share during the workshop is the genesis of Navajo weaving. According to Diné teachings, Spider Woman was taught to weave by the spider. She then came down from Spider Rock, 800 feet high in Canyon de Chelly, and shared her knowledge with the Diné. The loom, which was made by Spider Man, used cross poles of sky and warp sticks of sunrays. Spindles were made of lightning.

Navajo weavers, afraid of trapping their creativity in one rug, traditionally leave a single line of contrasting thread running from the background color through the border to the edge. Called a "weaver's pathway" or a "spirit line," the errant thread is often mistaken as a flaw. In truth, it's carefully crafted as an escape route for the weaver's spirit and creativity.

intuitively that by passing along what was in danger of becoming a dying art, she could not only preserve her beloved craft, but she could share her culture with people who craved the quiet mind and the peace that Navajo weaving instills. Now, of course, Navajo weaving is taught all over the place, and Sarah is recognized as being the pioneer that she always has been.

During the weeklong workshops, held in May and late September, Natani shares Navajo weaving techniques, but more importantly, she also passes down Diné legends, lore, and wisdom (see sidebar). In the process, students learn how to prepare fleece (you will help shear sheep) and how to wash, card, spin, and dye it (only vegetable dyes allowed). She also teaches students how to warp a loom, weave stripes, and use the "S" and "Z" twist. Field trips to nearby trading posts are included, as well.

Although the Natani hospitality is open to weavers of all levels, don't come with unrealistic expectations. Natani's hogan is not a resort. It has dirt floors and is heated with a coal-burning stove. There's no room service, the only bathroom is an outhouse, and, besides the other weavers, you'll be sharing the family ranch with Natani's several dozen head of churro sheep (their wool is highly prized for rugmaking), a couple of cows, a llama, three chihuahuas, some stray cats, a few ponies, and a horse.

As Kathleen Burhnam, the volunteer organizer for the fall trip, says, "This is a weaver's workshop, not a convenient excuse to take a friend and vacation in the Southwest. We live as the Navajo lived, however briefly and superficially, and in this way we develop an appreciation for their accomplishments, their enduring dignity, their grace and beauty in the face of adversity, and we come away with the glow of the Southwest sunsets in our hearts."

The price for the weeklong workshop is $350, with lab fees ranging from $50 to $125. Natani is often invited to lead weaving workshops at locations around the country; check her website for upcoming venues.

HOW TO GET IN TOUCH

Sarah Natani, P.O. Box 2270, Shiprock, NM 87420, 505-368-4906. For the May workshop, contact Judy Ness, 541 E. 47th Avenue, Eugene, OR 97405, 541-465-1236, judyness@uoregon.edu; for the fall workshop, contact Kathleen Burhnam, 831-588-5806, www.navajovalues.com/natani/nataniworkshop.htm.

CHAPTER 2

volunteer vacations

We've GOT to make noise in greater amounts!
So, open your mouth, lad! For every voice counts!
—Horton, in Dr. Seuss's *Horton Hears a Who*

Most folks think they want to *get* something from a vacation—time off from work, a break from their normal ho-hum, maybe a tan. But here's the deal: What you *really* want from a vacation is to *give* something.

I hate to be the one to break it to you, but you know you don't really care about five-star hotels and Coppertone tans and exclusive tours of the French Riviera. Not really. You care about what happens to our children. To our oceans. To the great big, beautiful dream of freedom and wildness and a chicken in every pot. You long to make the world a better place.

Granted, it's a cliché, but deep down, you know it's the truth. It's that little voice that continually nags at you anytime you stop long enough to listen: "Isn't there something more?"

That's what this chapter is about: The *something more*. Read through the following volunteer vacation listings and see which one speaks to you. One of them will call to you, "Psst, over here. This is yours to do."

With all the problems in the world, finding your own way to help can seem overwhelming. How can you, one person, stop the forces of environmental destruction? How can you, a single mom, solve the homeless epidemic? Well, you can't. But you can help a defenseless sea turtle make it to the ocean. Or hand a chocolate chip cookie to a kid on the street. And each time you make these seemingly tiny contributions, the world becomes a tiny bit sweeter, a tad bit closer to heaven.

blaze a new trail

NEW MEXICO, COLORADO, WYOMING, IDAHO, MONTANA

Few have ever had the opportunity to be a part of something
as grand as the creation of a pristine trail across
America's most precious landscape. In creating the CDT,
we are providing the public an opportunity to taste history.
—Steve Fausel, CDTA honorary board cochair

25 In 1978 Congress officially opened a new hiking trail to join the great American treks that already included the Appalachian Trail, the Pacific Rim Trail, and other long interstate trails that only the most avid outdoorsperson would ever consider undertaking in their entirety.

The Continental Divide Trail stretches from Canada to Mexico. It crosses five states, three national parks (including Yellowstone), 20 wilderness areas, and five very distinct ecosystems. Measuring 3,100 miles in length, it's the longest of all trails in the U.S. trail system. It has been dubbed "the king of trails" and "the backbone of America." It's also received a few other choice epithets bestowed by would-be thru-hikers who are forced to bail out before finishing. Given its seriously rough terrain, only a couple dozen hikers are able to traverse it from end to end each year. To give you some perspective, 800 people—out of the 4,000 who try—succeed in thru-hiking the Appalachian Trail in an average year. But that doesn't mean you can't tackle one gorgeous segment or another—the Bridger Wilderness section in Wyoming, for instance, or Baker Gulch in Rocky Mountain National Park.

So what's the problem? The Continental Divide Trail isn't finished yet. Congress, while acknowledging that the trail is worthy of preserving, didn't allocate enough funds to complete it. Nearly 1,400 miles of the proposed route are yet to be built. People who do attempt to thru-hike it end up following paved roads or, worse, lost in the woods.

To remedy such Hansel-and-Gretel mishaps, the Continental Divide Trail

Alliance (CDTA), a nonprofit organization formed in 1995, has come up with a plan to finish the trail by 2008, just in time for its 30th anniversary (and even if the trail is finished by then, there will be trail maintenance for eternities). The group's challenge is to stitch together existing segments with new trails through federal lands, state lands, and private ranchlands. But since the CDTA depends on private donations and volunteer labor, they need your help in this historic undertaking.

From April through October since 1996, the CDTA has hosted volunteer trail-building projects. Since they began, more than 7,500 volunteers have built 1,355 miles of trails, 32 bridges, and 46 trailheads.

Keep in mind that the work is all done in the backcountry, in places where you can't just skip over to the convenience store for a hot coffee. If you volunteer for one of CDTA's 40-plus annual projects, you'll be sleeping in a tent, eating from a camp stove, and hiking each day just to get to your work site. Suffice it to say, there's no cell phone reception.

The work is demanding, but the rewards are immense. For one thing, the scenery is spectacular. Most of the trail is above 8,000 feet in elevation. You'll see vistas the average person sees only on postcards. And since CDTA volunteers range from investment bankers to rodeo bull riders to highway crew workers, the after-dinner chats can get mighty interesting. Roxanne McKay, a cardiothoracic surgeon in her 60s who has volunteered on the trail for two years in a row, said the post-dinner fireside chats ranged from "previous trail projects, the Vietnam War, and Peace Corps experiences in Uzbekistan to opinions on stock investments and the latest camping gear."

Best of all, you get the chance to make history, to open a trail that accesses the wildest and most remote parts of our country. You'll get a glimpse of the West as it was when Lewis and Clark traversed its wild tracts, before our overdeveloped,

THE BIG LEAGUE OF HIKING

Hiking the Continental Divide Trail is not for the weak of heart. It's remote and wild, posing numerous hazards. Watch out for everything from grizzly bears and charging moose to fickle weather complete with lightning strikes. On large stretches of the trail, you'll be above timberline. One hiker joked that his friends argued about who would get dibs on his gear once his body was found—if his body was found.

WHY THIS EFFORT
IS IMPORTANT

Eighty percent of Americans live in cities and urban areas. The Continental Divide Trail is a way of giving urban dwellers a place to connect to the wilderness.

overstimulated society decided to turn every other mountain into a ski resort or a condominium development.

Volunteer opportunities are plentiful. If you choose one of the many organized projects (they range from building a new trail on Berthoud Pass in Colorado to replacing a bridge in Bridger Wilderness in Wyoming), you can sign up to be a crew leader, a crew chef (you'll get a budget and lots of backcountry cooking gear), or just one of the gofers that rakes up underbrush, clears out rocks and roots, and helps inventory the trail.

Or maybe you'd rather sign up for CDTA's Explorer Program, which invites volunteers to scout the backcountry for new routes. In other words, you'll literally explore virgin territory. Heather Gordon, for example, recently blazed a new 15-mile segment between Big Spring and Antelope Spring in the Cibola National Forest of New Mexico. Before her work, hikers on the trail were forced to take a forestry road they shared with diesel-belching logging trucks.

Although you will be responsible for getting yourself to the designated meeting place (you'll get a letter explaining everything once you register), there is no cost to volunteer on one of the CDTA projects.

HOW TO GET IN TOUCH
Continental Divide Trail Alliance, P.O. Box 628, Pine, CO 80470, 888-909-2382 or 303-838-3760, www.cdtrail.org.

help out on the blackfeet reservation

BROWNING, MONTANA

Occasionally in life, you get to do something amazing.
—Michele Gran, cofounder of Global Volunteers

26 The Native American story is full of tragedy, as various tribes were pushed onto reservations to subsist and generally be forgotten. Global Volunteers offers a unique weeklong stint to learn more about these disregarded cultures and peoples. Specifically, every year, the organization sends nine or ten teams to the Blackfeet Reservation in northwestern Montana. Each project is different—"We try to do what the communities ask us to do," says Barb DeGroot, spokesperson for Global Volunteers—but you can know that you're helping out a strong and resilient Native American tribe that faces geographic and social isolation, poverty, and loss of cultural traditions. "In many respects," DeGroot says, "volunteering on the Blackfeet Reservation is like experiencing the struggles of a developing country right here in the United States."

Since 1999, Global Volunteers has done all sorts of things on the reservation, from landscaping and making playgrounds to building community centers and befriending at-risk youth. And the Blackfeet warmly welcome the Global Volunteer participants to partake of their heritage. Volunteers are often invited to participate in sweat lodges, powwows, and other Blackfeet ceremonies. You can even swim in their beautiful, pure rivers.

Global Volunteers organizes international volunteers in 20 countries. And it all started because of a honeymoon. In December 1979, Michele Gran and Bud Philbrook were planning a barefoot honeymoon cruise in the Caribbean. "It was the era of the Vietnamese boat people," Philbrook recalls. "Michele didn't want to play while people were on the same water, fighting for their lives." So they compromised: five days at Disney World, Philbrook's childhood dream, and five days in rural Guatemala, helping villagers obtain funds for an irrigation project.

WHILE YOU'RE IN THE NEIGHBORHOOD

You may have heard of Glacier National Park. Well, all those pristine forests, alpine meadows, rugged mountains, lakes, and 700 miles of trails used to be Blackfeet land. The tribe sold the 1,013,572 acres of this amazing national park to the U.S. government in 1896 for a paltry $1.5 million, 25 times less than the price tag on Brad Pitt and Jennifer Aniston's former Beverly Hills home.

After the local newspaper wrote a story about their unusual honeymoon, people started hounding them for info: How can we do the same thing? In 1984, Bud and Michelle established Global Volunteers to provide people with an opportunity to make a difference in the lives of others around the globe. Since then, they have hooked up more than 20,000 volunteers with hundreds of projects, ranging from building schools in Ghana to caring for orphans in Romania to teaching English to kids in China.

Individual costs for Global Volunteer trips range from $795 for this weeklong program on the Blackfeet Reservation to as much as $2,750 for international programs. The tax-deductible fee includes food, lodging, and ground transportation. Volunteers pay their own way to their destinations.

HOW TO GET IN TOUCH

Global Volunteers, 375 E. Little Canada Road, St. Paul, MN 55117, 800-487-1074, www.globalvolunteers.org.

teach english to villagers in mexico

MAZUNTE, MEXICO

Nobody made a greater mistake than he who did nothing because he could do only a little.
—Edmund Burke, British statesman

27 It's easy to spout off about ecology and conservation and saving the whales when you live in the developed world. But what do you do when your entire livelihood depends on an endangered species?

Case in point: Mazunte, Mexico. For centuries, the families in this little Pacific coast town lived off the now illegal sea turtle and turtle egg trade. They're willing to admit that the turtle deserves to be saved, but that begs a pretty important question: How are they going to feed their families? When the turtle slaughterhouse was closed in 1990, the year the Mexican government officially banned the killing of sea turtles, it was apparent to everyone that something had to give.

Enter ecotourism. Why not earn a living selling services—tours, food, lodging—to rich gringos who want to save turtles?

NO MORE TURTLE SOUP

Seven of the eight known sea turtle species (all threatened or endangered) nest on the coastline in southern Oaxaca. The state of Oaxaca also has 53 percent of the whole indigenous population in Mexico, with half of its population living close to the poverty line. A third of them still speak a native language.

So far, the scheme is working. The turtles are making a comeback, and tourists are paying five dollars a head (not a shabby sum in the state of Oaxaca) to visit the Centro Mexicano de la Tortuga, an aquarium-research facility right on the beach. And the admission price doesn't scratch the surface of the amounts these ecotourists are willing to pay for meals and lodging and tours through the mangrove swamps.

So what's the problem? Well, most of the locals don't speak English. That's not an issue when capturing and slaughtering the *tortugas*, but tourists like to be able to communicate—at least a little—with the folks who rent them their cabanas and feed them their shrimp pizza. And that's where you can help. Volunteers, who sign up for two-week trips (or can stay longer if they choose), tutor locals in how to communicate with their customers.

The volunteer organization that sponsors these trips, i-to-i, specializes in teaching English. The international organization was started in 1994 by Deirdre Bounds, a 40-something British backpacker who taught English in Japan, China, and Greece before coming home to her one-bedroom apartment to wonder "What am I going to do with the rest of my life?" She decided to go for her dream, which was helping others go "eye to eye" with fascinating cultures and travelers. Since then, Bounds's i-to-i has trained more than 15,000 people in TEFL (Teaching English as a Foreign Language) and organized more than 500 service projects in 23 countries.

On this trip, in addition to teaching English, you'll get the chance to work at a crocodile nursery in the nearby beach village of Ventanilla. Two miles west of Mazunte, Playa Ventanilla is a former coconut plantation with a beach that leads

WHILE YOU'RE IN THE NEIGHBORHOOD

Playa Zipolite, a town just a few miles east from Mazunte, is famous for having the only "officially sanctioned" nude beach in Mexico. This mile-long beach was pretty quiet in the 1970s, when it was visited by few but adventurous campers and back-to-the-landers, but it has grown in recent years. There's even Internet service and a yoga studio. Be careful: *Zipolite* is supposedly a Zapotec word that means "beach of the dead," a name inspired by the strong surf and undertow.

You can also take a tour of Cosmeticos Naturales de Mazunte (S. de S.S. Mazunte, Sta. Maria Tonameca, Oaxaca, 01-958-583-9656), a progressive cosmetics cooperative in Mazunte that uses unendangered local plants to make creams, shampoos, and body oils. Created by the founder of the Body Shop to stimulate sustainable agriculture, this cute little palm-shaded adobe factory has replaced dozens of jobs lost by the closing of the town's sole employer—Mexico's largest sea turtle slaughterhouse. And when the cosmetics factory became successful, its workers invested in other fair-trade and ecological projects in the area, including a chocolate-processing plant and a visitor center for the Ventanilla cooperative's crocodile farm.

all the way to Puerto Escondido, a famous surfing town in southern Oaxaca. After 1997's Hurricane Pauline devastated the area, 25 families settled in Ventanilla and started a cooperative. Not only do they give tours of their crocodile and iguana nurseries, but they've also started a community-owned restaurant, El Maíz Azul (Blue Corn), and a dugout-boat tour operation that takes tourists through the mangrove swamp.

i-to-i offers more than 500 other volunteer projects around the world, many centering around teaching English as a second language. Other i-to-i projects focus on community development (working with street children in the Philippines, for example), sports (coaching a soccer team in Costa Rica, say), conservation (preserving and protecting dolphins in South Africa, perhaps), and health (working in a prenatal care unit in Honduras, for instance).

The cost for the Mazunte trip is $1,165 for two weeks (with additional weeks available for $265) and includes TEFL instruction, two meals a day, and lodging in a community bungalow.

HOW TO GET IN TOUCH
i-to-i North America, 190 E. Ninth Avenue, Suite 350, Denver, CO 80203, 800-985-4864, www.i-to-i.com.

work on an organic farm

HAWAII

You should bring an open mind,
a sense of tolerance, a desire to help.
—Fran Whittle, WWOOF organizer

28 Whether you want to pick orchids, harvest coffee beans, or study the medicinal value of noni, a Polynesian shrub, consider a volunteer vacation with **WWOOF** Hawaii. While it sounds suspiciously canine, **WWOOF** actually stands for World-Wide Opportunities on Organic Farms. It's an international organization that assists travelers in visiting farms around the world.

In return for a few hours' work each day, WWOOFers, as volunteers like to call themselves, get free room and board and the chance to learn about organic farming in some of the most beautiful spots of the world. For some, being a **WWOOFer** is simply a cheap way to travel; others do it to learn sustainable-farming techniques, while for some it's an opportunity to meet "real" people.

Whatever the motivation, it's a win-win for everyone involved. Volunteers get firsthand experience of organic farming and gardening, and the hosts get much needed help. Since organic farms shun artificial fertilizers and pesticides, there's lots of extra labor involved. Your three to six hours a day of weeding, composting, planting, fencing, milking, feeding, or anything else your host family might need comes in handy. Plus, it's the perfect forum for organic growers to share their passion for natural foods.

PERKS OF WWOOF

- Travel to some of the most beautiful parts of Hawaii for far less than you'd pay for a hotel on Waikiki Beach.
- Learn skills that will last a lifetime.
- Come home fitter than you've ever been.
- Eat the most amazing food on Earth, all homegrown or homemade.
- Feel good knowing that by supporting organic gardening you're contributing to the health of the planet.

WWOOF was started in 1971 when a London secretary recognized the need for city folks like herself to experience the countryside. She organized a trial weekend at a farm in Sussex (WWOOF used to stand for Working Weekends on Organic Farms, among other things; see sidebar) for four people she met through a classified ad. It was a rousing success, and WWOOF quickly spread from England to Canada, Australia, New Zealand, Italy, Germany, Austria, the United States, and many other countries. Now, there are even host farms in Slovenia, Uganda, the Czech Republic, Turkey, and Ghana. Although there are loosely followed international guidelines, each country hosts its own list of farms and runs its operation separately.

WWOOF Hawaii was launched by the organizers of WWOOF Canada. There's also a WWOOF USA covering the rest of the United States if you'd rather work on the mainland. Hawaii, however, with the perfect growing climate, offers endless possibilities and a wide variety of farms. All told, there are more than a hundred organic farms, ranging from large plantations to small community gardens, located on five Hawaiian islands.

On Maui, for example, you can work on a tropical flower garden in the middle of the rain forest or on a bamboo farm that doubles as a meditation-and-retreat center. On Kauai, you can work on a small goat-cheese dairy farm or on a farm that runs a whole foods co-op. The Big Island offers the chance to work on the largest organic coffee farm in the United States or a 50-acre oceanside property that produces Hawaiian awa (also known as kava), used to make an age-old herbal drink with soothing effects, and noni, the fruit of which is believed by many to have healing properties. On Oahu, you can live in a barn and help grow avocados, bananas, and citrus or live in a 300-square-foot studio and help grow and sell a gourmet salad mix. Accommodations range

WHAT'S IN A NAME?

When the name WWOOF was innocently coined in 1971, it wasn't imagined that the word "work" would cause such serious problems for immigration authorities, who in some countries view WWOOF as a clandestine migrant worker organization. The WW part of the name was changed from Working Weekends to Willing Workers (when it grew past weekends) to the now accepted, World-Wide Opportunities. The phrase "to WWOOF" has become an accepted part of the vernacular in Europe and North America.

from an oceanfront cabin with mostly windows to a mosquito-proof tree house overlooking a waterfall.

To become a WWOOfer, simply fill out the application on the WWOOF Hawaii website and send $20 to the listed address. Upon receipt, organizers will send you a booklet with contact information for all the farms. Once you've got the list, sift through it and decide whether you want to pick nuts, keep bees, harvest medicinal herbs, grow flowers, or make soap and essential oils. In return for several hours work a day, you'll get accommodations (some hosts also offer meals), as much fruit as you can eat, and the chance to experience Hawaii far off the beaten track.

You're in charge of setting up the details. Most host farms welcome volunteers for a week or longer. Some require a minimum of two weeks. No farming experience necessary, but it does help to have a willingness to learn and to laugh.

HOW TO GET IN TOUCH
WWOOF Hawaii, 4429 Carlson Road, Nelson, BC V1L 6X3, Canada, 250-354-4417, www.wwoofhawaii.org.

create costumes for a historic outdoor theater

DANVILLE, KENTUCKY

I never used a blueprint. I would just put up a board and start nailing.
—Eben C. Henson, founder of the Pioneer Playhouse

29 In 1951, there were only two states with official performing arts commissions: New York and Kentucky. The Kentucky Arts Council led the country in progressive arts planning, thanks to a funky outdoor theater in the unlikely town of Danville (pop. 15,477).

It all started in 1950 when Col. Eben C. Henson, a Danville native who had briefly studied acting in New York, decided to turn a 200-acre cornfield into the Pioneer Playhouse. Lacking sufficient funds to build even so much as a stage, Henson talked a state mental hospital into hiring him to produce plays while he scrounged up used and abandoned materials for his theater. Often joking that he was the country's first recycler, Henson traded four bottles of rye whiskey for the main timber beams, scavenged lights from an ice-cream parlor, and somehow managed to incorporate a couple of World War II army barracks into the playhouse. He even hired prisoners from the local county jail to help him lay the first foundations.

His tenaciousness paid off. In the 1950s and '60s, Pioneer Playhouse became known as the "King of Summer Stocks." Although Henson passed away in 2004, the Pioneer Playhouse is going strong nearly six decades after its founding.

Every summer from early June to mid-August, Pioneer Playhouse stages five plays in ten weeks—and indeed they're still scrounging. The theater depends entirely on volunteers to make costumes, hang posters, usher, assist backstage, and basically do everything that needs doing to make sure the five-play season goes off without a hitch.

Every April, Henson's daughter Holly, a stand-up comedian in Minneapolis and the current artistic director, goes to New

BEFORE PULP FICTION

In 1969, when he was only 15, John Travolta appeared at Pioneer Playhouse in *The Ephraim McDowell Story*, an original play about a 19th-century Kentucky surgeon. Other actors who honed their skills at Pioneer include Lee Majors, Bo Hopkins, and Jim Varney. The real star at Pioneer Playhouse, though, was Colonel Henson, the string-tie wearing charmer who staged more than 300 plays. Other accomplishments from his wide-ranging and storied career include working as an alligator wrestler in Silver Springs, Florida; acting in dozens of movies, notably *Raintree County, April Love,* and *The Treasure of Matacumbe;* and performing in plays with Tony Curtis, Bea Arthur, and Harry Belafonte while studying drama in New York. In 2003, PBS aired a documentary about Henson and his world-famous Pioneer Playhouse.

York to audition actors for the summer season (they're the only ones who get paid). As Holly is quick to point out, "It's not for everyone. We're definitely off the beaten path. I always say we're looking for the anti-divas of the theater world."

Volunteers come in from around the country (one volunteer has been driving here from Nevada for five years), and they either camp at the campground on the 200-acre site or land a spot in one of the theater's rustic rooms. In return for four or five hours help a day Thursday through Saturday, they get three meals a day (except Sunday, when the cook gets a day off) and free tickets to all five performances. An outdoor preshow dinner of fried chicken, barbecue brisket, corn pudding, green beans, and other southern delights is served.

Besides the campground, the Pioneer Playhouse theater complex includes a drama school, a museum, a re-creation of an 18th-century Kentucky village, and a box office that was once the train station in MGM's Civil War epic *Raintree County*. There is no charge to volunteer at the Pioneer Playhouse.

HOW TO GET IN TOUCH
Pioneer Playhouse, 840 Stanford Road, Danville, KY 40422, 859-236-2747, www.pioneerplayhouse.com.

build a website
of ancient plants

WASHINGTON, D.C.

Most of the drugs currently available are derivatives of ancient medications.
—Irwin Ziment, clinician and author

30 The famous ancient Greek physician Hippocrates (author of the Hippocratic Oath that doctors today still take) accumulated a great deal of medical information in his lifetime, but his findings could not be widely disseminated until some 1,700 years after his death when Johann Gutenberg invented the printing press (around 1440). Not surprisingly, some of the first books to be published after the printing press became available were treatises on medicinal plants or "herbals" spanning the centuries back to classical times.

On this Earthwatch-sponsored expedition called "Behind the Scenes: Medicinal Plants of Antiquity," volunteers help record and catalog these ancient books, many of which are the basis of Western pharmacology. The program recovers therapies that were practiced by physicians from antiquity through the Middle Ages.

Working alongside principal investigator Dr. Alain Touwaide, a historian of sciences at the Smithsonian Institution (all Earthwatch projects are led by "principal investigators"), you can help build a website that features hundreds of rare and fragile books. This invaluable body of knowledge not only protects biodiversity and preserves ancient folklore but also has the potential to open new paths for medical research.

Although your home base will be the Smithsonian's National Museum of Natural History, the data you'll be compiling was collected by Touwaide over the course of 30 years' research. It comes from archaeological sites (such as inscriptions with cures from temples in Corinth, Greece), historical books (such as the plague of Athens as detailed in a books by historian Thucydides), and medical and scientific works by such authors as Hippocrates, Galen, and Pliny. Touwaide has also offered Earthwatch expeditions to Rome, where more than 150 volunteers inventoried ancient books from the Rare Book Room at the National Library of Rome.

SO WHAT IS EARTHWATCH?

"You don't have to know anything when you arrive,
but you'll feel like a Rhodes Scholar when you go home."
—Earthwatch motto

Founded in 1971, Earthwatch has supported more than 1,300 field research projects in 119 countries. These projects, run by respected members of the scientific community, have addressed problems ranging from public health to declining biodiversity. Earthwatch-supported work in the Peruvian rain forest canopy, for example, revised estimates for the total number of insect species from 1.5 million upward to 6 million. A decade-long botanical study in the highland forests of western Cameroon uncovered 50 new endemic plant species.

Earthwatch teams work in some of the most interesting places on Earth, oftentimes in areas inaccessible to tourists. Sites range from Inner Mongolia to the Outer Hebrides, from Hudson Bay to Uruguy. Most of these intense, hands-on research projects last 10 to 14 days, but there are also one-week, three-week, and weekend projects.

Accommodations on Earthwatch projects range from condos to hammocks. On one expedition to Mongolia, volunteers shared a communal brick bed in the home of a Mongolian goatherd. There may be hot showers or only a bucket of cold water. There may be private bathrooms or pit toilets. Food also runs the gamut from cheese sandwiches and an apple to fare from a four-star Hungarian restaurant with an extensive wine cellar.

Each project includes a detailed expedition briefing that explains logistics, as well as a history of the expedition, its research mission, its goals, the background of the researcher, reference maps, and a recommended reading list.

Volunteers on this stateside project will scan digital images, reformat slides, write descriptions of books, gather biographic material about authors, and type texts on significant plants. Your donation for the Medicinal Plants of Antiquity program is $849. Lunches and several dinners are included on this five-day experience, but you'll be responsible for securing your own accommodations. In the expedition brief, you'll be given names and numbers of several nearby options, including a B&B that charges prices starting at $15 a night.

HOW TO GET IN TOUCH
Earthwatch Institute, 3 Clock Tower Place, Maynard, MA 01754, 978-461-0081, www.earthwatch.org.

introduce a street kid to the wilderness

WILDLANDS ACROSS THE COUNTRY

As a reward, we saw our familiar trails through the eyes of kids who'd never heard the wind whistling through the trees overhead and whose idea of a Saturday outing was going to the mall. It was a gift of perspective that bagging all the 4,000-footers in New England could not provide.
—Craig Kelley, volunteer for the Massachusetts Sierra Club

31 John Muir, founder of the Sierra Club, believed that if you want people to go to bat for the environment, you've got to get them out into the wilderness. He said that if people "could be got into the woods, even for once, to hear the trees speak for themselves, all difficulties in the way of forest preservation would vanish."

The Sierra Club has taken its founder's advice to heart, offering hundreds of trips into the wilderness each year. A quick perusal of its website shows canoe trips, bicycle trips, dogsled trips, sailing trips, trips for families, trips for seniors, trips for activists, and on and on.

Although all their outings advocate the "exploration, enjoyment and protection of the planet," their service trips, roughly 90 of them per year, send volunteers across the country to do everything from researching whale calving grounds in Maui to assisting with prairie restoration in Iowa to building a trail along Arkansas rivers. The Sierra Club estimates that in man-hours alone, it contributes nearly a half million dollars a year to work projects in state and federal land agencies.

In terms of changing the mindset of the planet, the Sierra Club's Inner City Outings (ICO) may be one of the most important volunteer opportunities in the organization's busy lineup. Volunteers for ICO introduce inner-city kids—kids who probably have never seen a mountain or a stream, kids who spend all their free time on a computer or a playground—to the majesty of the Great Outdoors. These trips not only introduce wilderness newbies to the beauty of wildlands but

HOW I WROTE OFF MY SUMMER VACATION

Since some of the fees you pay for volunteer vacations are used to support research and other noble causes, they may qualify as a charitable contribution. That means the vacation is tax deductible. In fact, if you happen to be in the 28 percent tax bracket, Uncle Sam will foot more than a fourth of the cost of your volunteer vacation. As you may suspect, the IRS isn't keen on subsidizing fun and games, which is why volunteer organizations often recoil when their volunteer projects are called "tax-deductible vacations."

There's no question about the deductibility of the portion of the fee that supports the research. But travel costs qualify only if there's "no significant element of personal pleasure or vacation." Not that they'll disqualify you if you happen to have a good time. What it means is that if you tour the country before or afterward, you forfeit being able to deduct transportation costs.

---

also teach them survival skills, teamwork, and self-esteem. Kids who have rarely seen anything but concrete and man-made buildings learn what it's like to hike a trail, read a map, and get to the top of a peak, gaining an appreciation of the need for preservation of the environment.

Although many inner-city outings are one-day trips (hikes in a nearby state park, afternoons at a farm to see where milk comes from, day trips to a beach to collect shells), ICO volunteers also organize multiday backpacking trips, canoeing trips, and cross-country ski trips. All these community outreach trips are organized through local ICO groups.

On one ICO from New York City, for example, volunteers took a group of kids camping on Fire Island. They spent the weekend swimming, shell hunting, playing catch with Frisbees and baseballs, building a sand sphinx, and inventing games such as saltwater *Jeopardy!* where anyone who answers questions wrong gets dunked. Another ICO in San Francisco organized a nature photography workshop for kids at a housing project.

The Sierra Club San Francisco Bay chapter started the first ICO group in 1971 when it realized that many of San Francisco's kids had never even seen Golden Gate Park, let alone areas outside the city. Today, there's a dedicated core of volunteers in 50 cities across the United States. They work with local schools and social service agencies, and it's not just kids in housing projects who benefit, as volunteer Kate Mytron, founder of the ICO in New Orleans, emphasizes: "It's so incredibly rewarding to rediscover what it feels like to see frogs for the first time. The volunteers still talk about the good time we had."

To be a volunteer for Sierra Club's Inner City Outings, contact your local club. A list can be accessed at www.sierraclub.org/ico/national/websites.asp. In Atlanta, for example, the ICO group hosts nearly 30 trips a year, monthly meetings, and an annual fundraiser. Each volunteer must fill out an application, undergo a background check, and agree to the rules of the individual organizations.

There is no charge to volunteer with ICO, but for insurance purposes, each volunteer is required to join the Sierra Club, a $25 fee.

HOW TO GET IN TOUCH
Sierra Club Foundation/ICO, 85 Second Street, 2nd Floor, San Francisco, CA 94105, 415-977-5628, www.sierraclub.org/ico.

save the earth!

CAZADERO, CALIFORNIA

We love our wildlands. We believe that to know its beauty and feel its inner music is a human need, a need important to our hearts as well as our heritage.
—Wildlands Studies website

32 The buzz about the environment is everywhere: SUVs are polluting the air, accelerating glacial melt is threatening the sea level, species are dying out faster than you can say "Save the environment." Rather than standing by and wondering whether it's all hype or not, there's a unique opportunity to actually *do* something with Wildlands Studies.

Sponsored by the University of California, Santa Barbara, this organization has been conducting unbiased environmental research since 1980, research that addresses critical issues facing our wildlands and our wildlife. And, like Uncle Sam, they want you. This prestigious outfit invites interested citizens to join their backcountry field projects to help them "search for answers to important environmental problems."

Although many of the "field associates," as team members are called, are environmental studies students getting college credit, each of Wildlands Studies projects is open to any volunteer interested in environmental research. In fact, the only criterion for joining one of the ten or so yearly projects in the United States (they also conduct field research in several foreign countries) is submitting a statement of health.

If you can do that, you can help research scientists conduct field research on endangered species in Yellowstone National Park, on glaciers in Alaska's Wrangell Mountains, or on the changes in Hawaii's island ecosystems, to name just a few of Wildlands Studies ongoing projects. You can choose from more than 30 wildlife, wildland, and wildwater projects examining wildlife preservation, resource management, conservation ecology, and cultural sustainability issues.

"These projects provide boundless opportunities to observe patterns of wild nature without the usual controls that are imposed on a classroom or laboratory exercise," says Chris Carpenter, a Wildlands Studies program leader.

BEARLY THERE

When Lewis and Clark explored the West in the early 1800s, an estimated 50,000 grizzly bears roamed the wildlands between the Pacific Ocean and the Great Plains. Today, now that millions of humans have taken over those same lands, the grizzly population is down to an estimated 1,200 to 1,400.

In 1975, the U.S. Fish and Wildlife Service listed the grizzly bear as a threatened species in the Lower 48, placing the remaining six populations (of the original 37) under federal protection.

The grizzly is one of several species that Wildlands Studies observes in their annual "Wildlife Survival: The Yellowstone Endangered Species Project," along with the gray wolf, the bison, and the mountain goat.

Research teams are small (no more than 15 team members) and tend to fill up quickly. You'll be out in the field the entire time (no coffee shops or Internet access) and, while there's plenty of time for relaxation, you'll endure long days, uphill trails, and weather that is sometimes capricious. But look at it this way: It's a great chance to stand up for a noble cause.

No previous fieldwork experience is necessary. Requisite skills are taught on site. Research projects range from two weeks to all summer, and prices range from $700 to $1,700.

HOW TO GET IN TOUCH
Wildlands Studies, 3 Mosswood Circle, Cazadero, CA 95421, 707-632-5665, www.unex.ucsb.edu/wildlands.

build a house to replace a shack

MEXICO & WORLDWIDE

> I've published books, been on national TV, flown planes,
> met celebrities, built a car from a kit, had my picture in the
> *New York Times* . . . but on my deathbed, I'm betting I'm going to say,
> "Boy, I wish I'd built more Habitat houses!"
> —Chris Goodrich, coleader of a Global Village build in Isla, Mexico

33 Ever wonder why so many Mexicans try to cross the U.S. border? The average wage for more than half of Mexico's working population is less than $30 a month. Try paying a mortgage on that. For that matter, try buying meals—even one—for a family of five. No wonder more than ten million (or one out of every ten) Mexicans live in a house that can't withstand wind or rain, much less a hurricane.

Since 1988, Habitat for Humanity Mexico has been working to correct the disparity. In that time, its volunteers have built more than 16,000 homes in the country, many of these through the Global Village program.

Global Village volunteers enlist for building blitzes lasting anywhere from one to three weeks in Habitat locations around the globe. They work hand in hand with future homeowners and volunteers from all backgrounds, races, and religions. Global Village volunteers often describe their experience as life changing.

Every Global Village trip is different, but the itineraries are flexible and balanced between work, rest, and free time. Most teams spend a few days taking in the local culture. On an eight-day build in Isla, Mexico, for example, volunteers flew to Veracruz on a Saturday, toured the Catemaco Lake area on Sunday, built homes Monday through Friday, and then toured the Las Tuxtlas rain forests and Olmec ruins on the second Saturday before returning home Sunday.

Chris Goodrich, one of the leaders of that Global Village trip, claims he suffers from "infectious Habititis," an ailment that he describes as a "disease that lets you see giving *is* getting, that you can build your own American dream by helping less

THAT'S FORMER MR. PRESIDENT TO YOU

Dustin Hoffman, Robin Williams, and Desmond Tutu are just three Habitat for Humanity volunteers whose names you probably recognize. But the most famous Habitat volunteer is undoubtedly Jimmy Carter, who every year leads a work project for the organization. The former President first became involved with Habitat in 1984 when he and a group of volunteers renovated a six-story building in New York City. Every year since, he has donated a week of his time. He and his wife, Rosalynn, have lent their construction skills on a build in Lonavala, India, Los Angeles, Detroit, South Korea, Mexico, Alabama, and South Africa, to name a few.

lucky people build theirs." A full-time volunteer, Goodrich says, "I've been to the mall and drooled over those big-screen TVs, those flat-panel plasma 'entertainment centers' . . . but then I look at the price tag and say, 'Man, I could build a house in the Dominican Republic for that!'" Goodrich has even written a book, *Faith Is a Verb: On the Home Front with Habitat for Humanity and the Campaign to Rebuild America (and the World)*," about his time volunteering.

Since it was started in 1976, Habitat for Humanity's volunteers have built more than 200,000 homes in nearly a hundred countries. Millard Fuller, the nonprofit's founder, is the quintessential volunteer. A millionaire at age 29, he realized that all the money wasn't making him happy so he gave it all away and decided to look for a new focus. After several years at Koinonia Farm, a Christian community near Americus, Georgia, Fuller moved to Zaire and began building homes. He came back to the United States in 1976 and started Habitat, whose mission is to eliminate poverty housing worldwide.

The cost of Global Village trips depends on the area visited, the Habitat for Humanity host affiliate, and the length of the trip. Usually a 7- to 14-day trip (including everything except airfare) runs between $1,000 and $2,200. The trip to Mexico described above cost $1,210.

HOW TO GET IN TOUCH
Global Village, Habitat for Humanity International, 121 Habitat Street, P.O. Box 369, Americus, GA 31709, 800-422-4828 or 229-924-6935, www.habitat.org.

excavate george washington's whiskey distillery

MOUNT VERNON, VIRGINIA

I learn something new about George Washington every time
I volunteer with the archaeologists!
—Betsy Alexander, archaeology volunteer

34 You'd think by now they'd have already excavated everything on George Washington's Mount Vernon estate. Yet, according to Eleanor Breen, an archaeologist and volunteer coordinator for Mount Vernon archaeological projects, there will be artifacts to dig up for years to come.

If it weren't for volunteers, much of the 500-acre site (in the 18th century, Mount Vernon comprised 8,000 acres) would still be a mystery. Since 1987 when a permanent archaeology program was established on the estate, volunteers (with the help of their professional mentors) have uncovered everything from tobacco pipes and wig curlers to forks made from animal bones.

All of this was accomplished without help from your tax dollars. Mount Vernon receives no funding from the U.S. government. Instead, the "First Home" is maintained by the Mount Vernon Ladies' Association, the oldest historic preservation organization in the United States.

The association was founded in 1853 by Ann Pamela Cunningham, a South Carolina woman disabled after falling from a horse. Cunningham's mother, while taking a tour down the Potomac River, was shocked to see Mount Vernon's peeling paint, overgrown weeds, and columns so rotten that the famous portico was propped up with a sailing mast. She wrote a letter to her daughter describing the unacceptable condition of the first President's home, exhorting her to do something.

The governments of both the United States and Virginia had already turned down the offer to purchase Mount Vernon, and there was even some talk of demolishing the home. Cunningham decided that if the men of the country (at that

DIG IT!

The archaeological excavation at Mount Vernon is one of more than 250 field-work projects listed in the bulletin put out each year by the Archaeological Institute of America. If you want to volunteer for an archaeological excavation, the *Archaeological Fieldwork Opportunities Bulletin* is the best place to start. It lists hundreds of excavations from a Stone Age site in South Africa to a site on Easter Island in Chile. Each listing provides an in-depth description, including accommodations, price, and contact information. The yearly volume can be accessed on the institute's website (www.archaeological.org); a paperback version is also available each year from Oxbox/David Brown Books, 800-791-9354.

time, women didn't even have the right to vote) wouldn't renovate the historic site, the women would. Within five years, her women's group raised $200,000 and bought the mansion, the outbuildings, and 200 acres. There's an 1858 photo on their website that shows the dilapidated state of the famous home when they took over.

And take over they did. Using donations, private grants, admissions fees to the grounds (more than a million people show up every year), and volunteer help, this savvy outfit has restored 20 structures and 50 acres of gardens as they existed in 1799 (the year Washington died), the tombs of George and Martha, Washington's greenhouse, and a collection of artifacts dug up by staff archaeologists, interns, and volunteers. In late 2006, a state-of-the-art orientation center, museum, and education center opened with much fanfare. The museum boasts 23 galleries filled with fascinating multimedia exhibits, including a "forensic lab" that shows how the forensically correct figures of Washington displayed throughout the galleries were created.

The Archaeology Department at Mount Vernon has a wide range of volunteer opportunities involving both field and laboratory work. Needless to say, excavations vary from year to year. A recent project found volunteers processing and writing reports on artifacts dug up from Washington's distillery. In the 1700s, it was one of the country's largest whiskey distilleries, using five stills and a boiler and producing 11,000 gallons of whiskey a year.

Volunteers have also excavated Mount Vernon's laundry room, gristmill, gardens, a dung repository, and many other sites on the property. The Archaeology Lab exhibits finds from the Slave Quarters, the Blacksmith Shop, and the South Grove Midden. Recovered artifacts provide clues about the daily life of not only

ONE-DOLLAR PORTRAIT

Anyone who has ever seen a dollar bill knows what our first president looked like. Or do they? When the Mount Vernon Ladies' Association wanted exact likenesses of good old George for the new education center, they turned to a forensic anthropologist to figure out how the great general might have looked at ages 19, when he was a frontier surveyor; 45, when he served as commander-in-chief of the Continental Army; and 57, when he was sworn in as president. Although anthropologist Jeffrey H. Schwartz wasn't allowed to dig up Washington's bones, the easiest way to tackle such a task, he was able to reconstruct the first leader by examining his false teeth (on display at the museum—they were made of human teeth, ivory, and ox bone), a mask of Washington created by a French sculptor, letters, diaries, and old clothes. Turns out the familiar Gilbert Stuart portrait of Washington, called the "Athenaeum" portrait, the likeness of which was used on the one-dollar note, is not exactly accurate. Washington had a pockmark on his left cheek from the smallpox that afflicted him at 19. He also had taut lips from holding in dentures and, as he grew older, a chin slightly longer on one side than the other caused by bone loss associated with tooth loss.

Washington's family, who owned the property from 1726 until the Mount Vernon Ladies Association took it over in 1853, but also the slaves, craftspeople, and laborers who lived and worked on the plantation.

There is no fee to volunteer. Although the Archaeology Lab doesn't provide housing for its volunteers, there are many nearby hotels. Volunteers can work at excavation projects any Monday through Friday and will be given 50 percent off meals at the Mount Vernon Inn, the on-site restaurant serving typical colonial fare.

HOW TO GET IN TOUCH
Mount Vernon Ladies' Association, 3200 Mount Vernon Memorial Highway, Mount Vernon, VA 22121, 703-799-6314, www.mountvernon.org.

EXPLORATIONS IN TRAVEL

walk & feed abandoned pets

PUERTO RICO

There is lots to be done to make the world a better place.
No one can do everything, but each of us can do something.
Find what moves you and act on it.
—Debbie Jacobs, founder and president of Explorations in Travel

35 Vieques, a 21-mile-long island off Puerto Rico, has a population of fewer than 10,000. The abandoned pet population, however, has skyrocketed since the U.S. Navy gave up control of its bombing range there and pulled out on May 1, 2003. The good news is that there is a humane society. The bad news is that, like all humane societies, the Vieques Humane Society is underfunded, understaffed, and under constant pressure to save the growing number of homeless Fidos and Sparkys.

Luckily, Explorations in Travel, a travel company in Guilford, Vermont, organizes volunteers to help the tiny nonprofit. Debbie Jacobs, owner of Explorations in Travel, has a soft spot for pets, and when she first visited Puerto Rico in 1994, she was horrified to see dying dogs on the beaches, homeless kittens, and pet carcasses lying along the road. The first question she asked in Vieques was, "Where is animal welfare?" She was directed to Penny Miller, owner of the Seagate Hotel and a one-eyed basset hound named Jackie (as in Jacqueline Bassette). At that time, Penny was the main volunteer at the Vieques shelter.

At first, Jacobs arranged for the *satos* (Spanish for "street dogs") to be shipped to the mainland United States for adoption through local rescue organizations, but then she had a better idea. Since 1991, she and her husband, John Lee, a language teacher, have been organizing cross-cultural exchanges in Puerto Rico, mainly for students. She and her husband reasoned that as long as students were there experiencing a new culture, being involved in a community, why not have them repair a hiking trail, visit a school, plant some trees—or help build the Vieques Humane Society? Volunteer vacations, or what Jacobs calls "volunteer placements," sprang out of these visits.

CAN YOU SAY "BIOLUMINESCENT"?

After years of protests, the U.S. Navy finally relinquished its bombing range at Vieques Island, turning over its holdings, which covered two-thirds of the laid-back little island, to the U.S. Fish and Wildlife Service. That means Vieques, with its powdery white-sand beaches, will remain largely undeveloped, so when you're not walking dogs for the Humane Society, you'll be able to explore miles of beaches with no buildings, no T-shirt shops, and almost no tourists.

The one place you will find plenty of tourists is at Puerto Mosquito, on a shallow bay that is home to billions of luminescent organisms, a rare species of phytoplankton called *Pyrodinium bahamense,* that light up the waters at night like fireflies. Any underwater movement in the shallow waters of the bay, from waves slapping against a boat to darting schools of fish to a swimmer's simple scissors kick, causes these tiny creatures to glow and leave glittery, luminescent trails. The experience is eerie, and this is one of the few places in the world where you can see such a spectacle.

Now, Explorations in Travel works with volunteers of all ages, organizing volunteer placements in several countries. In Puerto Rico, for example, Jacobs also matches volunteers up with a small conservation group that's working to preserve a Caribbean rain forest.

The unique aspect about working with the Vieques Humane Society is that volunteers get hands-on experience in lots of things they probably wouldn't do back home. Stacy Morris, a volunteer from Seattle who had zero veterinary training before arriving in Puerto Rico, found herself giving injections, assisting with spaying and neutering, and conducting biopsies. She had so much fun that her five-month volunteer placement grew into a year's stay.

According to Jacobs, the volunteer placements offered through Explorations in Travel are designed for independent, self-disciplined folks who want flexibility not typically offered in group travel. Want to extend your two-week or two-month volunteer vacation? Not a problem. Want to come up with your own project? Just name it. In Vieques, for example, Explorations in Travel volunteers helped build and maintain the Humane Society's website. They have also worked in classroom and community education, teaching locals about the importance of sterilization, vaccinations, and heartworm protection.

Explorations in Travel charges a placement fee ranging from $775 to $975. As

Jacobs explains, "If you're only going for a week, it's not economical. But if you're staying for several weeks on up to a month, the price becomes reasonable."

For the placement fee, Jacob will set up all the arrangements with your host and provide you with information on where you'll be living (Volunteers at the Vieques Humane Society stay in a little house near the shelter with a 180-degree view of the ocean), the type of work you'll be doing, recommended clothing, an equipment list, and contact names and numbers.

HOW TO GET IN TOUCH

Explorations in Travel, 2458 River Road, Guilford, VT 05301, 802-257-0152, www.exploretravel.com.

restore a campground in "the bob"

There is one hope of repulsing the tyrannical ambition of civilization to conquer every niche on the whole Earth. That hope is the organization of spirited people who will fight for the freedom of the wilderness.
—Bob Marshall, author, conservationist, and big-time rabble-rouser

36 If your backyard had more than a million acres, you'd probably bring in help, too, to maintain trails and restore campgrounds. The Bob Marshall Foundation, a nonprofit organization that helps the U.S. Forest Service maintain the gargantuan wilderness known locally as "the Bob," organizes about a dozen volunteer trips each year. These day- to weeklong adventures, which start in June and run through November, backpack volunteers into one of the largest protected wilderness areas in the United States. If you add the million acres of the Bob Marshall Wilderness to adjoining Glacier National Park, you're talking a backyard that's roughly the size of Connecticut. Except that in this backyard, you're straddling the Continental Divide in an untrammeled wild vastness filled with high mountain lakes, alpine meadows, crystal clear lakes, remote valleys, and a giant wall that looks an awful lot like the man-made version over in China. The Bob's Chinese Wall, as it's called, towers 1,000 feet above the valley floor. Its limestone cliffs are not quite as long as its counterpart in Asia (that one is 4,000 miles long), but even at 22 miles, we're talking a big wall.

If you haven't figured it out by now, the volunteer trips into the Bob are not for sissies. Roads are outlawed in the Bob, and for miles the only living things, besides you and your fellow volunteers, will be grizzlies, lynx, mountain lions, wolverines, and gray wolves. The trips involve long hikes, camping, and work strenuous enough to give a lumberjack pause. You'll be restoring primitive campgrounds, bushwhacking trails, and removing trees. You'll be working with crosscut saws, axes, Pulaskis, shovels, loppers, and other primitive tools. Just

THEY DON'T MAKE 'EM LIKE THAT ANYMORE

In his short, not-quite-39-year life, Bob Marshall managed to protect 5.4 million acres of American wildland. Marshall, who died in 1939, managed to accomplish an awful lot in four decades. A few of the notches in his belt:

- His 1930 article in *Scientific Monthly* called "The Problem of the Wilderness" is credited with launching the wilderness movement.
- He regularly walked 30 miles a day.
- He made lists and ratings of everything from mountain and baseball statistics to books and girls. In fact, his elaborate rating system for women, with number values for such qualities as intellect, physical ability, interests, and sex appeal, may explain why he remained a bachelor.
- He had two graduate degrees.
- He wrote three books.
- He once departed a Washington soirée by descending the front steps on his hands.
- While visiting a Supreme Court chamber, he executed an impromptu somersault.
- Although he acquired a generous inheritance when his father died, he valued money only for the independence it provided. He never owned a house or a car.
- He climbed his first mountain when he was 14.
- He once climbed 14 Adirondack peaks in one day, and by the time he was 25, he and his brother George had become the first mountaineers to ascend all 46 Adirondack peaks above 4,000 feet.
- He called himself a socialist and believed in the abolition of profit and rent and in government ownership of natural resources. He was arrested for these beliefs and weathered several Red-baiting attacks when he worked as head of the Division of Forestry and Grazing for the Bureau of Indian Affairs.

getting to your work site may mean a hike of 10 or more miles and a 2,000- or 3,000-foot change in elevation.

The website recommends that you can pass the "Moderate Pack Test," a work-capacity test designed by the Forest Service. In a nutshell, it requires you to hike 2 miles in less than 35 minutes while wearing a 25-pound pack.

Look at it this way. The three dozen or so adventure outfitters that arrange trips into the Bob charge upward of $2,000 for a week of camping, while the Bob Marshall Wilderness Foundation will take you in for free. The scenery's the same, the food's pretty much the same (when there aren't any Denny's nearby, trip leaders have little choice but to backpack in the grub), and the accommodations are the same. The only difference, besides the sizable gap in your wallet outlay, is that after a volunteer trip with the foundation, you can pat yourself on the back for helping the world stay a little bit wilder.

"The Bob is one of the last best places in the country," says Shannon Freix, program director for the Bob Marshall Wilderness Foundation. "Unfortunately, because of budget cuts and shrinking resources, the forest service can't maintain all the things they'd like to do. And on these trips, especially at some of the campsite restoration trips, volunteers get to see in a tangible way the impact humans have. It helps keep everything in perspective."

There's no charge for a volunteer vacation in the Bob, but the foundation asks for a $50 deposit that you can either get back at the end of the trip or donate to the foundation's work.

HOW TO GET IN TOUCH
Bob Marshall Wilderness Foundation, P.O. Box 903, Whitefish, MT 59937, 406-863-5411, www.thebmwf.org.

preserve a piece of history

NATIONAL FORESTS NATIONWIDE

> I've never worked so hard, had so much fun, learned so much, or gotten so dirty in just one week! We feel guilty calling these experiences 'do-good vacations' because we have such a great time.
> —Martha Blair, volunteer with Passport in Time

37 Your chance to be a Deadhead has more or less expired. But there's still plenty of time to be a Pithead. That's what volunteers of the U.S. Forest Service's Passport in Time (PIT) program jokingly call themselves. PIT is a volunteer program giving everyday Joes and Janes the chance to assist professional archaeologists and historians in surveying, excavating, and restoring historic and archaeological sites.

Some Pitheads have more than 2,500 volunteer hours under their belt. They literally finish up one project and head to the next. PIT even keeps an honor roll on which volunteers (at last count, more than 350) with lots of contributed time get recognized. Obviously, being a Pithead can be addictive.

Eva and Don Peden of Landers, Wyoming, went on their first dig in 1992 after their daughter sent them a two-line classified ad she'd spotted in the back of a magazine. Now, they go on at least two digs every year and have logged more than 500 hours on the PIT honor roll. They've excavated tepee rings in Wyoming's Thunder Basin National Grasslands, uncovered bison bones in Nebraska, and dug through prehistoric sites in the Black Hills of South Dakota.

Once, while excavating a quarter-master dump at Fort Laramie,

CRASH COURSE

Archaeologists spend four years of college learning some of the skills you can pick up in just one PIT project. Some of the more common Pithead skills:

- Mapping
- GPS usage
- Compass reading
- Oral history gathering
- Rock art restoration
- Historic preservation
- Artifact cataloging

Wyoming, Eva found three rare round-bottom soda bottles. "They designed them that way to keep the corks from drying out," she explains. "Because of the round bottom, they had to be stored on their side."

"It has been an awesome experience," says Eva, who went on to serve two terms as president of the Wyoming Archaeological Foundation. "We have learned so much. The professional archaeologists are so willing to work with volunteers. They're open and friendly and seem to really appreciate the help."

PIT projects, which are listed on the website, vary from year to year. There are usually several dozen listed in a wide variety of states. One year, you could apply to restore an old gold miner's cabin in Colorado, and the next, you could record gravestone data from historical cemeteries in Vermont and New Hampshire. Pitheads have done everything from excavating ancient tools in Mississippi to surveying an old military road in Oregon to stabilizing cliff dwellings in New Mexico. Some projects even throw in the bone of college credit such as the Misty Fjords Monitoring and Inventory Program near Ketchikan, Alaska.

The idea for PIT originated with Gordon Peters, a former Forest Service archaeologist and University of Minnesota–Duluth instructor, who in 1988 ran out of help on a dig in the Superior National Forest. Already, nearby resorts were bringing guests to see "Indiana Jones" at work and when no one signed up for the field school that fateful year, the Forest Service offered to recruit volunteers if Peters would continue the archaeological research. Modeled after a similar program in Ontario, Canada, the regional program went nationwide three years later.

Unlike similar projects sponsored by Earthwatch Institute (see pp. 93–94 and 122–124) and Crow Canyon Archaeological Center (see pp. 198–200), Passport in Time charges no fee, requiring only that participants pay their way to the site. Once your application (downloadable from the PIT website) is approved, you'll get an official PIT passport that project leaders stamp and use to log your volunteer hours. Projects range from two days' to several months' duration.

HOW TO GET IN TOUCH
Passport in Time Clearinghouse, P.O. Box 15728, Rio Rancho, NM 87174, 800-281-9176 or 505-896-0734, www.passportintime.com.

protect america's wild places

WILDLANDS ACROSS THE COUNTRY

It feels great to get out and do some good honest physical labor. You work
in beautiful places, meet interesting people, get relief from the hustle-
bustle of daily life—and fresh perspective on what's really important.
—David Brooks, Wilderness Volunteers team leader

38 If you have a thing about America's wild places, like to backpack,
and could pass a Marine physical (well, almost), consider a volunteer
vacation with Wilderness Volunteers. This organization sends vigorous volunteers
(mainly in their 20s to 40s) into America's national and state parks to repair the
damage done by heedless visitors. They restore hiking trails, clean up debris, plant
strategically located trees and remove not-so-strategically located ones, and take
inventory of plant and wildlife species.

It's a cheap way to backpack America's remotest reaches. Twelve participants
per trip pay their way to the trailhead plus a modest $239 for a week of hearty
chow, good company, and the satisfaction of knowing they're contributing to the
preservation of public lands.

Wilderness Volunteers was founded in 1997 by Debbie Northcutt and a couple
of friends who all worked as coordinators for Sierra Club service projects. "The
Sierra Club kept getting more and more expensive and volunteers kept wondering
why they're paying so much to go out in the sun and sweat," explains Northcutt,
who now serves as executive director. "Plus our trips are much more diverse. We
might get someone from NRA or Ducks Unlimited, something you'd never find on
a Sierra Club trip. I led a trip to the Maroon Bells [Colorado] recently that had a
Mormon housewife, a Navy pilot, and a college president. By the end of the trip,
they were practically best friends."

On another trip, an older volunteer from Ohio looked askance at an 18-year-old
kid with spiked purple hair and piercings. "The guy from Ohio kept asking the kid
why his parents allowed him to walk around like that," Northcutt recalls. "By the
end of the week, however, he was seeking tips from the 18-year-old on how to relate

HOW TO BUY THE PERFECT TENT

- The fewer stakes the better. Stakes are heavy and easy to lose.
- Make sure the fly closes completely and has a vestibule for storing packs and boots out of the rain.
- A three-season tent is plenty. Unless you plan on extreme mountaineering (and you wouldn't be reading this sidebar if you were), you only need a three-season tent, which is much lighter.
- Find a big stuff sack for the tent so that you don't have to kill yourself cramming it into the bag, which could cause damage to the tent.
- Buy the lightest tent that meets your needs and budget.
- Take the sales reps' pitches with a grain of salt.
- The fewer seams on the tent bottom the better.
- Practice setting up your tent in the backyard *before* you're at your campsite.

to his own kids. When people pull together on a common goal, it creates a certain intimacy. By the end of the week of working, living, and cooking meals together, we've created a sort of family."

Wilderness Volunteers organizes about 50 trips a year to such beautiful and exotic places as Utah's Glen Canyon National Recreation Area (where you'll eradicate Russian olive trees along the Escalante River), Idaho's Seven Devils Mountains (where you'll clear deadfall from three high-country trails) and Hawaii's Hakalau Forest National Wildlife Refuge (where you'll plant native saplings). You'll get access to lots of places you'd never see otherwise. Plus, one or two of the seven days are spent exploring natural wonders. On the Denali National Park trip, for example, you'll clear brush from the 8-mile Triple Lakes Trail for five days and then get a free bus pass to view wildlife in the park's interior.

The group's website posts four trip ratings: easy, active, strenuous, and challenging. Take the rankings to heart. In fact, the joke is that the easy trip rating, described on the website as short walks on level terrain with minimal bending and lifting, are like the Easter Bunny and the tooth fairy—they don't exist.

Trips with challenging ratings often involve long hikes with backpacks, significant elevation changes, and occasional canoe portages. If you don't know that portaging means flipping the canoe over and placing it on your shoulders to walk a trail, your head inside with mosquitoes, flies, and zero visibility, then steer clear.

In other words, Wilderness Volunteer trips are not for wimps. Northcutt notes that "even on our front-country trips, there's lots of moving big rocks, digging and bending. Volunteers put in a full day of manual labor." If your body mass index is over 28 (and there *is* a place on the online application for listing your height and weight, so you *will* be busted), you will probably be turned down for most of the trips. But never fear, the website also lists tips for getting into shape. Northcutt suggest volunteers train before coming on a trip the way they would train to run a marathon.

Wilderness Volunteers trips fill up quickly. The spring trips, which are listed on the website at the beginning of October, are usually filled by the first of December. The yearlong schedule that goes up by December is often filled by March.

HOW TO GET IN TOUCH
Wilderness Volunteers, P.O. Box 22292, Flagstaff, AZ 86002, 928-556-0038, www.wildernessvolunteers.org.

track mountain lions

HUACHUCA MOUNTAINS, ARIZONA

People like John Muir and Rachel Carson—we look back at what they did and we're in awe. We laud them, we teach them in our schools— so why the hell aren't we doing the same thing?
—Susan Morse, one of the original founders of Sky Island Alliance

39 Mountain lions have gotten a bum rap in the past few years. These big cats, also called pumas, cougars, panthers, and a few other names with curse words thrown in, have inspired fear in whole communities, some demanding their immediate eradication.

Luckily, they're pretty crafty creatures that are active mostly at night. Plus, the stats show that their threat is overstated. Since 1900, only 18 deaths can be attributed to mountain lions, while dogs knock off 20 humans in an average year.

If you'd like to learn more about the elusive animals that hunt a 200-square-mile range, consider volunteering for Sky Island Alliance's annual mountain lion track count. It takes place the first week in June on the Fort Huachuca Military Reservation in southeastern Arizona's Sonoran Desert. It's the longest-running volunteer track count in the United States.

You'll camp and train with leading wildlife biologists and experienced trackers, then stalk the rugged Huachuca Mountains south of Tucson. If that sounds dangerous, Sky Island Alliance is quick to point out that you're not actually tailing the animal, but rather looking for what it leaves behind. Telltale signs of mountain lions include footprints, scat, fur, and the occasional kill,

WILDLIFE MESSAGE BOARDS

Mountain lions are territorial and make no bones about which "real estate" is theirs. If you're savvy, you can read the visual and olfactory messages. Male mountain lions swipe their hind feet backward to create two parallel furrows at the edge of their turf, and then, in case you're too dense to take that clue, they spray urine on top of the mounds at the end of each furrow. What they're trying to say is: "Keep Out!"

WHILE YOU'RE IN SOUTHEASTERN ARIZONA

Besides preserving wildlife, Arizona has a folklore preserve. It was started by Dolan Ellis, Arizona's official state balladeer and an original member of the New Christy Minstrels. The mission of this unique place is to preserve useful and fascinating stories, songs, and legends of successful (and not-so-successful) Arizona moments for future generations. Each Saturday and Sunday, the preserve offers a delightful program of acoustic and folk entertainment at a beautiful theater along Ramsey Creek. *Arizona Folklore Preserve, 56 Folklore Trail, Hereford, AZ 85615, 520-378-6165, www.arizonafolklore.com.*

all of which gets fed into an ongoing population study. Not scientifically perfect, perhaps, but an important starting gate for wildlife conservation.

Letting average citizens track wild animals suits Susan Morse just fine. A renowned tracker from Vermont and one of three original organizers of the Arizona mountain lion track count, Morse believes that if laymen get involved in tracking wildlife, it creates momentum for influencing the political process. The mountain lion track count, for example, gives Sky Island Alliance a leg up when campaigning against urban development, misplaced highways, Border Patrol fences, and other things that aren't amenable to your average mountain lion.

The term "sky islands," in case you're wondering, describes isolated mountain ranges separated by valleys of grassland or, in the case of Arizona and Mexico, a "sea of desert." The 40 ranges of Arizona's Sky Island System are among the most unusual ecosystems in North America. They're home to four or possibly five species of native wildcats.

The Fort Huachuca Military Reservation, where the actual count takes place, has been around since 1877, when the cavalry set up camp to protect travelers in the San Pedro Valley from raiding Apache. In 1886, it was headquarters for the military campaign against Geronimo. Although many forts from that era have been shut down, Fort Huachuca survived budget cuts and even thrived. In 1954, it became Ground Zero for testing electronics and communications equipment and today serves as an intelligence school. Base environmentalists, thanks to Stone, Shaw and Morse, got involved in mountain lion tracking as far back as 1989.

Sky Island Alliance has been hosting the annual track for the past five years. And for overachievers, Sky Island Alliance offers a year-round volunteer tracking program that tracks not only mountain lions but also bobcats, jaguars, bears, gray wolves, and other carnivores. To participate in Sky Island's year-round tracking program, the organization offers an intensive five-day training, after which time you and your team of three or four volunteer trackers will adopt a transect, a 1- to 1.5-mile walking route located in such wildlife movement corridors as washes and ridge tops. You're responsible for monitoring the transect once every six weeks, with all data reported regularly to the program coordinator.

Besides monitoring mountain lions, Sky Island Alliance offers a full schedule of volunteer "field trips," from mapping roads to collecting plant data.

There is no charge to participate in the annual mountain lion track count. Training for the year-round program costs $75.

HOW TO GET IN TOUCH
Sky Island Alliance, P.O. Box 41165, Tucson, AZ 85717, 738 N. Fifth Avenue, Suite 201, Tucson, AZ 85705, 520-624-7080, www.skyislandalliance.org.

care for the homeless

After ten days of service, education, sightseeing, and interaction with trip
members, I have watched my stereotypes on homelessness crumble. And
I have made a difference—a small one, but a difference all the same.
—Rose Mutiso, Amizade volunteer

40 With more than 3.5 million homeless people in America, you can
easily volunteer at a soup kitchen right in your own neighborhood.
But if you'd like to spend a whole week challenging your preexisting stereotypes,
consider a volunteer vacation with Amizade, an international agency that organizes
dozens of volunteer programs in 11 countries.

Although Amizade's volunteer programs vary widely—from renovating a health
clinic in the Bolivian Andes to building a community center in Australia to tutoring
kids on a Navajo reservation—the purpose for all of them remains the same: to
bridge cultures and make the world a better place.

At each project site, Amizade teams with a community partner, a group or
nonprofit that is just as committed to sustainable development and poverty-
elimination projects as it is. In Washington, D.C., that community partner is the
D.C. Central Kitchen (DCCK), which, among other things, runs the world's largest
entirely volunteer-run homeless shelter. It's the national model for more than 60
community kitchens in the United States.

During this unique program, conducted three times a year in the nation's
capital, you'll learn about the root causes of homelessness, hear guest speakers, and
participate in discussions and reflection sessions about what can be done. Prepare
to push your comfort zone.

Every day, DCCK recovers nearly 3,000 pounds of food—its motto is "Waste
is wrong, be it food, money, or potential"—and provides 4,000 meals. Besides
offering street-level meal service, DCCK also has a catering project, a campus
kitchens project, and a nationally recognized culinary school. The culinary school
has graduated more than 500 chefs, most of them men and women whose résumés

were limited to drug addictions, prison, and lengthy joblessness. For many, their completion certificate represents the first success of their lives.

During this volunteer vacation, you'll visit the 10,000-square-foot training kitchen, as well as work at soup kitchens and homeless shelters. Some of your duties will be preparing and distributing food, hanging out with kids at the shelter, and performing such maintenance tasks as painting or hammering. You'll also get to know many of the DCCK clients on a first-name basis.

Although housing for Amizade projects varies from tents to community buildings, volunteers for the D.C. program stay at First Trinity Lutheran Church. Bring a sleeping bag.

The seeds for Amizade (it means "friendship" in Portuguese) were planted in 1992 by Dan Weiss, who on his own volunteer vacation in Brazil couldn't help but notice that volunteers were working out of straw huts. Realizing that those fragile huts didn't stand a chance of surviving the rainy season, he pitched the idea of a permanent volunteer organization to several large nonprofits. When none stepped up to the plate, he decided to do it on his own. Weiss started Amizade in 1994 with an orthopedic shoe and prosthetics workshop in Santarem, Brazil. To say it has been a success is an understatement. Since its inception, Amizade has connected thousands of volunteers ages 13 to 79 with dozens of community service projects.

Amizade's program fees for the weeklong D.C. trip is $610, including all lodging, meals, recreational activities, cultural activities, and transportation to and from the local airport.

HOW TO GET IN TOUCH

Amizade, P.O. Box 110107, Pittsburgh, PA 15232, 888-973-4443 or 412-441-6655, www.amizade.org.

uncover the ice age

HOT SPRINGS, SOUTH DAKOTA

Macrauchenia No. 1: Well, why don't they call it The Big Chill? Or The
Nippy Era? I'm just sayin', how do we know it's an Ice Age?
Macrauchenia No. 2: Because … of all the ice.
—From the movie *Ice Age*

41 About 26,000 years ago, a large group of teenage mammoths, faced with the choice of sweeping off new snowfall to eat last year's dead grass or going for the green vegetation around a thermal pond, decided to go for the "salad bar." Unfortunately for them, they stumbled over the edge of the sinkhole at the pond and got trapped in the muddy bottom. Eventually, the deadly sinkhole filled in, preserving at least a hundred unlucky dead mammoths. For millennia, their graves went unmarked.

In 1974, when a bulldozer was leveling a hill for a planned housing development, it sliced through what looked like a tusk. The operator of the bulldozer showed the tusk and other bones to his son, who invited his former geology professor, Dr. Larry Agenbroad, to take a look. At first, Agenbroad thought it was a mammoth kill, a site where hunters took down some much needed meat, but radiocarbon dating of the bones ruled out that theory. It seems that the mammoths died long before humans arrived in North America 15,000 years ago.

The Columbian mammoths, like their better known cousins the woolly mammoths, inhabited North America for well over a million years before dying out about 11,000 years ago. Taller and heavier than the woollies, typically standing 13 feet high at the shoulder and weighing nine tons, they looked like an overgrown version of today's Asian elephants.

The owner of the land, Phil Anderson, postponed the housing project and gave Agenbroad three years to explore the hill. The following summer, Agenbroad spent the only grant money he could secure, $500, to feed his students as they began the site's inaugural excavation. A year later, he began his association with Earthwatch (see sidebar p. 94). When it became clear that the little town at the southern tip

SCIENTIST, SCHMIENTIST

"You don't need a Ph.D. to look at your watch and say
the monkey has been sleeping for 10 minutes."
—Alison Jolly, a Princeton primatologist who since 1983
has been using Earthwatch volunteers to study lemurs in
Madagascar

Some scientists scoff at the idea of using unpaid volunteers who walk in off the street. According to Dr. Larry Agenbroad, professor emeritus of geology at Northern Arizona University and principal investigator for the Hot Springs mammoth dig, however, volunteers are extremely motivated. And because they're afraid to do anything wrong, they pay strict attention to his instructions, something that can't always be said for grad students.

"My colleagues used to give me a lot of flak about [using volunteers]," Agenbroad says, "but after picking crews every way you can—grade point average, experience, degrees—I'm happy with the volunteers."

Some scientists claim volunteer funding is better than government funding. "You don't have political people breathing down your neck, and you can do whatever you damn please," says Harold Edgerton, an MIT emeritus professor who is now on the Earthwatch board of advisors.

Jane Phillips-Conroy, who studies baboons in Ethiopia, says volunteers sometimes teach her a thing or two. The best tooth casts she ever collected were made by a dentist who volunteered for the expedition.

So agree with the volunteer concept or not—no one can argue with the results. Since Earthwatch was started in 1971, the research the volunteers have contributed has resulted in 12 new national parks and reserves, hundreds of new species discovered, dozens of endangered species rescued from extinction, and health services and sustainable agriculture brought to remote villages in more than 20 countries.

---

of the Black Hills possessed an enormous mammoth graveyard, Anderson sold the land at cost to the Mammoth Site of Hot Springs, a nonprofit corporation set up to let Agenbroad develop the graveyard.

More than three decades later, you can help Agenbroad continue to investigate the New World's largest natural deposit of Columbian mammoth remains. Since 1976, dozens of Earthwatch crews (it was one of Earthwatch's first projects) have excavated more than 52 mammoths, as well as camels, llamas, and the first wolf and giant short-faced bear fossils found in the north-central plains.

Working with Agenbroad and his field staff, you'll learn how to excavate, record, and preserve bone fragments in plaster casts, map where bones are discovered, screen earth for small fossils of other species, and estimate a mammoth's age by measuring its teeth. If you come for the first of the two 14-day expeditions, held every year in July, you'll even get to take part in the Hot Springs Fourth of July parade.

You'll also share your knowledge with the more than 100,000 visitors who come each year to the site, now a $1.1 million museum and a national natural landmark. Expect a warm welcome from Hot Springs locals, who are proud of their mammoths.

A master at building esprit de corps, Agenbroad will give you a complete education on prehistoric environments and Pleistocene extinctions. He also throws in good food, field trips, afternoon Popsicle breaks, and hilarious lectures.

After digging through 20,000-year-old sediments, you'll welcome showers at a comfortable motel near the site. Hearty meals prepared by a local ranch woman are served family style. Team members and staff rotate kitchen duties.

The contribution for participation is $2,449.

HOW TO GET IN TOUCH
Earthwatch Institute, 3 Clock Tower Place, Maynard, MA 01754, 978-461-0081, www.earthwatch.org or www.mammothsite.com.

rebuild the big easy

NEW ORLEANS, LOUISIANA

We work 9 to 3, then shower and walk into the French Quarter. We have our stools reserved now at the Crescent City Brewhouse. Every afternoon we look at each other and say, "This was a good idea."
—Fred Schenck and Makoto Ogura, volunteers with ACORN

42 Unless you've been in a cave, you know that on August 29, 2005, the greatest natural disaster in U.S. history occurred in southeast Louisiana. Hurricane Katrina ripped families to pieces, destroyed homes, took lives, and shook our social order to the very core.

What Katrina couldn't demolish was the will of a great American city.

New Orleans looks different today. In many places, it's still a surreal landscape with splintered houses and moldy rubble. But amid that bleak landscape, a new brand of grassroots service organization has sprung up. In fact, New Orleans is giving whole new meaning to the term "voluntourism."

Frustrated by the Federal Emergency Management Agency's foot-dragging, government gridlock, and the mess they saw on their TV screens, voluntourists began showing up soon after Katrina left. This new breed of hardy tourist reports for duty during the day and parties it up in the French Quarter at night, nobly putting money back into the struggling economy.

For the foreseeable future, there is no shortage of volunteer jobs. New Orleans needs every kind of skilled and unskilled volunteer who is willing to show up. Obviously, construction and medical skills are needed, but there are volunteer jobs in everything from child care to food preparation to conducting needs assessment surveys. For a while, City Hall even accepted volunteers to answer city phones.

Some volunteer groups are able to house and feed their volunteers in makeshift camps or at churches or surviving community centers, but if you can afford it and really want to "make a difference," consider paying for hotels, eating out at restaurants, and using free time to patronize local attractions. Not only does this arrangement help local businesses stay open, but it also reduces the burden on relief organizations. Many New Orleans hotels even offer special packages for volunteers. The Windsor Court on the edge of the French Quarter, for example, provides rides to volunteer sites with the Habitat for Humanity Package, as well as free Cajun cooking classes to volunteer groups of ten or more.

The following is a short list of some of the grassroots organizations that would gladly welcome your shining face. In addition, the Louisiana governor's office has a blanket website for volunteers at www.volunteerlouisiana.gov, or call 866-286-3835 or 225-342-3070.

ACORN. The Association of Community Organizations for Reform Now is the nation's largest community group of low- and moderate-income families. Its mission is working together for social justice and stronger communities. It's been around since 1970 and has chapters in 75 U.S. cities. Since Katrina, much of its volunteer work has been refocused to New Orleans, where it has been instrumental in gutting and cleaning low-income housing. Every weekday, volunteers meet at 7:30 a.m. and work until 2:30 p.m.

ACORN, 1016 Elysian Fields Avenue, New Orleans, LA 70117, 617-359-7240, www.acorn.org.

Common Ground Collective. Just days after Katrina, this grassroots group started providing medical assistance and supplies to hurricane victims. Now its activities are varied and shift with the seasons. Besides cleanup and rebuilding, it offers a health clinic and a women's shelter. Its members even tutor kids, refurbish churches, and have a wetlands reparation program. Operating out of an abandoned Ninth Ward school, the organization has hosted volunteers from more than a hundred countries. You'll get free room and board at St. Mary of the Angels School.

    Common Ground Relief, 2225 Congress, New Orleans, LA 70017, 504-218-6613, www.commongroundrelief.org.

Emergency Communities. EC needs volunteers for its makeshift café (you may have heard about the Made with Love Café, which opened in St. Bernard Parish right after Katrina) and community center in Buras. EC was founded by a group of self-described hippies who were adept at setting up large-scale outdoor kitchens at concerts, conventions, and forest gatherings. They reasoned they could apply that skill to disaster zones.

    After Katrina, EC was one of the first organizations to arrive on the Gulf Coast and start feeding people. Its café feeds thousands of relief workers and residents and has become a popular meeting place. "A volunteer might do anything from gut a house to cook a meal to play with kids," says volunteer coordinator Katherine Pangaro.

    Emergency Communities, 4316 Baronne Street, Suite D, New Orleans, LA 70115, 347-351-9559, www.emergencycommunities.org.

help out at a national park

AT A NATIONAL PARK NEAR (OR FAR FROM) YOU

People ask all the time how many more years we'll keep returning to Glacier. . . . I like to say, "Until we die, until we die!"
—Mary and Joe McGeehan,
summer campground hosts at Glacier National Park

43 They're not exactly on the endangered species list yet, but America's national parks are getting sucker punched by budget cuts. With so much of our national budget going to the military, visitor centers at national parks are being forced to cut back hours, retiring rangers are not being replaced, roads that were once open to the public are now restricted, and trail maintenance is being neglected.

Fort Necessity National Battlefield in Pennsylvania, for example, has cut back on grass-cutting in the 900-acre park from once every two weeks to once a month. Olympic National Park in Washington has been forced to close its main visitor center two days a week.

In fact, the national parks are taking such a beating that, in the northwest United States, volunteers are giving talks about threats to the National Park System along with talks about shrinking salmon habitats.

So, you can write your representatives in Congress, but if you *really* want to help, spend a week or a month or a whole summer volunteering in one of America's nearly 400 national parks. Earthwatch (see pp. 93–94 and 122–124), Wilderness Volunteers (see pp. 114–116), and other outfits offer volunteer vacations in national parks, but you can also go straight to the source and become a VIP—which, while it certainly qualifies you as a "very important

HOME SWEET HOME

Another option for preserving our legacy is to volunteer at a state park. Like their national cousins, most state parks offer a volunteer program. Contact your state's park service for more details.

person," in this case stands for Volunteers in Parks. The VIP program deploys volunteers in virtually every one of our national parks.

Although you would certainly be appreciated at a park in your own neighborhood, many VIPs choose to work in a favorite park away from home. Needless to say, your "office" would be among the most amazing on the planet. Decor selections include mountains, deserts, seacoasts, lakeshores, assorted wildlife, geysers, glaciers, and more.

The jobs, of course, are as diverse as the parks. You could lead history tours of Ellis Island or cave tours in the Ozarks. You could be a lightkeeper on Wisconsin's Apostle Islands, work a remote duty station in the Teton Wilderness, tend livestock in Nevada, or create exhibits at the Desert Discovery Center in California's Mojave Desert. Or, if you like history, you might choose to wear period clothing and interpret life on a canalboat at Maryland's C&O National Historical Park.

There are hundreds of established volunteer positions listed on the National Park Service website, and you can even propose your own volunteer job, coming up with a way to utilize your own unique talents. Jim Black, for example, the great-grandson of a Navajo who escaped the horrors of the Long Walk, a forced 300-mile trek in the mid-1800s across New Mexico from Canyon de Chelly to Fort Sumner, leads interpretive hikes at Navajo National Monument, an ancient Betatakin Indian ruin in Arizona. A couple from Maryland, along with their greyhounds Micha and Jericho, lead tours and monitor trails at Maryland's Monocacy National Battlefield.

Owning your own motor home is certainly a leg up, especially if you'd like to volunteer as a campground host, but sometimes the park will offer a cabin, as Death Valley did when a photographer offered to document petroglyphs in the park.

Generally, you'll be asked for a commitment of time that will vary from part of the season to the full season. Park seasons vary as well. For instance, the Glacier National Park season runs three to four months, while Big Bend is open year-round.

HOW TO GET IN TOUCH

You can download an application and view a list of volunteer openings at www.nps. gov/volunteer, or contact the VIP coordinator at a specific park at which you are interested in volunteering.

contribute to an international work camp

THE UNITED STATES & WORLDWIDE

These days, people are more inclined to use travel as a way to affirm their connection to humanity, to measure the things we all have in common. It's less about being jolted out of your own world than about feeling bolted to the wider one.
—*Newsweek*

44 Stage a challenge race for the disabled from Fairbanks to Anchorage. Or help set up Solar Fest, a renewable energy fair that takes place on a horse farm in Tinmouth, Vermont. These are just two of the thousands of volunteer camps that Volunteers for Peace (VFP) sets up each year. Other projects might be tagging sea turtles in Mexico or tutoring Native populations in British Columbia. Name a topic you're interested in or a country you're interested in visiting, and VFP will undoubtedly have a work camp that fits.

Volunteers for Peace is a nonprofit organization that enlists volunteers for United Nations–sanctioned community projects all over the world. At last count, there were about 3,000 programs held in more than a hundred countries. Projects range from historic preservation and archaeology to ecology and social work.

You'll work in what VFP calls a "work camp," a group of between 2 and 20 international volunteers who come to help a local community with a project on which the community needs help, typically for two or three weeks. At the Sadler's Ultra Challenge Camp in Alaska, for example, you might drive the wheelchair athletes' pilot cars, assist them with food and clothing, and learn about disabled athletes. At the Solar Fest Camp, held each year in July, you would help clear the brush on the horse farm where it's held and make sure it's ready for the thousands of folks who come to sing, dance, and celebrate renewable energy.

You'll work about 30 hours a week and live in cooperative living environments, sometimes in a school or a church and other times in private homes or at a

A TEENSY SAMPLE TO WHET YOUR APPETITE

There are lots of perks to signing up for Volunteers for Peace work camps. The two best are dirt-cheap trips to foreign countries and geographically diverse coworkers. Even if you choose a work camp near your own home, you're guaranteed to hear accents from across the globe. At a recent VFP work camp in Wells, Maine, for example, volunteers hailed from Germany, Northern Ireland, South Korea, Japan, and Serbia. During their two-week work camp, these international volunteers maintained the 7 miles of trails through the Wells National Estuarine Research Reserve coastal reserve and helped with the annual Laudholm Nature Crafts Festival, a two-day arts-and-crafts festival.

As for the dirt-cheap part, how does $250 for a two- to three-week vacation sound, room and board included? Granted, you won't be staying in a four-star hotel and, of course, you're expected to donate some elbow grease, but what could be more meaningful and fun than contributing to the betterment of the planet?

Because this book focuses on the best vacations in North America, here are a few more examples of recent work camps on this continent:

- Each fall, the snow geese migrate to Cap-St.-Ignace, a small town on the St. Lawrence River in Quebec. A work camp of international volunteers came for three weeks in early fall to lay out a paved path for cyclists, Rollerbladers, and hikers, and, of course, to witness the spectacle of tens of thousands of snow geese.
- A work camp in Flagstaff, Arizona, asked volunteers to construct trails, build fences, plant native species, and work on other aspects of wildlife restoration. Free time included a trip to the Grand Canyon.
- In Willits, California, volunteers worked at the Mendocino Ecological Learning Center learning about permaculture, ecological design, and natural building. Daily yoga was included.
- In Zihuatanejo, Mexico, volunteers living in beachside cabins collected data on sea turtles.
- On a ranch in Oaxaca, Mexico, volunteers built dorms, kitchens, dining rooms, and classrooms for a children's home for orphans.

community center. Volunteers themselves coordinate and share the day-to-day activities of food preparation and free time.

Because volunteers usually come from several different countries, you get the rare chance to build bonds with people from diverse cultural backgrounds. Think of it as a mini UN right there in the work camp. The idea is that the better we get to know folks from other countries and the more we practice working together, the easier it will be to create world peace.

International work camps emerged in Europe right after World War II. The Vermont VFP, which serves as an affiliate of UNESCO's Coordinating Committee for International Voluntary Service, an umbrella organization for nongovernmental volunteer agencies, sprang up in 1982.

More than 85 percent of the work camps are set up between July and September, and at least a fourth of volunteers register for several work camps, thus giving them a whole summer abroad. With so many camps to choose from, you can name a month you want to travel and it's almost guaranteed you'll find a VFP project that will appeal. The *International Work Camp Directory* (nearly 300 pages of projects) is posted on the website in March and available for mailing in early April. Send $20 to the address below for a hard copy.

A $250 registration fee per two- to three-week camp covers room and board. Transportation is arranged and paid for by the volunteer. Each volunteer must also pay a mandatory onetime VFP membership of $20.

HOW TO GET IN TOUCH
Volunteers for Peace, 1034 Tiffany Road, Belmont, VT 05730, 802-259-2759, www.vfp.org.

protect loggerhead sea turtles

WASSAW NATIONAL WILDLIFE RESERVE, GEORGIA

For most of the wild things on Earth, the future
must depend upon the conscience of mankind.
—Archie Carr, scientist and author who almost single-handedly
turned the tide on the extinction of sea turtles

45 The dinosaurs didn't make it. But giant sea turtles, which have survived for 175 million years, still have a fighting chance, even though they're endangered. The days when hunters nearly killed them off are mostly in the past, but today high-rise condominiums are taking over their nesting grounds and the mammoth sea turtles are laying eggs on shaky ground.

Since 1978, *Caretta caretta*—better known as the loggerhead turtle—which nests largely in the southeastern United States, has been on the threatened species list. Their numbers have been in steep decline since humans began vacationing on their nesting grounds. The good news is that, even before the Federal Endangered Species Act added the loggerheads to the list, the Caretta Research Project on Wassaw Island, one of Georgia's many barrier islands, has been tagging them and doing their best to protect the vulnerable creatures.

And that's where you come in. Between May and September, the research facility invites volunteers to Wassaw Island to help scientists patrol the beach. Each week, six volunteers come to tag and measure female turtles as they emerge from the sea to lay their eggs, move the nests if they're too close to the tide line, and protect them from raccoons, feral hogs, and other predators. Volunteers even cheer on the tiny 2-inch hatchlings when

ADOPT A TURTLE

If you can't make it to Wassaw Island, consider adopting a loggerhead sea turtle, nest, or hatchling. During the summer, you can even log onto the Caretta Research Project website and track your adopted turtle's nesting activity. For your $25 adoption fee, you'll receive a list of adoptees and an adoption form, a semiannual newsletter, and a Caretta Research Project bumper sticker.

LOGGERHEAD STATS

- While hatchlings are a mere 2 inches in length, adults can be up to 3 feet long and weigh as much as 350 pounds.
- Only 1 in 1,000 hatchlings survives to adulthood.
- Females, which lay as many as ten clutches at a time, lay eggs only every two or three years.
- The average loggerhead lives 50 to 75 years.
- The loggerhead's name comes from the turtle's unusually large head.
- Even though loggerheads don't reach maturity for 20 or 25 years, they somehow remember where they were born and return to the same place two decades later to lay their eggs.
- Loggerhead turtles migrate more than 8,000 miles—alone, without other turtles guiding the way. The journey, which takes them across the Atlantic past the Azores, takes five to ten years to complete.
- Although their streamlined bodies and flippers are perfect for the ocean, they are nearsighted and defenseless on land.
- When loggerhead hatchlings break out of their shells at night, they instinctively crawl toward the brightest light on the horizon. On an undeveloped beach, that's the moon's reflection off the surf. However, on a developed beach, the brightest light can be a light from a nearby disco.
- An estimated 14,000 females nest in the southeastern United States each year.

they finally peck their way out of their shells 60 days after mom deposits her eggs in the sand.

Working in cooperation with the U.S. Fish and Wildlife Service, the Savannah Science Museum, and the Wassaw Island Trust, the Caretta Research Project has been around since 1972. It's one of the longest running marine turtle tracking projects in the United States. And while scientists are slow to take credit, there is striking evidence suggesting the project has been successful. The number of loggerhead clutches on Wassaw has gone from 50 or 60 in the mid-1980s to more than 100 in recent years.

Wassaw Island is a 10,053-acre national wildlife refuge with rolling dunes, live oaks, vast salt marshes, and a 6-mile-long beach where the female loggerheads sneak in each summer to lay nests of 120 eggs the size of Ping-Pong balls. Getting there requires a 45-minute boat ride from Landings Harbor Marina on Skidaway Island.

Volunteers stay in a rustic cabin (no air-conditioning or indoor showers). Because turtles lay their eggs at night—it's safer that way—turtle patrol usually begins around nightfall and lasts until roughly 5 a.m. Daytime is when you'll sleep and have free time to explore, hike the island's many dirt roads, swim in the pool, and go bird-watching. Not only does Wassaw support rookeries for egrets and herons, but a variety of wading birds also show up each summer.

Volunteers pay $650 per week. This includes a cabin bunk and all meals.

HOW TO GET IN TOUCH
Caretta Research Project, P.O. Box 9841, Savannah, GA 31412, 912-447-8655, www.carettaresearchproject.org.

HEIFER INTERNATIONAL
teach sustainable agriculture

PERRYVILLE, ARKANSAS

You give this gift to Third World countries—a cow, a sheep—and they start breeding and selling them, and suddenly they have a livelihood.
—comedienne Ellen Degeneres, at a fundraiser
for Heifer International's Six Villages campaign

46 Heifer International, one of the country's most visible charities thanks to its colorful catalogs and support from dozens of movie stars, was based on the well-known adage "Give a man a fish, you feed him today; teach a man to fish, you feed him for a lifetime." Rather than give money or sacks of grain to help people only in the short term, Heifer International gives breeding animals (27 different species at last count) that poor families in underdeveloped countries can use to start their own herds and feed their families over the long haul.

The idea was incubated in 1939 when Indiana farmer Dan West, a relief worker in the Spanish Civil War, was passing out cups of powdered milk to orphans and refugees in Spain. Moved by their plight, he came up with his own version of the popular proverb: "Give a cow, not a cup."

CELEBRITY DONORS

Here is a list of celebs who donate to Heifer International:
• Ed Asner • Bill Clinton • Walter Cronkite • Ted Danson • Ellen Degeneres • Jane Kaczmarek • Barbara Kingsolver • Heath Ledger • Susan Sarandon • David Spade • Bradley Whitford

Upon returning to the United States, West started Heifers for Relief, dedicated to providing permanent freedom from hunger by giving struggling families livestock, training, and the ability to support themselves. The first 17 heifers—young dairy cows that could be a continual source of milk, offspring, and fertilizer—were shipped from York, Pennsylvania,

COWABUNGA

Besides your standard cows, sheep, and goats, Heifer International gives out two dozen other types of breeding animals, each chosen for their appropriateness to local ecologies and economies. Some of the offerings over the years: earthworms, edible snails, bees, silkworms, crayfish, ostriches, guinea pigs, alpacas, grasshoppers, water buffalo, yaks, and, in two Thai projects, elephants. In Ghana, Heifer is raising a large edible rodent called the grasscutter, and in Ukraine, they're reintroducing Hutsul horses, descendants of the wild tarpan.

to Puerto Rico in 1944. The project grew exponentially until thousands of cows aboard converted World War II cargo vessels were being escorted by volunteer "cowboys" to war-ravaged Europe.

In recent years, Heifer International has taken the fish adage a step further: Teach donors about their own impact on the planet and then we'll make some real changes. You see, it's one thing to donate a cow or a flock of goats, but to really understand how we, the developing world, affect issues of hunger and poverty is a whole different ball of wax. If Heifer International has its way, those of us who "have it all" will understand our imprint on the planet and realize our responsibilities are greater than simply writing a check.

Heifer International is so committed to educating the developed nations on issues of poverty and sustainability that it has opened three learning centers. Its demonstration farm and visitor center in Perryville, Arkansas, has not only a convention facility but also demonstration gardens and a "global village" of seven plots, each containing a small house or shanty and landscaped to resemble living conditions in one of the organization's project areas. The other learning centers are Overlook Farm near Rutland, Massachusetts, and the Ceres Center in California.

Although each of these learning centers hires paid employees, the bulk of the work is done by volunteers. With more than 28,000 annual visitors to Perryville alone, you can imagine there's a lot to be accomplished—from tending the organic gardens to caring for the livestock to facilitating the many educational programs. Residential volunteers get housing and noon meals plus stipends, with a one month commitment, in exchange for helping run Heifer's programs, which range from two-hour tours to weeklong experiences.

A shorter volunteer option is to take an Adult Service Journey, in which you'll visit for a week and help with such activities as building a greenhouse or sprucing up the ranch for the Global Village Day celebration. Each of the adult service journeys revolves around a particular theme. On a recent "From Bees to Honey" journey, for example, volunteers helped with everything from extracting honey from honey boxes to bottling and labeling the honey for sale. Tuition for the adult service journeys is $406, including all meals and lodging as well as a hayride tour of the ranch and other programs.

HOW TO GET IN TOUCH
Heifer International, 1 World Avenue, Little Rock, AR 72202, 800-422-0474 or 501-907-2600, www.heifer.org.

help transform health care

HILLSBORO, WEST VIRGINIA

It often falls to the court jester to speak the truth
that those in power need to hear.
—Bernie Siegel, M.D.

47 The fact that comedian Robin Williams was chosen to play Patch Adams in the eponymous 1998 movie about his life should be your first clue that Dr. Adams is not your average M.D. and that the Gesundheit Institute that he started in rural West Virginia is not your run-of-the-mill hospital. Situated amid beautiful mountains, hardwood forests, and at least three waterfalls, Gesundheit is a holistic hospital and health-care community based on the radical notion that medicine should actually be fun and free.

Whether you saw the movie or not, it's probably obvious by now that a volunteer vacation to Patch's 317-acre institute promises to be unorthodox and extraordinary. Although the "silly hospital" that Patch envisioned is still on the drawing board, there's an active community of artists, dreamers, healers, and clowns interested in changing the medical paradigm. They're living at the institute, preparing the

NUT-WORKING

For more than 20 years, Patch Adams has been involved in what he calls "clown healing work." He and a posse of clowns have visited hospitals on every continent. For nearly 20 years, he has taken clowns to Russia for two weeks of clowning in hospitals, orphanages, prisons, and nursing homes. In 2006, Patch and 45 clowns and 8 builders constructed a seven-room clinic in Perquin, El Salvador. He and 22 clowns from six continents took ten tons of aid into the war of Afghanistan. He has taken clowns into the war in Bosnia, the Kosovo refugee camps, Romanian AIDS orphanages, African refugee camps, and tsunami relief camps in Sri Lanka.

WACKY HOSPITAL

The 40-room Gesundheit Hospital will be completely free, with no malpractice insurance and no third-party insurance. If you think that's wacky, you ought to get a load of the architectural blueprints. A giant ear sticks off one end of the building and giant feet mark the entrance. Below the main hospital floor, there's a waterway that allows people to travel from one end to the other via paddle-boat. Beautiful murals cover the walls, toys line the floors, and secret doorways and slides add mystique and amusement.

land, and building the community that will sustain the hospital once it is built. Volunteers of all stripes are welcome.

A significant component of the Gesundheit experience is education. Programs are based on Patch's vision for world peace, social justice, and the recognition that the health of the individual cannot be separated from the health of the community. The idea is that volunteers should learn about Gesundheit's utopian ideas so they can return to their homes and spread the vision.

While living at Gesundheit, volunteers might prepare fresh whole food for the three dozen or so attendees of the institute's annual School for Designing a Society or build a deck on the back of the barn or collect buckets of sugar maple sap. For their community service projects, they might don red noses for clowning at the Pocahontas Care Center in Marlinton or pick up trash along U.S. 219 between Locust Creek Road and Hillsboro.

Every year, the institute hosts three four-day visitor weekends in April, July, and September (where volunteers work for a day or two), as well as an increasing number of educational offerings. For example, medical students come each year to learn about medicinal herbs, health-care clowning, and other topics pertinent to Patch's vision of integrating medicine with fun, art, and friendship.

Patch's big, crazy dream began in 1971 when he and a couple of other doctors opened a free hospital in Arlington, Virginia. It was a six-bedroom house where Patch and 20 adults (including two other docs) lived and practiced medicine. Their "zany hospital" was open 24/7, for all manner of medical problems. They saw 500 to 1,000 people each month, including many who took up residence. Patch called the pilot project "ecstatic, fascinating, and stimulating." After nine years of no donations and being refused for some 1,400 foundation grants, the project was finally disbanded. Dr. Adams, of course, persevered, making, as he describes it, a deal with "the devil"—to cooperate with the movie and get some publicity for his project.

Volunteers are needed at Gesundheit from April through October with a minimum commitment of one month. In exchange for 35 hours per week, Gesundheit provides room and board. Some of the positions include gardeners, cooks, builders, and housekeepers. If you can't spare a month, consider the Visitor Weekend Program, which could involve such service work as ecological restoration, construction, and grounds maintenance. Either option is—you guessed it—completely free.

HOW TO GET IN TOUCH

Gesundheit! Institoot, P.O. Box 268, Hillsboro, WV 24946, 304-653-4338, www.patchadams.org.

save the whales

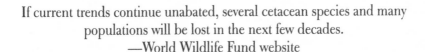

QUEBEC, CANADA

If current trends continue unabated, several cetacean species and many populations will be lost in the next few decades.
—World Wildlife Fund website

48 If studying whales at a research station on the St. Lawrence Gulf sounds like something you'd like to do, then get ready to run to the nearest phone. The four Ecovolunteer summer trips helping scientists in Les Bergeronnes, Quebec, study minke whales fill up fast, sometimes a whole year in advance. Marine biologists at the Swiss Foundation for Marine Environment Research study all 11 species of baleen whales, but their focus is on minke whales, a fast-swimming, little-studied whale that is most often targeted by whaling fleets.

Even though whales have been internationally protected since 1986, the drumbeat of the whaling lobby is getting louder and faster. The International Whaling Commission is being hounded by lobbyists from Norway, Japan, and Iceland who are demanding a resumption of commercial whaling. Even without permission, hunters are bagging an average of a thousand minke whales a year.

As a member of the research team, you'll bunk in a wooden cabin at the research station and be out on the water four to six hours a day, documenting the distribution and behavior of these 35-foot behemoths. You'll get to know Confucius, Crab Claw, Double Scoop, Hang Nail, and other minke whales that come to eastern Canada for the summer feeding season. More than 13 species of marine mammals frequent the area, ranging from the smallest cetacean, the harbor porpoise, to the largest animal on the planet, the blue whale. You'll also see three species of seals and several types of whales, including finbacks, humpbacks, sperm whales, and even belugas in their most southerly population outside Arctic waters.

Your research will measure the effects of industrial development, commercial river traffic, and even whale-watching boats (which have exploded in the region during the past two decades) on the 200-plus minkes that feed in the area. While on the water, you'll collect data in a Dictaphone (the whales appear and disappear too quickly to do it any other way) and learn to distinguish behaviors and identification marks. On land, you'll process the data and listen to lectures by marine biologists. You'll also have plenty of time to read, relax, and visit a whale museum in the nearby village of Tadoussac.

The research center is based in a hundred-year-old farmhouse overlooking the St. Lawrence River. You'll bunk in one of two wooden cabins next door. A biking-hiking trail along the shore connects the harbor with an impressive glacial overlook at Cap Bon Désir. The research facility even owns two bikes you can borrow.

Cost for the two-week volunteer trips is about $1,400 ($1,648 Canadian). Meals are estimated to be an extra $40 to $60 ($47 to 71 Canadian) per week.

HOW TO GET IN TOUCH

Great Canadian Travel Company, 158 Fort Street, Winnipeg, MB R3C 1C9, Canada, 800-661-3830 or 204-949-0199, www.ecovolunteer.org, or **Foundation for Marine Environment Research,** P.O. Box 117, 215, Route 138, Les Bergeronnes, QC G0T 1G0, Canada, 418-232-6422, www.ores.ch.

help run a booming tourist town

MEDORA, NORTH DAKOTA

Medora is a place where people can connect with history,
entertainment and other people.
—Annika Nelson,
Theodore Roosevelt Medora Foundation Development Assistant

49 To hear Teddy Roosevelt tell it, Medora, a ranching town in western North Dakota, was the "romance of his life." In fact, he used to say that if it wasn't for his experience in North Dakota, he'd have never been elected President. Roosevelt first showed up in the North Dakota badlands for a buffalo hunt in 1883, when he was a young New York politician. He liked the area so much that he bought two ranches, the Maltese Cross, just south of Medora, and Elkhorn, 35 miles north.

Medora today is still a mystical place where people come because, like Roosevelt said, it has the power to change your life. In the winter, the little community has barely a hundred people, mostly folks who ranch or manage the Theodore Roosevelt National Park or the government business of being the Billings County seat. But in the summer, when folks are out of school or off work, they flock from all over the country to Medora in droves. Something like 300,000 show up any given summer.

Needless to say, that's too big a crowd for the permanent residents to feed and house and sell souvenirs to. So, in 1998, the Theodore Roosevelt Medora Foundation, a nonprofit organization that promotes the area, came up with the brilliant scheme of bringing in volunteers who could serve the locally famous pitchfork fondue (steaks speared on pitchforks and cooked over fire); usher at the Burning Hills Amphitheater, a 2,900-seat theater that since 1958 has been presenting the high-energy *Medora Musical;* clear tables at the Chuckwagon Buffet; and greet tourists at the Information Center.

In return for roughly six hours of work a day, the foundation provides these
volunteers with a room at the Bunkhouse Motel and a name badge (complete with
a personal photo) that allows them to eat free at the Chuckwagon's all-you-can eat
buffet, the Maltese Burger, or the Badlands Pizza Parlor.

The volunteer season runs from mid-May to mid-September and is divided into
three segments. If you come in mid-May, you'll be in charge of painting, planting
flowers, and sprucing up the little town with its wooden sidewalks, split-rail fences,
barn-board buildings, and wooden benches. This perfectly coiffed town could easily
double as Disneyland's Frontierland. Those volunteer stints run for five days.

Starting in June when the musical kicks off, volunteers come for eight-day
"terms" to do everything from answering questions at the Medora Doll House—an
antique doll museum housed in the old home of the Marquis de Mores, the guy
who founded Medora back in 1883—to passing out programs at the Old Town
Hall Theater for the one-man show on the life of Roosevelt, aptly entitled *Bully*.
Around August 15, after the college kids have all returned to school, volunteers
even take over such end-of-season duties as catering, running the Bully Pulpit Golf
Course, and managing the retail establishments.

When the volunteer program was first launched in 1998, there were 44 applications for the 16 positions. Today, more than 400 volunteers show up, 22 per week from early June through the first of September.

There is no charge to volunteer, but get your dibs in early. More than 800 people are already on the volunteer list.

HOW TO GET IN TOUCH
Theodore Roosevelt Medora Foundation, P.O. Box 198, 301 Fifth Street, Medora, ND 58645, 800-633-6721 or 701-623-4444, www.medora.com.

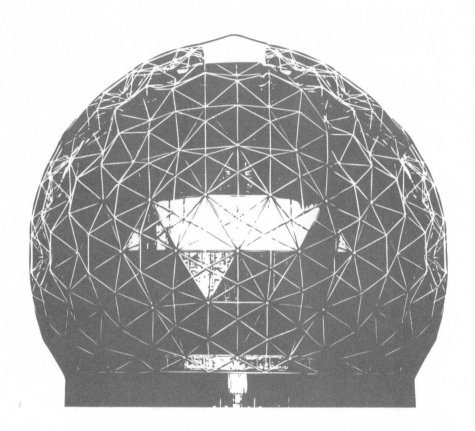

CHAPTER

3

brain retreats

*I always say to myself, what is the most important thing
we can think about in this extraordinary moment?*
—R. Buckminster Fuller, American visionary, architect, and inventor

When you were five, you wanted the answers to everything. You wanted to know where rain came from, why some people were bald, how music came out of that little box called a radio. Back then, it was okay not to know everything. It was perfectly acceptable to ask questions, wonder why, want to know more. But at some point, you figured out it wasn't "cool" to admit you didn't know something. You learned to keep your questions to yourself.

Or you began asking different questions. Instead of asking "What's the most extraordinary thing I could think about today?" you began asking "What was the closing price of Janus Worldwide?" Instead of asking if that star out your bedroom window is really Mars, you wanted to know which top looked best with your gray skirt.

Scientists estimate the average human being has 60,000 thoughts per day—a pretty impressive statistic until you hear this next one: All but 2 percent of those 60,000 thoughts are the same ones you had yesterday.

Just think what you could do if you used a little more of that other 98 percent to think up new ideas, to dive into life's mysteries, to ask those questions that still burn in your heart. That's what this chapter is about: diving into life's mysteries. We offer a selection of vacations that will encourage you to think, to begin asking those questions you've been keeping to yourself, the questions you've been holding in because . . . well, because you're a "responsible adult" now.

study yellowstone's wolves, geysers, & bears

YELLOWSTONE NATIONAL PARK

You're not going to get the full experience
of Yellowstone through the windshield.
—Jeff Brown, director of education
at the Yellowstone Association Institute

50 Here's the itinerary of most of the three million visitors to Yellowstone: Snap a photo of Aunt Edna in front of Old Faithful, buy a T-shirt of a bear and a bison for the niece and nephew, snap another picture of Aunt Edna beside the Roosevelt Arch, get in the RV, and go home.

There's another breed of tourist, however, who knows how to "break on through to the other side," a group that has figured out how to leave behind the mob scene and get back to the primordial pull that Yellowstone is really all about. These folks come to take classes, to sit at the feet (rather, walk behind the day pack) of Yellowstone biologists, naturalists, and park rangers.

These tourists come for the field school sponsored by the Yellowstone Association Institute (YAI). Established in 1976, the YAI provides in-depth courses on the natural and cultural history of Yellowstone. Most of the courses last from one to five days, have 12 or less students, and include both field and classroom sessions. Play your cards right and you can even get academic credit through Colorado State University.

Here are some of your options:

• **Field seminars.** These intensive educational experiences provide a closer look at a specific subject in the areas of wildlife, geology, ecology, history, plant life, art, or outdoor skills. The hundred or so yearly seminars are taught by the top experts in their field. "Wolves of the World," for example, is taught by Dr. Doug Smith, the project leader for the Yellowstone Gray Wolf Restoration Project. "Mammal Tracking" is taught by Dr. Jim Halfpenny, a prominent tracker and author of a

NO ADULT—OR CHILD—LEFT INSIDE

Yellowstone is not the only national park to offer field schools. In fact, it might be easier to list the national parks that don't offer courses. With packages ranging from afternoon lectures to a week's backpacking trip, these roving classrooms are geared for all ages. Here's a short list of some of the best:

Glacier Institute. With the slogan "Learning Gone Wild," this top-notch institute affiliated with Montana's Glacier National Park has been providing hands-on, field-based education adventures since 1983. Classes include everything from nature journaling to stalking grizzly bears. Many packages offer lodging in comfy cabins. Packages run from $55 to $415. *Glacier Institute, 137 Main Street, P.O. Box 1887, Kalispell, MT 59903, 406-755-1211, www.glacierinstitute.org.*

Grand Canyon Field Institute. With lots of multiday backpack trips, this relative newcomer to the field school community teaches everything from the geology of Red Canyon to the inner workings of the Havasupai Indian tribe. Scheduled courses are offered March through November with the option of a "You Pick the Dates" class offering hikes all months of the year. Prices from $95 per person for a daylong class to between $400 and $550 for a multiday backpack course. *Grand Canyon Field Institute, P.O. Box 399, Grand Canyon, AZ 86023, 866-471-4435, www.grandcanyon.org/fieldinstitute.*

North Cascades Institute. Offering more than a dozen field seminars, this field school at Washington's North Cascades National Park covers such topics as geology, history, wildlife, and art. Instructors include scientists, poets, photographers, loggers, and rangers. Year-round courses range from $75 for a one-day seminar to $425 for a four-day naturalist retreat. *North Cascades Institute, 810 State Route 20, Sedro Woolley, WA 98284, 360-856-5700, ext. 209, www.ncascades.org.*

Smoky Mountain Field School. Run in conjunction with the University of Tennessee, this school in Great Smoky Mountains National Park has courses for everyone. There are strenuous five-day hikes along the Appalachian Trail as well as nature sketching and wilderness orienteering, Courses are offered March through November and average $49. *Smoky Mountain Field School, 600 Henley Street, Suite 105, Knoxville, TN 37996, 865-974-0150, www.outreach.utk.edu/smoky.*

Teton Science Schools. Founded in 1967, this stellar school has four locations, including one in Grand Teton National Park, two in Jackson Hole, and the newest one in Jackson. Prices range from $20 for a four-hour family bird-banding and breakfast seminar in summer to $400 for a five-day course for a child at the Teton Junior Science School in June to August. Science School classes fill up fast, so try to register no later than February. Also available are several Elderhostel programs offered between June and early September for people age 55 and over; a five-day residence program runs about $900. *Teton Science Schools, 700 Coyote Canyon Road, Jackson, WY 83001, 307-733-1313, www.tetonscience.org.*

popular tracking field guide, and the "Yellowstone Volcano" class is led by the two scientists featured in the popular BBC docudrama *Supervolcano*. Although workshops are held throughout the park, the home base for a majority of the field seminars is the Lamar Buffalo Ranch, a comfortable field campus in the park's northeast corner. Overlooking the Lamar Valley, a haven for elk, bison, mule deer, and bighorn sheep, the ranch was the site of the park's bison recovery project in the early 20th century. "The ranch is right in the middle of one of the richest wildlife habitats in North America," says Jeff Brown, director of education for the institute. "You can literally walk out your front porch to a spotting scope that's pointed at a wolf." Participants stay in a rustic log cabin that has kitchen facilities and a nearby bathhouse. Rates average $80 per day, plus $25 per person for a cabin.

- **Lodging and Learning Programs.** This is the option for folks whose idea of roughing it is more along the lines of not being able to plug in a hotel blow-dryer. You'll get the same expert teachers during the day, but at night you'll return to one of the park's historic hotels for a meal and a comfy bed complete with room service. One phone call sets it all up. Programs run from May through September, and prices start at $783 for single occupancy, $579 per person for double occupancy.

- **Backcountry courses.** In these courses, you'll learn about wilderness travel, low-impact camping, and bear safety. And that's just the orientation. You'll pick a topic that ranges from tracking grizzlies to field journaling to glacier ecology. You'll be provided tents, stoves, and other group equipment, but you need to bring your own sleeping bag, backpack, and food. Courses are offered from the end of May through mid-September and average $100 a day.

- **Yellowstone Ed-ventures.** This option is for a family or small group that wants its own private naturalist guide. You'll meet early in the morning at a designated location (usually at Mammoth Hot Springs or in Gardiner, Montana) and spend eight hours watching wildlife or hiking. Four programs are available for all ages; figure $495 for up to 5 people, $625 for 6 to 14 people, and $1,250 for 15 to 28 people.

HOW TO GET IN TOUCH

Yellowstone Association Institute, P.O. Box 117, Yellowstone National Park, WY 82190, 307-344-5566 (Field Seminars and Lodging and Learning Programs), 307-344-2294 (Backcountry courses and Ed-ventures), www.yellowstoneassociation.org/institute.

experience marine life at an island campus

APPLEDORE ISLAND, MAINE

How I wish that somewhere there existed an island
for those who are wise and of good will.
—Albert Einstein

51 Most of the four dorms on 95-acre Appledore Island, the largest of the nine Isles of Shoals, are filled with college students getting course credit for such classes as coastal ecology, oceanic law, field marine biology, and forensics for marine biologists. Several times a year, however, the remote "research island," located 6 miles off the coast of Portsmouth, New Hampshire, invites the public out for three- to five-day adult education programs ranging from marine science to bird study. Shoals Marine Laboratory (SML) has even been known to throw in a watercolor painting or nature photography class or perhaps a kayak instruction session. The classes are all taught by professors from Cornell University or the University of New Hampshire (UNH), which jointly manage the granite island campus.

Appledore, with its pristine marine and terrestrial habitats and its rocky intertidal and gravel beaches, makes an ideal natural lab. There are a resident gull colony and a heron rookery (as well as more than a hundred migrant warblers, shorebirds, and sparrows), lobsters, fish, seaweed flora, and a whole range of marine mammals that swim in the Gulf of Maine, one of the world's most biologically productive ecosystems.

You'll get to the island on one of the lab's research vessels (they maintain a daily schedule during the summer season from June to late September), stay in one of the dorms, share meals at Kiggins Commons, the hub of the campus, and take field trips to the other islands in the archipelago on the lab's small fleet of Boston Whalers, inflatable boats, a 19-foot sailboat, and the 47-foot R/V *John M. Kingsbury*.

Although Appledore Island has been a research station for more than 30 years, it once served as a gathering ground for such literati as Mark Twain and Ralph Waldo Emerson, who came to stay at the summer hotel built by the father of poet Celia Thaxter. That hotel, one of the first built on the New England coast, burned to the ground in 1914, but Thaxter's Garden, a fabulous mess of poppies, sweet peas, hollyhocks, asters, and clematis that was immortalized in her 1894 book *An Island Garden,* is still there—or rather was re-created in 1977 by Dr. John Kingsbury, the founder and first director of the marine laboratory. Some of her original plants are still there, but many are raised in greenhouses on the UNH campus. Visits are limited to Wednesdays and reservations are required.

The rest of the island, other than the lab facilities and the migration banding station (which uses volunteers nicknamed "Band-Aids"), remains in a pristine state, far enough offshore to escape the major effects of coastal pollution and light-years away from the normal distraction of mainland life. There are no cars, no movieplexes, and nothing to distract you from the island's 3 miles of rocky shoreline—unless you count the live underwater lobster webcam.

Cornell biology professor Kingsbury founded Shoals Marine Laboratory in

WHILE YOU'RE IN THE NEIGHBORHOOD

All nine of the Isles of Shoals are privately owned. The only hotel is the Oceanic, a historic cluster of buildings built along a wooden walkway on Star Island, and only attendees of summer conferences can stay there. For more than a century, the Star Island Corporation, which also owns 90 percent of Appledore (it leases the island to Cornell and UNH), has been hosting a series of weeklong conferences at the Oceanic. Each week, the conferees challenge the Penguins (the nickname for the young college kids who work at the Oceanic) to a rousing softball game. Not only does the quirky softball field have a centuries-old graveyard in left field (any ball hit there is a ground rule double) and a tree near first base, but powerful hitters have been known to whack their balls into the ocean.

The Shoal island known as Smuttynose was the site of a famous 1873 murder of two Norwegian immigrants. The murder was dramatized in the book *The Weight of Water* by Anita Shreve and a movie of the same name starring Sean Penn and Elizabeth Hurley.

1973, partly in frustration at the lack of hands-on research opportunities for his budding students. Before World War II, when the military seized Appledore Island to use as an observation post, UNH had operated a marine zoology lab there. Somehow Kingsbury managed to cut through red tape and got his university and UNH to join forces. Today, SML is a self-sufficient community that generates its own power, maintains its own fresh-, salt-, and wastewater systems, and runs this campus that attracts students from all over the world.

Prices for the three-day programs are about $400 and include transportation, three meals a day (except on Sunday when there's only a late morning brunch and dinner), a shared room in one of the dorms, and all instruction.

HOW TO GET IN TOUCH
Shoals Marine Laboratory, G-14 Stimson Hall, Cornell University, Ithaca, NY 14853, 607-255-3717, www.sml.cornell.edu.

step inside the pages of a literary classic

TORONTO, ONTARIO

*Give me books, fruit, French wine and fine weather and a little music
out of doors, played by someone I do not know.*
—John Keats, great English poet

52

Tour operators have made a killing in the last few years selling *Da Vinci Code* tours of Paris and London. But long before Dan Brown penned the popular page-turner, Ann Kirkland was organizing book tours centered around literary classics (sorry, Dan, your book has yet to make her list). Her Toronto-based company, Classical Pursuits, specializes in learning vacations with a literary theme. On a tour called "Irish Literary Genius," for example, Kirkland shows off Dublin, Galway, and the Aran Islands to readers enjoying James Joyce's *Ulysses*, Oscar Wilde's *The Importance of Being Earnest*, and the poetry and plays of Martin McDonough, W. B. Yeats, and John Millington Synge.

"We offer the opportunity to travel through both space and time to destinations like Dante's Italy, Hemingway's Paris, or Dickens's London," Kirkland says. "We explore great works of literature in the places where they are set."

Arranged in collaboration with the Great Books Foundation of Chicago, each of the tours has a walking guide (expect to put some miles on your Keds), a local expert (on a theater tour to New York, for instance, Kirkland arranged a discussion with playwright Elizabeth Sharland who was Yul Brynner's personal assistant before turning to writing plays), and an experienced discussion leader. Although leaders often provide substantive commentary on, say, Carlos Fuentes's *Old Gringo* (one of three books on a tour to Mexico's Yucatán Peninsula) or Wallace Stegner's *The Angle of Repose* (for a tour to the desert Southwest), their primary mission is to make sure the discussions are lively and thought provoking. They'll help you grapple with the meaning of a book, painting, or opera, not tell you what it is.

Kirkland's flagship program, "Toronto Pursuits," is a one-week program held each summer at the University of Toronto's St. Michael's College. It's a chance to leave behind your Day-Timer and immerse yourself for an entire week in the great classics of music, philosophy, and literature. Each participant chooses one of 12 seminars (some of the choices in 2007 were Goethe's *Faust*, Tolstoy's *Anna Karenina*, Melville's *Moby-Dick*, Bach's *St. Matthew Passion*, the Book of Genesis, and Iranian cinema) to bone up on before coming. The two-hour morning sessions are followed each day by a leisurely lunch, where conversation continues. Afternoons and evenings offer a wide choice of cultural and social activities, including chamber concerts, guided walks through Toronto's back alleys, yoga classes, escorted visits to local museums, and theater performances.

The program fee for "Toronto Pursuits" is $925 and includes seminars, lunches, and most activities. For a moderate fee, accommodations can be arranged at the University of Toronto's Sorbara Hall. Fees for the learning vacations range from $1,500 to more than $3,000. The books are sent to you before your departure, and you are strongly encouraged to read them before catching your flight.

HOW TO GET IN TOUCH

Classical Pursuits, 349 Palmerston Boulevard, Toronto, ON M6G 2N5, 877-633-2555 or 416-892-3580, www.classicalpursuits.com.

get your sea legs on a sailboat

ANYWHERE THERE'S AN OCEAN, LAKE, RIVER, OR INLET

> It was such a good reminder that you're in control
> of a lot of your destiny. You just set your course,
> adjust your sails, and keep moving forward.
> —Katherine Souka, participant in a Womanship sailing school

53 For years, sailing was considered an inherited passion, the exclusive preserve of Ivy Leaguers in white linen pants, navy blazers, and boat shoes. Not anymore. At last count, there were something like 500 sailing schools in the United States alone, ranging from huge operations that offer ocean classrooms at eight current locations around the country to mom-and-pop schools docked at one luxurious resort allowing students to spend half their day mastering sailing skills and the other half golfing or lounging around the pool, mai tai in hand. Many of the schools offer live-aboard courses, which means you'll sample the delights of galley cooking, take showers in the head, and rarely leave your classroom for the week.

Before you sign up, it's wise to decide how serious a sailor you want to become and what you'd like to accomplish. Although most schools offer beginning courses where you literally start with "This is a boat . . . ," there are also courses in racing, cruising, bareboat chartering, and celestial navigation. The big vacation sailing schools offer a variety of courses, so half the vacationers may be brushing up on racing strategies while the other half familiarize themselves with the bare bones.

NAUTICAL LINGO

- A "ketch" is a two-masted sailboat, not something you do with a ball.
- They're *sheets* or "lines," not ropes.
- They're "shrouds" or "stays," not wires.
- It's "port" and "starboard," not left and right.
- It's *fore* and *aft*, not front and back

For those just wanting to get their boat shoes slightly wet—so to speak—start with a beginners' learn-to-sail course that usually combines classroom lectures with hands-on-the-tiller instruction. You'll learn the vocabulary (they may *look* like ropes, but they're actually called "lines"), how to rig the sails, how to read the direction of the wind, and how to set a course. You'll master the basics of water safety, knot tying, and navigation and get lots of practice coming about and jibing (that's sailor speak for changing course into the wind).

Beginner classes are ordinarily taught on stable, idiot-proof keelboats. While a false step can still pitch you into the drink—an embarrassing blunder, no doubt—the boats themselves are virtually impossible to capsize. Cruising courses focus on navigation, teaching you how to read charts, operate, and make basic repairs on all manner of shipboard equipment, from engines to depth finders.

Both the American Sailing Association (www.american-sailing.com) and the U.S. Sailing (www.ussailing.org) maintain rosters of approved North American sailing schools. You can also consult *Yachting* magazine's annual boat buyers' guide. In the meantime, here's a short list of well-known schools with stellar reputations, an impressive variety of courses, and decades-long track records.

Annapolis Sailing School. With two locations, Annapolis is the oldest salt among the sailing schools. It has been in business since 1959, and more than 150,000 students have learned to sail and cruise in its straightforward, step-by-step classes. Packages offered at both the Annapolis, Maryland, and St. Petersburg, Florida, campuses range from the "Become a Sailor in One Weekend" course at $375 for the Annapolis location or $525 for St. Petersburg (with a bigger boat) to the five-day "Preparation for Bareboat Chartering" at $1,045.

Annapolis Sailing School, 7001 Bembe Beach Road, Annapolis, MD 21403, 800-638-9192 or 410-267-8082, www.annapolissailing.com.

J World. Calling itself "the performance sailing school," J World has traditionally been renowned for its racing instruction, but it also offers corporate teambuilding events and sailing vacations to such exotic locales at Tortola, British Virgin Islands. With courses in Key West, Annapolis, Newport, San Diego, and San Francisco, J World offers everything from five-day "Learn to Sail" classes at $995 to seven-day live-aboard adventures for $2,690.

J World, 2240 Shelter Island Drive, San Diego, CA 92106, 800-666-1050 or 619-224-4774, www.jworldschool.com.

Offshore Sailing School. You can sign up for classes with Offshore in ten resort locations. Owned by former Olympic racer Steve Colgate and his wife Doris (who founded the National Women's Sailing Association), the school was started in 1964 and is considered the toniest of the sailing schools. Basic training is aboard the sleek but unsinkable Colgate 26, designed by Steve himself. A typical three-day learn-to-sail week on Florida's west coast at Captiva Island costs $1,500 based on double occupancy. For that, you get 20 hours of instruction and three nights at the luxurious South Seas Island Resort. Offshore also offers weeklong racing and cruising courses where you race all day, every day, against other sailors.

Offshore Sailing School, 16731 McGregor Boulevard, Fort Myers, FL 33908, 800-221-4326 or 239-454-1700, www.offshoresailing.com.

Womanship. Not a typical sailing school, Womanship offers women-only courses and aims to "empower" women as well as merely giving lessons in how to handle a boat. "Tacking and jibing are means to a greater end," says Suzanne Pogell, who started the school in 1984. "We've had women write and tell us that this was the most incredible experience they've had other than the birth of their children." With eight current locations from Vancouver to the Florida Keys, Womanship offers live-aboard programs ranging from 3 days in New England for $1,175 to 12 days in Turkey at $4,250.

Womanship, 137 Conduit Street, Annapolis, MD 21401, 800-342-9295 or 410-267-6661, www.womanship.com.

learn spanish in mexico

SAN MIGUEL DE ALLENDE, MEXICO

I learned more Spanish in one month
than I did in two years at my local community college.
—Sherry, student at Instituto Allende's Language School

54 Sure, you could pick up a few Spanish words and phrases at any number of language schools in this country, but why not go for an immersion? Learning Spanish in Mexico is more organic. Not only are you surrounded by Spanish—on the TV, menus, bus schedules, and signs—but you get the opportunity to use it in real-life situations.

San Miguel de Allende is a charming, 16th-century cobblestone street of a town about three hours north of Mexico City. Spanish, of course, is the predominant language, but because more than 5,000 Americans have chosen to retire there (something about the weather resembling early spring 352 days of the year), it's a great place to expose yourself to a new language without feeling like you're on another planet.

There are at least a half-dozen Spanish language schools in San Miguel, all offering inexpensive group or one-on-one lessons. The most popular and well established school is the Instituto Allende, housed in the sprawling former palace of the Counts of Canal. In existence since 1950, this prestigious school offers about every type of Spanish class you could ever think of: informal conversation classes up to accredited, semester-long courses. The institute will even set you up to live with a local family if you want to speak Spanish all day long. Because the institute's historic buildings and garden patios are often used for art openings, poetry readings, and other cultural events, you get to learn about the culture at the same time you're practicing pronouncing it.

Groups of 3 to 12 can take Spanish lessons that last four weeks and range from $145 for one hour of instruction a day to $520 for four hours. The institute also offers what it calls "Total Impact Spanish," one- to six-hour private lessons for $14 an hour. It can organize housing as well.

Instituto Allende, Ancha de San Antonio 22, San Miguel de Allende, Gto, 37700, México, 52-415-152-0190, www.instituto-allende.edu.mx.

TALE OF ONE CITY

Founded in 1542 by a barefoot Franciscan priest named Juan de San Miguel, this hip, artsy town is famous for luring foreigners who come for a vacation and end up staying for a lifetime. Soon after World War II, American GIs, realizing that their postwar education grants stretched further here, began showing up to learn Spanish and take arts courses. The Instituto Allende, along with the Bellas Artes, a government cultural center that also offers year-round arts, dance, and music classes, lured the expats and launched the town's reputation as a happening artist colony.

Unlike Cancun or Acapulco, where uber resorts, American fast food joints, and discos dominate, San Miguel de Allende still feels like old-time Mexico. It's full of winding cobblestone streets, high walls with bougainvillea pouring over them, big courtyards, bubbling fountains, stone arches, and carved wooden doors. Way back in 1926, the Mexican government declared the whole town a national monument (thanks to its starring role in the Mexican revolution), so traffic lights, billboards, flashing neon signs, and chains are major no-nos. Things you definitely don't want to miss:

- **El Jardin Principal.** The main square in town, it is San Miguel's social heartbeat. Shaded by trees, it has cantinas, art galleries, boutiques, and strolling mariachis; the glorious scents of corn tortillas, carnitas, and churros; and the landmark Parroquia de San Miguel Arcangel, an elaborate parish church with neo-Gothic sandstone arches and a lighted crucifix.
- **Tuesday Flea Market.** On a hill above the center of town, the sprawling flea market has anything you might ever need, from fresh guavas to Mexican vanilla to black Lab puppies to parts for your margarita blender. It's a great place to practice your Spanish because most vendors, selling their wares under makeshift tents, don't speak English.
- **Mercado de Artesanías.** Huichol Indian bead bracelets, Oaxacan crafts, tin folk art, papier-mâché, carved gourds, and woven rugs are just a few of the arts-and-crafts items available at this street market.
- **La Gruta Hot Springs.** With four spring-fed pools, this thermal hot springs, one of several in the area, is the favorite of locals. You can swim in a series of outdoor pools or be baptized in a grotto with a natural waterfall springing from a hole in the cave's wall.

give it the old college try

NATIONWIDE

Bring together wonderful people, stellar teachers, great settings, and terrific logistical support, and presto, the experience is exhilarating (some say magical).
—Cornell's Adult University website

55 Back when you were eating dorm food, cramming for finals, and reading about dead Greek guys, you couldn't wait to get away from your college campus. "Best years of my life? Who are you kidding?" But now, with a few years of the "real world" under your belt, you have come to realize that a college campus, with its erudite professors, stimulating assignments, and all-night gabfests, ranks right up there on your list of happiest memories. What wouldn't you give to go back?

Now you can. Sprinkled across America are universities that offer summer classes for adults. You get to stay in the dorms, eat at the cafeterias, and use the gyms, swimming pools, and other facilities (Cornell University even has a Robert Trent–designed golf course) and take advantage of all those bright minds you failed to fully appreciate back when you were 18. Best of all, there are no entrance exams, no tests, no nothing except the chance to spend a whole week thinking about a topic that's near and dear to your heart.

Some universities open their campuses for just a short time. Indiana University's Mini University, for example, offers about a hundred noncredit classes during a single week every mid-June (see p. 185). Other universities offer weeklong adult learning opportunities, such as St. John's College in Santa Fe, New Mexico, which conducts three weeks of summer classics (see pp. 165–166), or **Skidmore College** in Saratoga Springs, New York (815 North Broadway, Saratoga Springs, NY, 12866, 518-580-5590, www. skidmore.edu), which offers a four-week adult writing institute. **New York University** (Office of Summer Sessions,

7 E. 12th Street, 6th Floor, New York, NY 10003, 212-998-2292, www.nyu.edu/summer) offers summer adult workshops in filmmaking, and **Moravian College** in Bethlehem, Pennsylvania (Music Department, 1200 Main Street, Bethlehem, PA 18018, 610-861-1650, www.julyjazzgetaway.org), offers a weeklong jazz workshop every July.

Still others utilize their professors to lead off-site educational and cultural tours. The **University of Vermont** (UVM), for instance, books more than a dozen tours per year. A recent example is the "Fair Trade Coffee Tour," which took participants to a coffee cooperative in Veracruz, Mexico. Led by two UVM instructors, participants worked on a coffee farm, witnessed how fair trade impacts local communities, and examined sustainable agriculture. (**UVM Learning Adventures,** 460 S. Prospect Street, Burlington, VT 05401, 800-639-3210 or 802-656-1085, www.uvm.edu.)

There's a good chance your alma mater offers a summer adult institute, but if not, here are five of the best:

Colby College. Every August for more than 50 years, Colby College in Waterville, Maine, has been hosting the Great Books Summer Institute, an in-depth discussion and workshop on six selected classic books. Although courses change every year, recent examples are Thomas Mann's *The Magic Mountain,* Fritjof Capra's *The Tao of Physics,* or Cervantes's *Don Quixote.* It's a great bargain—only $480—for tuition, lodging, all meals (including a Maine clambake), and the six books, which will be sent to you four months in advance.

    Colby Summer Institute, 4730 Mayflower Hill Drive, Waterville, ME 04901, 207-872-3386, www.colby.edu/spec.prog/other/great_books/index.shtml.

Cornell's Adult University. Perhaps the most ambitious, Cornell University offers four one-week sessions each July in a wide variety of disciplines. You can study such diverse topics as "Life on a Thread: An Introduction to Spider Biology," "The Rise, Decline, and Resurgence of Islamic Culture," and "Understanding the Science of Everyday Things." There are also workshops in landscape design, writing, golf, and tennis. For between $1,355 and $1,535, you get tuition, lodging, 16 meals, and use of Cornell's facilities.

    Cornell Adult University and Summer Programs, 626 Thurston Avenue, Ithaca, NY 14850, 607-255-4987, www.cau.cornell.edu.

MR. LAKE GOES TO COLLEGE

Steve Lake, a Las Vegas casino pit boss, is on a mission to visit 500 college campuses. He began his unique odyssey after his 1984 honeymoon to Boston. He and his new wife visited Harvard and a light bulb went on: "Wow, there's some beautiful schools out there! I really missed out on something." It's not that Lake didn't attend college, but as he says about Concordia, the Montreal university where he got his marketing degree, "It didn't really have a campus, not 1 inch of grass. It was a 12-story office building."

On each of his campus visits, Lake walks around campus, inspects the architecture, reads the student newspaper, checks out the bulletin boards, eats at the campus dining hall, and when he can, sits in on a class. If the classrooms are empty, he'll leave his mark on the chalkboard: his name, the date, and the number of campuses in his count.

Lake, who admits to being a tad bit obsessive-compulsive, has also collected a few other milestones. He has visited every U.S. state, its capital, and its capitol; he's seen a game at every major league ballpark; and by 1980 he had achieved life master status in contract bridge. Number of campuses? 384 and counting.

Mini University, Indiana University. Since 1972, Mini University has been offering this reasonably priced week of classes that draws summer scholars from all over the world. For a mere $215 (on-campus lodging at the Union Biddle Hotel & Conference Center is extra), you can take up to 15 classes that are from one to two hours long on everything from "Life of a CIA Operations Officer" to "Is Wal-Mart Good for America" to "Eugenics: Then and Now." They're delivered by volunteer IU faculty. At night, Mini University stages picnics, films, theater trips, and other social gatherings. And you don't have to be an alum.

IU Alumni Association, Virgil T. DeVault Alumni Center, 1000 E. 17th Street, Bloomington, IN 47408, 800-824-3044 or 812-855-4822, www.alumni.indiana.edu/events/miniu/.

St. John's Summer Classic Series. With a series of three weeklong seminars, you'll delve into such classics as Dostoevsky's *The Brothers Karamazov*, Tolstoy's *War and Peace*, Milton's *Paradise Lost*, Joseph Conrad's *Nostromo*, and the operas of Benjamin Britten. In groups of 17, you'll attend morning and afternoon sessions.

Seminars go for $1,100 and include tuition, books, lunch, course materials, and special events. Accommodation on campus including all meals can be arranged for $510 per week.

Summer Classics, St. John's College, 1160 Camino Cruz Blanca, Santa Fe, NM 87505, 505-984-6117, www.stjohnscollege.edu (click on Educational Outreach).

University of North Carolina. Since 1979, the University of North Carolina's (UNC) Program in the Humanities and Human Values has been offering seminars, workshops, and conferences "to enrich the life of the mind and contribute to the development of a more humane world." For a while, it was called "Vacation College" and offered five weeklong sessions of classes. It has morphed into about 30 weekends throughout the year (with the occasional Wednesday) called "Adventures in Ideas." Recent offerings include "Empires across Time," "God, Religion, and Evil," and "Moral Philosophy: An Introduction to Kant and Mill." Although you don't bunk on campus, the UNC Humanities Program website has a listing of comfortable hotels around town. Tuition ranges from $105 to $185. Special rates are available for first-timers and teachers.

UNC Humanities Program, CB #3425, University of North Carolina, Chapel Hill, NC 27599, 919-962-1544, http://adventuresinideas.unc.edu.

HISTORYAMERICA TOURS

take a magical
mystery history tour

Anybody can make history; only a great man can write it.
—Oscar Wilde

56 It has been said we study history to avoid repeating the mistakes of the past. Others claim history gives us a context to understand the present, that it gives us an identity, a moral compass. While all those things might be true, the reason people study history with HistoryAmerica Tours, a company that has been giving riveting history tours since 1991, is because it's so much fun. Not to mention, you will be learning from some very fascinating people.

On a past HistoryAmerica tour called "Six Seconds in Dallas," for example, the assassination of JFK was explored by the FBI agent who coordinated the investigation, a reporter who covered it for the *Dallas News*, a police detective who questioned Lee Harvey Oswald and witnessed his shooting by Jack Ruby, an employee for the Texas School Book Depository who gave Oswald a ride to work that fateful morning, and the Yale-educated author who wrote the classic reference work about the case. On a different tour, Jim McPherson, a professor of American history at Princeton University and author of the Pulitzer Prize–winning book *Battle Cry of Freedom: The Civil War Era*, led guests around the battlefields of Gettysburg and Antietam, providing insider information on these battlegrounds that changed the course of American history.

HistoryAmerica Tours has a knack for finding the absolute best historian guides, as they call the experts, scholars, and authors who lead their tours. And it's not just the Pulitzer Prizes and Ivy League credentials that make them so special. It's their unique ability to breathe life into a particular slice of historical pie. HistoryAmerica's historian guides are so engaging, so riveting, that many of the company's customers have found something in common with their junior high granddaughters, at least the ones who follow the latest boy bands. Like film buffs

WALK INTO THE PAST

Walking tours of historic centers are an excellent way to get the buzz about a neighborhood's past. Here are some popular ones:

Joyce Gold History Tours of New York. Walk the streets of New York with fascinating historian Joyce Gold, who offers such diverse tours as "Gangs of New York and the Bloody Five Points," "Harlem—Keystone of African America," "Fifth Avenue Gold Coast," and "Central Park: The Big Back Yard of the City." Tours last 2.5 hours and cost $15 per person. Rain or shine. *Joyce Gold History Tours of New York, 141 West 17th Street, New York, New York 10011, 212-242-5762, www.nyctours.com.*

Original Charleston Walks. Explore the Old and Historic District, getting the lowdown on King Charles, the Merry Monarch; pirate attacks; and the invasion of the Union army during the Civil War. Tours include "Ghosts and Legends" (led in the evening, of course), "Slavery and Freedom," and "Pirates and Buccaneers." Tickets between $18.50 and $29.50. *Original Charleston Walks, 866-550-8939, www.charlestonwalks.com.*

San Francisco History Guides. Free history and architectural walking tours led by volunteers, including "1906 Earthquake & Fire," "Art Deco Marina," "Coit Tower Murals," which takes in some of the city's famous (and sometimes controversial) Depression-era murals; "Gold Rush City," which explores the haunts of the original 49ers; and "Landmark Victorians of Alamo Square," showcasing the beautifully restored Painted Ladies on the world-famous Postcard Row. Walks last between 1.5 to 2 hours. *San Francisco History Guides, 415-557-4266 www.sfcityguides.org.*

Washington Walks. A plethora of walking tours includes a hike through Arlington National Cemetery, the "White House 'Un-Tour,'" a one-hour walk *around* the nation's most famous residence; a nighttime exploration of the National Mall's monuments; and the "Blossom Secret Stroll," which delves into the history and lore behind the Tidal Basin's fabled Japanese cherry trees. The Washington Walks season runs April 1 through October 31. Most walks last an hour, begin near a Metro station, and cost (most walks) $10 per person. *Washington Walks, 202-484-1565, www.washingtonwalks.com.*

---

who count the days until the next Scorsese film or the next Woody Allen offering, HistoryAmerica's devoted fans end up hopelessly smitten, following their historian guides around like paparazzi.

"Some people take every tour a particular guide offers," says Georgia O'Connor, one of the new owners who bought HistoryAmerica Tours from Pete and Julia Brown. "Yesterday while writing a confirmation, I checked the computer on this guy and figured I'd made a mistake. It said he'd signed up for four tours last year. But sure enough, I checked the roster and he'd taken every one."

The Browns started the company in 1991. Inspired by the massive popularity of Ken Burns's PBS special on the Civil War, Pete decided to see if he could round up some other history buffs who might enjoy traveling to the spots they loved reading about. The first year, they offered two tours. By 2000, their roster of history tours listed 29. Although HistoryAmerica's offerings are currently slimmer (seven tours and three cruises in 2007), it's only because the new owners, taking over the reins in late 2006, wanted some time to get adjusted.

Over the years, HistoryAmerica has offered tours on a broad spectrum of subjects, from "Great Love Stories of the Civil War" to tours looking into the Cherokee Nation's Trail of Tears and Benedict Arnold's role in the American Revolution. For several years, they worked with the History Channel to offer such trips as "Take Me Out to the Ballgame" (spring training in Florida) and "Historic Hawaii." The Apache Wars, Crazy Horse and Custer, World War II in the South Pacific, and the War of 1812 on Lake Erie are all subjects that HistoryAmerica has tackled with enlightenment and fun.

The six- to eight-day tours, which include accommodations, transportation, all admissions, breakfast, and about half the lunches and dinners run from $2,095 to $2,695. The "Antietam and Gettysburg: Killing Grounds That Changed America" tour detailed on p. 169 goes for $2,165 per person, based on double occupancy ($2,595 single). Besides the historian guide, you'll get a professional tour director and a reading list.

HOW TO GET IN TOUCH
HistoryAmerica Tours, 4265 Peridot Lane, Rapid City, SD 57702, 800-628-8542 or 605-348-2250, www.historyamerica.com.

reach for the stars

MOUNT LEMMON, TUCSON, ARIZONA

We had the sky up there, all speckled with stars,
and we used to lay on our backs and look up at them,
and discuss about whether they was made or only just happened.
—Mark Twain, American humorist, writer, and lecturer

57 Amateurs can't exactly take on particle physics or molecular genetics, but when it comes to astronomy, there's not much everyday people can't do—given the right telescopes and an enthusiastic teacher. Maybe that's why the University of Arizona's Astronomy Camp has become so popular. In these three- to four-day programs for adults and seven- to eight-day programs for teens, stargazers find themselves observing, photographing, and electronically imaging various celestial objects through professional-grade telescopes, devising theories on globular clusters, and identifying near-Earth asteroids that only astronomy professors usually know about.

The enthusiastic teacher, Don McCarthy, the University of Arizona professor who heads the programs, is so much fun (he has a whole collection of music about stars—for example, from *Annie, Phantom of the Opera,* and *Cats)* and has such a knack for explaining complex theories that past campers keep coming back year after year. In fact, Lisa Roubal, codirector of the program, jokes that she practically has to beg Astronomy Camp alumni to wait a year before returning so there will be room for new campers.

Astronomy Camp, which has been going strong since 1988, takes place at Mount Lemmon, a mountaintop observatory just north of Tucson. Although the bulk of the programs are geared for teenagers, the adult programs are scheduled around the phases of the moon and are held several times a year in the spring through fall.

You'll sleep in an old Air Force barracks, eat with the scientists working at Mount Lemmon, and use the same telescopes they use in their research projects. You'll have access to six telescopes at Mount Lemmon (including a 40-inch and two 60-inch reflectors) and the 61-inch reflector that was built for NASA's Apollo program at nearby Mount Bigelow. You'll observe the sun through a variety of instruments, spot Venus with your naked eye, hear talks by well-known astronomers, catch the green flash, and even conduct your own research projects.

You'll also get to dissect obsolete astronomical instruments, develop film, play volleyball and billiards, hike the forests surrounding the observatory, and tour Kitt Peak and Mount Graham or Mount Hopkins observatories and the Steward Observatory Mirror Laboratory.

"The camps are not meant to produce future astronomers or even scientists," McCarthy says. "Instead, they are designed to promote a lifelong love of learning and an understanding of our cosmic environment."

Tuition is $550 or $700 per person, depending on the camp's length, and includes meals, lodging, and transportation. The only thing it doesn't include is a guarantee of clear nights (although that's not usually a problem in this desert environment).

HOW TO GET IN TOUCH

University of Arizona, 933 N. Cherry Avenue, Tucson, AZ 85721, 520-621-4079, www.astronomycamp.org.

WHILE YOU'RE IN THE NEIGHBORHOOD

Before there was John Wayne, Roy Rogers, or even the state of Arizona for that matter, there was Tanque Verde, a sprawling cattle ranch on the outskirts of Tucson. While most of the guests of this 640-acre spread–turned–guest ranch come to don Stetsons and practice their yippee-ti-yo-ti-yeas, there's a little-known contingent who come each year to sit at the heels of Jerry Brewer, a herpetologist who turns nature walking into the very highest form of entertainment.

Brewer, a half Cherokee–half Choctaw who was asked by owner Bob Cote to develop the nature center a half dozen years ago, doesn't miss a thing on his near-daily walks. And he makes sure guests don't either, introducing them to everything from rattlesnakes on a stick (a walking stick he holds at a safe distance) to scorpions and cochineel beetles that were once used to dye the red coats of early British soldiers.

"I'm a seven-year-old boy in a 54-year-old body," Brewer says. His enthusiasm is contagious. Engaging all the senses, guests on Brewer's walks eat wild hackberries, smell canyon ragweed that reeks of turpentine, and hear the call of dozens of birds. According to Brewer, "Most people miss 98 percent of their lives." But not here. *Tanque Verde Nature Center, 14301 East Speedway, Tucson, AZ 85748, 520-296-6275, www.tanqueverderanch.com.*

---

sit at the feet of the masters

CHAUTAUQUA, NEW YORK

It has mythic force, Chautauqua does. There is no place like it.
No resort. No spa. Not anywhere else in the country,
or anywhere else in the world.
—Historian David McCullough, Chautauqua speaker in 1995

58 Former Supreme Court justice Sandra Day O'Connor is not one to mince words. Asked to name her favorite vacation spot, she doesn't blink an eye: the Chautauqua Institution, of course. Unless you've experienced the intimate summer community in the southwestern tip of New York, it's hard to explain Chautauqua. Part arts colony, part summer camp, part college campus, part village square—"nirvana" is a word that springs to mind.

During its nine-week summer session, Chautauqua offers more than 400 special studies courses on just about any topic you can name. Want to learn the mountain dulcimer? Master astronomy? Perfect your Hebrew? Here, you can.

In fact, when it was started in 1874 as a summer training program for Methodist Sunday School teachers, it was the first place in the country, probably the world, to encourage and articulate a philosophy of self-improvement and lifelong learning. Its motto declares that everyone "has as right to be all that he can be—to know all that he can know."

More than 8,000 people are in residence on any given day during the season, taking classes, listening to the daily 10:45 a.m. lectures, and enjoying the nightly arts performances. The daily lecture series, always about burning issues of the day, is the lifeblood of Chautauqua. Each of the nine weeks is themed. Recent examples include "The Meteoric Rise of China and India," "21st-Century Cities," "Healthy Aging," and the Middle East. Experts on these topics are brought in to speak and lead discussions Monday through Friday.

Some of the names you might recognize who have been speakers here are Helen Keller, Jane Goodall, Rudyard Kipling, Thurgood Marshall, Margaret Mead, Tom Ridge, Kurt Vonnegut, Susan B. Anthony, Alexander Graham Bell, and Jonas

11 THINGS YOU MAY NOT KNOW ABOUT CHAUTAUQUA

- Franklin D. Roosevelt delivered his "I Hate War" speech from the amphitheater platform in 1936.
- Ronald Reagan addressed the Third General Chautauqua Conference on U.S.–Soviet Relations via satellite in 1987.
- Thomas Edison was the son-in-law of Chautauqua cofounder Lewis Miller.
- George Gershwin finished his composition of his Concerto in F in a Chautauqua practice shack in 1925.
- The Athenaeum Hotel was one of the first hotels to have electric lights.
- Abba, Kenny Rogers, the Village People, Lucille Ball, Willie Nelson, and Peter, Paul, and Mary all have performed at Chautauqua.
- The oldest continuous book club in America, the Chautauqua Literary and Scientific Circle, has enrolled at least a half million readers and at one time sponsored 10,000 reading circles throughout the country.
- Chautauqua has two 18-hole golf courses.
- Thanks to its huge bat population, Chautauqua is practically mosquito free.
- New York University conducted summer courses at Chautauqua for approximately 30 years.
- Chautauqua's Palestine Park is a large-scale model of the Holy Land.

Salk. With a pedigree like that, it's not surprising that Chautauqua Institution is a national historic landmark (designated in 1989), noted for its landscapes, historic architecture, beautiful gardens, and significance to American education. Not only did it pioneer continuing adult education, correspondence courses, and Great Books curricula, but it spawned a whole Chautauqua Movement, as well. During the late 1800s and early 1900s, traveling chautauquas toured the country, offering speakers and demonstrations in large open-air tents.

Chautauqua is set on a large natural lake in New York's wine country. Its 750 acres include stately homes, Victorian gingerbread cottages, winding brick roads, huge maple trees, art galleries, interesting little churches, and all the amenities of a rural village. Cars are discouraged.

There's a special energy at Chautauqua that defies words. People are excited, inquisitive, and hungry for more than they hear from the nightly drone of their TVs. They treat each other with friendliness and civility. Nobody locks their doors. There's a restorative, peaceful atmosphere. Theodore Roosevelt, in fact, pronounced Chautauqua as "America at its best."

Chautauqua has its own opera company, orchestra, theater company, movie house, and ballet. Nightly performances are held in the 5,000-seat, open-air, covered amphitheater, the oldest and largest of its kind still in use in the country.

The institution offers one-week, multiweek, and entire season packages. Some families have been gathering here for seven generations. There's a wide range of accommodations, from the stately Athenaeum Hotel to quaint B&Bs in lovely old Victorian homes. There are also many grand private homes that owners gladly rent out. Weekly classes vary in price, but most run in the $60 to $90 range. There's a onetime gate admission ($15 for a day ticket, $47.50 for a day/evening ticket) that allows entry into various lectures, readings, and rehearsals. A one-week ticket is $305 and includes admission to everything (lectures, symphony, popular entertainments, and so forth *except* theater, opera, and special studies courses). Accommodations range from $49 a night for a room to $5,000 per week for a house.

HOW TO GET IN TOUCH

Chautauqua Institution, P.O. Box 28, Chautauqua, NY 14722, 800-836-2787 or 716-357-6250 (box office), www.ciweb.org.

take a radical sabbatical

IN THE UNITED STATES & WORLDWIDE

When you come to a fork in the road, take it.
—Yogi Berra

59 Rather than supplying information—the purpose of most intellectual sojourns—a "radical sabbatical" is designed to seek information. From you. You'll be asked the kinds of questions that tend to get pushed to the back burner in our busy lives: "What do you stand for?" "Why are you here?" "What makes you want to get on the table and dance?"

Radical sabbaticals are offered by Horizon & Co., a high-end boutique travel company. Its goal is to transport its customers—not in the obvious, prosaic sense, but in a more lyrical, metaphysical way. For example, on Horizon's "Diamond Adventures" trip, customers literally fly into the tundra of the Northwest Territories to scout for diamonds. (In case you hadn't heard, diamonds were discovered on the shores of the Northern Territories' Point Lake in 1991. There were enough pristine-quality specimens to propel Canada into third place in the diamond-production rankings.) Not only do you learn about diamond processing, but you also dogsled, stay in a wilderness lodge, and dine on such delicacies as musk oxen and arctic char.

Horizon's radical sabbaticals, designed to push people out of their comfort zones, are led by Steve Zikman, a former attorney who quit his high-powered career to take a three-year, round-the-world escapade. The author of *The Power of Travel* and *Chicken Soup for the Traveler's Soul*, Zikman believes that travel, approached properly, is the catalyst for unlocking creative potential and innovative thinking. He says that his trips take people where conventional thinking just doesn't work. They're designed for people who are at a crossroads, people who are searching for deeper meaning, a higher purpose. Using a salon-like approach, Zikman pushes people to think, to ask the tough questions, to find that elusive balance between life and work.

In this case, being shoved from your comfort zone doesn't mean enduring physical hardship or partaking in such torments as oxygen-gulping ropes courses.

MAYBE IT'S THE WEATHER

Far be it from us to suggest that after a radical sabbatical you'll want to break free from the confines of your current job. Just as a warning, you should know that Santa Barbara, where several radical sabbaticals are staged, seems to be breeding ground for entrepreneurs. It spawned the success of Motel 6, the largest company-owned and -operated lodging chain in the United States (the first Motel 6, opened in Santa Barbara in 1962, rented rooms for six dollars a night); Big Dog Sportswear (with 200 nationwide locations, it was launched by a couple of Santa Barbara college students on a rafting trip); and Kinko's, which was started in a taco stand on the University of California, Santa Barbara campus with a single copy machine. In addition, one of the first film studios, Flying A, once sat at the corner of State and Mission Streets. Started by the American Film Company in 1909, Flying A produced more than 1,200 films, mostly Westerns and black-and-whites. Cecil B. DeMille worked as a carpenter there, and Charlie Chaplin liked the area so much that he moved to Montecito and built the still popular Montecito Inn.

Horizon's radical sabbaticals are every bit as posh as its other four-star programs. They're more about challenging your internal limits of daring.

Before you begin, you'll be asked to come up with a purpose for your sabbatical—an intention or a question that focuses on an aspect of your life you'd like to change. By using travel as a metaphor for life, a mirror that reflects your attitude toward change and dealing with adversity, you'll dramatically alter the way you think, feel, and act.

Many of Zikman's Next Fork vacations take place in California, where he lives. On the five-day "Sideways Wisdom in Santa Barbara's Wine Country," for example, you tour the wineries (of course), walk a labyrinth, participate in impromptu Zikman-led roundtables, and take workshops on exploring your life path. He also takes seekers to such exotic locales as far afield as Chile, Iceland, Myanmar (or Burma), and Bhutan.

Costs for the tours vary widely. The Santa Barbara trip is priced at $2,250 and includes accommodations, most meals, entrance fees, and challenging questions from Zikman himself.

HOW TO GET IN TOUCH
Horizon & Co., 478 Queen Street East, Suite 400, Toronto, ON M5A 1T7, Canada, 800-387-2977, www.horizon-co.com.

tour the canadian maritimes aboard a luxury train

MONTREAL TO HALIFAX

I have travelled around the globe. I have seen the Canadian and American Rockies, the Andes, the Alps and the Highlands of Scotland, but for simple beauty, Cape Breton outrivals them all.
—Alexander Graham Bell (1847–1922), inventor of the telephone and former resident of Baddeck, Nova Scotia

60 For more than a hundred years, Canada's longest running train, the *Ocean*, has been transporting passengers from Montreal to Halifax. This 21-hour journey takes passengers through New Brunswick and much of Nova Scotia, providing them with awesome glimpses of the Canadian Maritime Provinces.

A couple of years ago, VIA Rail, the national rail service of Canada, decided to take this service one step further by redecorating the cars, providing gourmet meals, and adding what they call the "Easterly Class: A Maritime Learning Experience." This unique trip combines the best of luxury train travel (think Marilyn Monroe strumming the ukulele in an old Pullman car) with the kind of educational component that travelers today tell marketing people they expect from their vacations.

WHILE YOU'RE IN THE NEIGHBORHOOD

If you've got a few extra days, Sackville, New Brunswick, on the *Ocean*'s route, is a nice stop-off thanks to its location on the Tantramar Marshes. Make sure to check out Mel's Tea Room, a diner with a general store and a soda fountain. Mel's has been around since 1919, when Mel Goodwin opened it soon after World War I. The quirky place is still in the family, now run by Roger Goodwin, Mel's grandson. It's a popular hangout for students from Mount Allison University. *Mel's Tea Room, 17 Bridge Street, Sackville, NB E4L 3N6, 506-536-1251.*

While chugging along the St. Lawrence Seaway next to pastoral farms, you'll get 10- to 15-minute vignettes, half-hour presentations, and longer hands-on learning experiences about this storied region. For example, a seafood vignette might include a demonstration of a lobster trap.

You'll have your own learning coordinator, who presents lectures on a wide range of topics, from culture and history to geography and regional cuisine. You'll hear riveting stories about French-English warfare, privateers, and shipwrecks; learn how to make fishing nets; or perhaps partake in Maritime cooking classes. Impromptu history conversations might spring to life when, say, you stop in Springhill, Nova Scotia, the scene of Canada's worst mining disaster. The learning coordinator and his or her team often dress in themed costumes while presenting workshops, short movie viewings, and off-the-cuff presentations.

Included in this package are three meals featuring Maritime cooking. You might have pan-seared Atlantic halibut or crispy crab cakes, for example, or imbibe some of the Maritime wines or Propeller Bitter, a dark, Halifax-made microbrew.

All your workshops and presentations will take place in the *Ocean*'s double-decker Park Car, a throwback to the old days of luxury railroad travel. With elegant curved windows, this old car from the 1950s has two lounges (the Mural Lounge, so-named because of a wall mural by a Canadian artist, and the Bullet Lounge) and a panoramic observation deck with windows in every direction so you'll have a 360-degree view of the beautiful passing scenery. Your accommodations for this unique vacation are a cozy sleeper car complete with duvet comforter and chocolate on your pillow.

The Easterly Class runs every day except Tuesdays. If you want the full nostalgic package, make sure to ask for the stainless-steel HEP cars; until recently, the entire train used these cars, which are of the same vintage as the Park Car, but recently they've added what they call Renaissance cars.

The price for the package is $355 ($406 Canadian) and includes three meals, exclusive access to the Park Car, and comfy seats for viewing all those blue seascapes, green spruce forests, and pink Tantramar salt marshes.

HOW TO GET IN TOUCH
VIA Rail, P.O. Box 8116, Station "A," Montreal, QC H3C 3N3, Canada, 888-842-7245, www.viarail.ca.

monitor active volcanoes

HILO, HAWAII

We don't do drive-by tourism. We don't ever sit in a bus
and say, 'This is Rainbow Falls.' We experience it.
—Judith Fox-Goldstein, director of Hawaiian EDventures

61 There are 500 active volcanoes in the world, and two of the most active are on Hawaii's Big Island—which makes it a great place to study lava, ash flows, tephra, and other volcanic ejecta that burst forth from the conical mountains. Thanks to the University of Hawaii–Hilo, which has teamed up with Destination Hilo and the state's Department of Business, Economic Development, and Tourism, you can spend an entire week learning about volcanoes. One of the first things you'll learn is that Mauna Kea, one of the three active volcanoes on your itinerary, is taller than Mount Everest: If you measure it from its base on the ocean floor to its summit, it rises 33,476 feet (Mount Everest towers 29,035 feet from sea level). You'll also learn that the Hawaiian Islands, as well as 80 percent of the rest of the world, wouldn't be here if it weren't for volcanoes.

On this three-island, three-volcano "EDventure," you'll study with scientists from the University of Hawaii–Hilo, the Hawaiian Volcano Observatory, and the Center for the Study of Active Volcanoes, exploring lava tubes, trekking across historic lava flows, and learning basic field methods in volcano monitoring. You'll collect seismic, geodetic, and geochemical data and learn how to interpret it. But volcanoes aren't the only thing you can study through Hawaiian EDventures, which custom designs each new adventure.

"A typical day can consist of any number of activities, depending on what you're interested in learning," says Judith Fox-Goldstein, director of the program, which has won several travel and business awards. "You can learn how to weave lauhala baskets and string lei with *Kupuna* (elders), study the stars at the Mauna Kea Observatory, or plant taro with farmers in Waipio Valley."

In 1990, Hawaiian EDventures began to offer programs that "you can't do as a regular visitor." At last count, there were more than 75 programs, each integrating

SOME ENCHANTED ISLAND TRIVIA

- Every day, on average, the Big Island of Hawaii gains an extra 3 or 4 square feet of real estate thanks to regular eruptions by the Kilauea volcano.
- With miles of black lava fields, the Big Island—at least on the west side—could easily play body double for the moon. In fact, Gemini and Apollo astronauts used to train there. Locals leave creative graffiti by strategically placing chunks of white coral.
- Before modern science came along, ancient Romans believed volcanoes were the chimney of the forge where the thunderbolts for the god Jupiter were made. Jupiter's blacksmith was named Vulcan, hence "volcano." In Hawaii, people attributed eruptive activity to Pele, the goddess of violence.

academic, cultural, and recreational activities. Most run from one to three weeks, with themes ranging from birding and natural history to health and wellness. On a weeklong marine science course, for example, you'll take guided tide-pool walks and snorkeling expeditions, attend lectures on marine ecology, and help with coastal cleanup projects.

Astronomy enthusiasts can sign up for an EDventure that includes stargazing at the Onizuka Visitor Center (elevation 9,000 feet) or at the observatories on the summit of Mauna Kea (13,000 feet). The facilities on top of the volcano support the largest collection of telescopes anywhere.

One of the most popular EDventures is an 8-day trip that includes one day each studying the following disciplines: birds and plants, volcanology, astronomy, agriculture, marine biology, art, geology, and business. Each area of study is integrated with all the other topics and reflects the teachings and traditions of Hawaii's Kupuna.

The cost for an EDventure varies depending on the experience, the length of the program, and the focus of the trip. All programs are adapted to fit within budgetary requirements and include meals, accommodations, ground transportation, field instruction, and educational materials.

HOW TO GET IN TOUCH

Hawaiian EDventure Program, University of Hawaii–Hilo Conference Center, 200 W. Kawili Street, Hilo, HI 96720, 808-974-7555, http://conference.uhh.hawaii.edu/edventure.html.

walk a battlefield with ed bearss

FAMOUS U.S. BATTLEFIELDS

A battlefield tour with Ed Bearss is a transcendental experience.
—Dennis Frye, historian

62 This entry doesn't have a company or an organization attached to it, because Ed Bearss, the chief historian emeritus for the National Park Service, gives battlefield history tours for many different organizations—National Geographic Expeditions, Smithsonian Journeys, and the National Trust for Historic Preservation, to name a few illustrious ones that have enlisted his services over the years. To tell you the truth, if you're lucky enough to get Bearss (pronounced Bars) as your tour leader, it's not going to matter who organizes the tour—you could sleep in a tent and eat beans from a can as long as the "Pied Piper of History," as Bearss has been called, is your trusty leader.

Although Bearss is often pegged as a Civil War historian thanks to his prominent role in Ken Burns's popular PBS documentary series, he can also give what the *Washington Post* described as "Homeric monologues" on the Revolutionary War, the Mexican War, World War I, World War II, and probably any war since. As he said in the preface to his book *Fields of Honor,* "I served in the United States Marine Corps and know how a battlefield feels, sounds and smells." And after a Bearss-led tour, so will you. Just Google his name and you'll find several options for studying under this indefatigable tour leader.

Born on a ranch in Montana in 1923, Bearss has been obsessed with the Civil War since he was a boy. His dad read him bedtime stories about the Civil War, and he named his favorite dairy cow Antietam. After graduating from high school in 1941, he thumbed around the country visiting Civil War sites for a few months before joining the Marines.

THE NEW BATTLE

"If I'm interested in something, I don't get tired."
—Ed Bearss

When he's not giving tours, Bearss is busy advocating for preservation of historic sites. As he says, "Development is advancing more irresistibly than Grant's army did on Richmond." At Gettysburg, for example, the once idyllic vista of the battlefield is broken by a water tower for an industrial park. For a while, there were plans for a casino. Bearss has seen 19th-century forts bulldozed to make way for malls. His bus tours often get stalled in shopping center traffic. As he says, "The battles are going to be played out in the next 10 to 20 years, because by then the battlefield parks will be islands in urban corridors of the United States, in a sea of sprawling shopping malls."

After some nasty mortar fire in the Pacific Theater of World War II left him wounded, he spent his 26-month recovery reading everything he could find about the Civil War. He then used the GI bill to get a degree in foreign service from Georgetown University (he also has a master's in history from Indiana University) and eventually went to work for the National Park Service. "It was a dream," he says, "getting paid for doing what I would have done on my own."

In fact, it was at Vicksburg, Mississippi, his first Park Service assignment, that he began giving interpretive tours. For years, he led eight one-hour tours a day around the Vicksburg battlefields. Even after he was promoted and was no longer required to give tours, he kept it up as a hobby on weekends. After retiring from his post as chief historian for the National Park Service, he went freelance, traveling and leading groups up to 300 days a year.

Always the consummate tour guide, Bearss brings history alive to visitors of all knowledge levels. For years, he gave an annual tour of Vicksburg to the Louisiana School for the Blind and Deaf. Not only has he visited virtually every battlefield in the country, but he also has an encyclopedic memory, enormous personal energy, and groupies who literally follow him from tour to tour. Not bad for a guy with 80 or so candles on his birthday cake.

As for the groupies, some of them have taken as many as 40 tours with him. They've been known to wear badges identifying themselves as the "Bearss Brigade."

Some wear T-shirts depicting his face on Mount Rushmore or transposed onto Elvis's white jumpsuit. One couple first met on one of his buses, got engaged, and then invited him to their wedding (he went).

HOW TO GET IN TOUCH

Some of the places to catch a Bearss gig:

HistoryAmerica Tours offers a menu of programs from "The Sioux Wars" ($2,095 based on double occupancy) to a two-week World War II South Pacific cruise (ranging from $9,300–$12,850). 4265 Peridot Lane, Rapid City, SD 57702, 800-628-8542 or 605-348-2250, www.historyamerica.com.

The National Trust for Historic Preservation runs Bearss-led tours to various battlefield sites regularly every year. 1785 Massachusetts Avenue, NW, Washington, DC 20036, 800-944-6847 or 202-588-6300, www.nationaltrust.org.

Smithsonian Journeys offers several Bearss events yearly, including a five-day tour of Gettysburg ($1,395 for double occupancy, $1,535 single). P.O. Box 23182, Washington, DC 20077, 877-338-8687, www.smithsonianjourneys.org.

try a frontier science workshop

PETALUMA, CALIFORNIA

It's an obligation for science to begin to look,
and look critically but open mindedly, at the possibility
that our minds are more powerful than we previously understood.
—Marilyn Schlitz, director of research
at the Institute of Noetic Sciences

63 Perhaps the biggest sleeper hit of 2004 was the indie film *What the Bleep Do We Know!?*, which imaginatively explained the emerging science of quantum physics. By word of mouth alone, it grossed more than $12 million and sold more than a million DVDs. The movie's runaway success didn't surprise the Institute of Noetic Sciences (IONS), though. This organization has been doing major scientific research in consciousness and human possibility for more than 30 years.

The institute also happens to have a 200-acre retreat and education center in Petaluma, California, just north of San Francisco, where you can take workshops on creativity, intuition, and other leading-edge ideas to learn how your beliefs, thoughts, and intentions affect the physical world. Lest you think this is some airy-fairy New Age mumbo jumbo, be advised that everything taught at the institute is backed by years of solid science. It works with more than 65 universities and has its own labs and staff of research scientists.

Apollo astronaut Capt. Edgar Mitchell, an MIT grad and nominee for the Nobel Prize in 2005, founded the institute in 1973. Two years earlier, the pragmatic young test pilot, strapped to his seat on the Apollo 14 mission to the moon, had had what he described as an epiphany. Looking back at Planet Earth, he became engulfed by a profound sense of universal connectedness. He knew from the depths of his being that reality was far more complex, subtle, and inexorably mysterious than conventional science had led him to believe. Upon his return, he devoted himself to exploring what he called the "next frontier": the uncharted territory of the human mind. He gathered a group of scientists whose mission became to explore the inner cosmos of the mind with the same level of rigor and commitment that had previously been applied to understanding the physical universe.

Noetic sciences further the explorations of conventional science by rigorous inquiry into aspects of reality—such as mind, consciousness, and spirit—that go beyond physical phenomena. Over the years, IONS has sponsored hundreds of research studies on such topics as the healing power of prayer, the physical and psychological effects of meditation, and distant healing. During the 1970s, for example, it supported Carl and Stephanie Simonton, whose groundbreaking work proved that meditation and biofeedback can positively affect terminal cancer patients, and in the 1990s it helped develop the *Heart of Healing* book and PBS-TV series.

IONS also is a membership organization that collaborates with other groups committed to personal and societal transformation. Many of these groups offer public workshops, retreats, and conferences at the 200-acre IONS campus, which is set among oaks, hiking trails, and rolling Sonoma County hills. Workshops range from a weekend of shamanic journeys to weeklong workshops exploring states of consciousness. Room and board runs from $108 to $135 per day. Because IONS' programs are so diverse and because the visiting organization leading a workshop or retreat determines the price, the cost of instruction varies.

HOW TO GET IN TOUCH
Institute of Noetic Sciences, 101 San Antonio Road, Petaluma, CA 94952, 707-775-3500, www.noetic.org.

learn the legislative process

WASHINGTON, D.C.

There can be no daily democracy without daily citizenship.
—Ralph Nader

64 Most people think of politics as a spectator sport, something to watch from the sidelines. It never occurs to them that developing an informed option about government policy is at least as important as whether their football team wins on Sunday. But the Close Up Foundation is out to change all that.

Close Up, a Virginia-based nonprofit, was started in 1971 by Stephen Janger to give young Americans a sense of direction and of purpose. At the time, he was organizing tours of Europe for high school students, and he noticed that a lot of his young charges were against the "establishment," but that they had no real idea of what the establishment was or how it really worked. He decided to show middle school and high school students that the "system" they were railing against *did* accept input and that change *could* happen if they simply understood the inner workings of politics and took the time to get involved.

The Close Up Foundation added weeklong adult programs in civics education in 1984. On one of these programs, you'll learn not only how public policy impacts every facet of your life, but also how, by getting involved, you can have a say and actually make a difference. Through seminars, tours, and daily briefings,

---

CLOSE UP'S BELIEFS

- Informed and engaged individuals are the foundation of strong communities and a vital democracy. Community-wide participation is essential; no one should be left out.
- Ignorance, cynicism, and apathy are persistent threats to our democratic system of government.
- Gaining the knowledge and practicing the skills necessary for civic and community involvement are lifelong commitments.
- One person *can* make a difference.

FOR OVERACHIEVERS—CAMP WELLSTONE

Oops! You went to a Close Up Foundation program and now you want to run for political office. Consider a visit to Camp Wellstone, a three-day traveling crash course on the nuts and bolts of political advocacy and grassroots organizing. Camp Wellstone is run by Mark and David Wellstone, sons of Paul Wellstone, a progressive Minnesota senator who was killed in a 2002 plane crash while running for reelection. Camp attendees apply the skills they learn with hands-on exercises like delivering a one-minute stump speech, developing a sample campaign budget, and participating in a simulated press conference. Since it began, Wellstone Action has sponsored Camp Wellstones in 27 states, training about 8,000 people in the essentials of effective political action. And since 2004, more than 110 Camp Wellstone graduates have won elective office and thousands of others have worked on campaigns or issue-organizing efforts. Camp Wellstone's courses are offered year-round on the weekends for $100 (or $50 for students and low-income participants), including meals. You can find the locations and dates on the website. *Camp Wellstone,* 821 Raymond Avenue, Suite 260, St. Paul, MN 55114, 651-645-3939, www.wellstone.org.

you'll learn your rights as a citizen as well as your responsibilities. Not only will you tour all the most famous Washington landmarks on this trip, but you'll also meet face to face with Washington insiders, get a behind-the-scenes peek at Capitol Hill, and observe sessions of Congress and the Supreme Court. You'll attend workshops and seminars given by such Washington players as Karen Tumulty, *Time* magazine's White House correspondent; Brian Lamb, CEO of C-Span; James Woolsey, the former director of the CIA; and Chris Matthews, host of MSNBC's *Hardball*.

Watch out, though. Alumni from Close Up's programs have gone home so energized that they staged rousing races for office. Mary L. Landrieu, now a U.S. senator from Louisiana, for example, turned her weeklong education on democracy into a full-fledged political career.

Close Up has programs for students, teachers, and seniors that are arranged through Elderhostel. These trips include all scheduled program activities and entrance fees, most meals, hotel accommodations, all gratuities, program instruction, and in-town transportation to all scheduled Close Up activities. Teachers and students have to set up programs through Close Up, and these programs range in price between $1,000 and $1,400 for seven days and six nights. The senior programs, which can be scheduled only through Elderhostel, are offered year-round and cost $800 to $1,500 for five or six days. You can also take an adult program by chaperoning a student group.

HOW TO GET IN TOUCH
Close Up Foundation, 44 Canal Center Plaza, Alexandria, VA 22314, 800-256-7387, www.closeup.org and **Elderhostel,** 11 Avenue de Lafayette, Boston, MA 02111, 800-454-5768, www.elderhostel.com.

discover & reflect
at a campus in the woods

ELLISON BAY, WISCONSIN

*It's beautiful. You have to really see it and smell it
to get the whole picture.*
—Mike Schneider, executive director of The Clearing

65 You can learn about mushrooms, birds, great books, or environmentally responsible development at The Clearing, a rustic outdoor folk school in Door County, Wisconsin. But the real reason people take classes at this school in the woods is because they want to connect with nature, with themselves, and with a community of people who realize there is joy in doing things with your heart and with your hands.

Unlike most schools where grades, competition, and dog-eat-dog strategies are employed, this school cheers on every sincere endeavor. The only thing that matters is that each student is engaged and growing as a human being. Conversation, nature study, and hands-on work are emphasized, rather than a bunch of stagnant texts. Of course, you'll likely read and write about the topic you choose, but you will also draw pictures of the mushrooms you're identifying, for example, or debate with fellow classmates on why Virginia Woolf's *To the Lighthouse* was written for nonacademics.

Jens Jensen, the world-famous Danish landscape architect who launched the school, modeled The Clearing after the Danish folk schools he attended as a youth. Rather than sitting in a classroom, students at a folk school get out into nature, work with their hands, and engage in lively discussions. Like the Danish folk schools, students at The Clearing live communally (although you *can* pay extra for a private room) and eat family-style meals together.

"It's a safe place to try something new," says Mike Schneider, the Clearing's executive director. "It's very informal and cozy and there's no competition. I hear from people that it's very freeing, that it gives them new direction, a new view of the world."

That was certainly Jensen's intention. He envisioned the Clearing as a place for people to reassess their lives. He figured that if you spend an entire vacation examining what's important to you, reconnecting with the natural world, and learning about topics you tend to overlook during your workaday life, you'll probably get a truer vision of what's important.

Jensen started the school in 1935 when he was 75 years old. Even then, he was able to predict that cars would take over his adopted country and that most Americans would live in cities and suburbs, far from the wisdom of nature. He envisioned The Clearing as a "school of the soil" where people could renew their inner selves and develop meaningful values for their lives and professions.

Although Jensen, who spearheaded the Illinois state park system and designed the estates of Armour, Florsheim, Ford, and other American industrialists, died in 1951, his school for growing a life is alive and thriving. The Clearing has been an independent nonprofit since 1988 after being run for years by the Wisconsin Farm Bureau with help from the University of Chicago, which took up the mantle after Jensen's death.

The summer program, which runs from May through October and offers weeklong classes with 25 to 35 students all living and learning together, is The Clearing's oldest school and the one that most closely resembles Jensen's original folk school vision. The summer program offers Sunday-through-Saturday workshops on natural sciences, literature, philosophy, and arts and crafts. The Clearing also offers a winter program with more than a hundred classes in January and February, but those are taught by volunteers and often offered off-site.

Why would you want to go anywhere else? Situated on the Niagara Escarpment on a limestone cliff near the tip of Wisconsin's Door Peninsula, overlooking Lake Michigan's Green Bay, The Clearing has amazing views, spectacular sunsets, and 128 acres of forests, meadows, hiking trails, and historic stone-and-log buildings, all of which have been added to the National Register of Historic Places.

A weeklong stay at The Clearing, including all meals and a bed in a cabin or dorm (all outfitted with handmade quilts), ranges from $750 to $1,085.

HOW TO GET IN TOUCH
The Clearing, 12171 Garrett Bay Road, P.O. Box 65, Ellison Bay, WI 54210, 877-854-3225 or 920-854-4088, www.theclearing.org.

take a cultural history cruise

HUDSON RIVER VALLEY, NEW YORK, & MORE

I haven't been everywhere, but it's on my list.
—Susan Sontag

66 Going on a cruise with the National Trust for Historic Preservation is like getting Eva Longoria to lead a tour of the *Desperate Housewives'* set—chock full of inside, front-row information not available to the average tourist. On a recent Hudson Valley Fall Foliage Cruise, for example, National Trust precruise participants got to tour Philip Johnson's famous Glass House in New Canaan, Connecticut, before it was opened to the public. They also got a personal tour of Edgewater, the residence of Richard Jenrette, a trustee who opens his charming river estate once a year for the cruise.

On this popular cruise aboard the *American Glory*, a cozy 49-passenger ship with 200-square-foot cabins, 14 of them with private balconies, you'll tour the Hudson River Valley, recognized as a national heritage area. And don't forget, the Hudson River itself has been designated one of 14 Great American Rivers. Led by stellar study leader Richard Barons, you'll get inside glimpses of Val-Kill, Eleanor Roosevelt's stone cottage on the banks of Fall-Kill Creek; Kykuit, the hilltop paradise where four generations of Rockefellers lived; the U.S. Military Academy at West Point; and the private home of Hudson River school painter Jasper F. Cropsey. If you do the precruise trip, an insiders' view of New York's theater scene, you'll get a private dinner with the grandson of Oscar Hammerstein II.

Even though the National Trust recently changed the name of its "study tours" to the less daunting "National Trust tours," you can be assured that the nearly 65 programs it offers each year are all led by accomplished scholars of history and architecture. The Hudson River Valley cruise, for example, has been led by Richard Barons, the director of the Southampton Historical Museum, who has been described by past participants as "marvelous," "know-

WE'LL LEAVE THE LIGHTS ON

The National Trust for Historic Preservation keeps a list of more than 200 hotels that have faithfully maintained their historic architecture and ambience. To be selected for the Historic Hotels of America program, a hotel has to be at least 50 years old, be listed in or eligible for the National Register of Historic Places, and be recognized locally as having historic significance. Here are just a couple on the list:

• **Biltmore Hotel, Coral Gables, Florida.** Not only does this historic resort have the largest hotel swimming pool in the continental United States, but it's where Esther Williams hosted her famous aqua shows in the 1930s. The Biltmore made its debut in January 1926 with a newsmaking inaugural that lured Northerners down on trains marked "Miami Biltmore Specials." In its heyday, the Biltmore played host to the Duke and Duchess of Windsor, Ginger Rogers, Judy Garland, Bing Crosby, Al Capone, and assorted Roosevelts and Vanderbilts.

During World War II, the Biltmore was converted to a hospital and even became the University of Miami's first School of Medicine. It then served as a VA hospital until 1968. Fast forward to 1992, when the city of Coral Gables reopened it as the first-class hotel and resort it was and is again today. A historic Biltmore package, which includes a copy of the Biltmore's 208-page illustrated history book, a free hotel tour, and a carriage ride through historic Coral Gables, costs between $130 and $149 per person, depending on the time of year. *Biltmore Hotel, 1200 Anastasia Avenue, Coral Gables, FL 33134, 800-727-1926, www.biltmorehotel.com.*

• **The Stanley Hotel, Estes Park, Colorado.** When Stanley Kubrick filmed *The Shining* with Jack Nicholson, he annoyed Stephen King, who wrote the novel, by not using the hotel that inspired the book. Maybe that's why Stephen King came back to The Stanley, the historic hotel in Estes Park, to film the TV miniseries.

According to the haunted hotel tour that takes place daily (reservations required), King's fictitious caretaker is not the only one to have seen ghosts at The Stanley. Three-quarters of the hotel staff report having seen or heard something otherworldly: lights flickering on and off, doors opening and closing by themselves, rooms getting tidied up by themselves, a big cache of items that were reported lost turning up in Room 203, or strange "sit prints" on newly made beds. The entire fourth floor (once the servants' quarters) is allegedly filled with the sounds of children running and laughing through the halls. King himself supposedly heard a child calling out for his nanny. It's also reported that the ghosts of F. O. and Flora Stanley, as well as Lord Dunraven, from whom they bought the land, also haunt the hotel. Room rates range between $109 and $189 per night. *The Stanley Hotel, 333 E. Wonderview Avenue, Estes Park, CO 80517, 800-976-1377 or 970-586-3371, www.stanleyhotel.com.*

ledgeable," and "lots of fun." On its tour of the antebellum South, the trust hired famed architectural historian John Meffert, past director of the Preservation Society of Charleston.

For more than 35 years, the National Trust for Historic Preservation has led its members (individual memberships start at $20) to domestic and international destinations to explore cultures of the world (its international tours go to destinations from Antarctica to Timbuktu), experience their artistic and architectural treasures, and gain a greater appreciation for historic preservation. In fact, getting folks out to see the historic sites and properties (including more than 200 hotels that have made the trust's list of Historic Hotels of America) is part of the trust's mission. Established in 1949 by congressional legislation, the National Trust is the premier nonprofit preservation organization in the United States. Historic, or what they call "heritage," tourism is an important part of the approach. As the trust likes to say, "Every time you enjoy a historic place, you are not only helping to preserve it—you are helping to improve the quality of life for residents and visitors alike."

Of the domestic National Trust tours, nearly half are aboard ships. That means you'll enjoy the comforts (and the food) of a cruise line while learning about, say, the military history of Vicksburg or the journey of Lewis and Clark. Some of the trips are even aboard historically recognized ships such as the 1927 *Delta Queen* steamboat that's used for the "Cruising the Mighty Mississippi Tour."

The cost of the Hudson River Valley tour ranges from $2,875 to $3,695.

HOW TO GET IN TOUCH

National Trust for Historic Preservation, 1785 Massachusetts Avenue, NW, Washington, DC 20036, 800-944-6847 or 202-588-6300, www.nationaltrust.org.

bone up on the opera

NEW YORK, NEW YORK ·

My soul grows a little bit each time I take a Smithsonian tour.
They are not vacations; they are personal journeys
of exploration and adventure.
—Janis Archer, past Smithsonian tour participant

67 Many of the big opera houses now offer captioning, either above the stage or on the back of the seats, which helps when watching those Italian masterpieces—but if you *really* want to understand opera, consider a study trip with Smithsonian Journeys. Every year, this tour company associated with the world-renowned Smithsonian Institution offers about a half-dozen educational opera tours, ranging from a primer for beginners who barely know the difference between a diva and a divan to behind-the-scenes opera tours for those who have seen *La Traviata* a zillion times and can convincingly discuss the pros and cons of casting renowned soprano Renée Fleming.

OPERA CLIFFSNOTES

Cornerstones, a website developed by Opera America, lists the top 20 most performed operas in North America, along with a synopsis, a composer biography, photos, and audio clips (www.operaamerica.org; look under audiences/lifelong learning/cornerstones). You'll also see suggestions for further reading, listening, and viewing as well as a listing of upcoming performances for more than a hundred opera companies. So, what are the top 20 most performed operas?

1. *Madama Butterfly*
2. *La Bohème*
3. *La Traviata*
4. *Carmen*
5. *The Barber of Seville*
6. *The Marriage of Figaro*
7. *Don Giovanni*
8. *Tosca*
9. *Rigoletto*
10. *The Magic Flute*
11. *La Cenerentola*
12. *Turandot*
13. *Lucia di Lammermoor*
14. *Pagliacci*
15. *Così Fan Tutte*
16. *Aida*
17. *Il Trovatore*
18. *Faust*
19. *Die Fledermaus*
20. *The Elixir of Love*

WORLDS LESS TRAVELED

The Smithsonian is not the only institution to offer educational enlightenment from a suitcase. Museum travel programs are being promoted by every venue from the Santa Barbara Museum of Art to the Textile Museum in Washington, D.C., but the Smithsonian is probably the largest, with 180 signature "journeys" a year. Although you have to be a member of the Smithsonian (something that's easily taken care of with a $36 donation) and the trips don't come cheap (a recent trip to India rang in at $15,000), participants in Smithsonian Journeys gain access to the museum's sizable network of scholars, private dig sites, preservation labs, and other normally off-limits places. There are examples to taking trips from educational institutions. Your average tour operator, for example, could never show you the inside of SpaceShipOne, the first privately financed space plane, or get astrophysicists and astronauts as tour leaders like the American Museum of Natural History did on its recent "Earth Orbit 2006: Inside the U.S. and Russian Space Programs." Price for that two-continent trip? A mere $37,900 per person.

All Smithsonian Journeys are led by study leaders, fascinating experts in various fields of study, and the opera tours are no exception. Fred Plotkin, who leads most of the trips to New York's Metropolitan Opera, has not only written the go-to book on opera (it's called *Opera 101*, of course, and novelist Ann Patchett said it was Plotkin's book that enabled her to write so convincingly about the opera in *Bel Canto*) but also has worked for both the Met and Milan's La Scala. When he leads a tour on Wagner's Ring Cycle (which he regularly does in New York), he knows every nuance of the four-opera epic from the first E-flat chord to the final river scene. And he should—he's seen it 39 times.

Because Plotkin is so connected to the New York opera scene, his tours always include lectures and conversations with Met insiders such as the Opera's house doctor, who might speak about his work behind the scenes keeping the divas' throats healthy, or James Conlon, the famous conductor who has worked in all the great opera houses.

Another perk of studying opera with Plotkin is that he also happens to be a food and wine expert and knows all the best restaurants in Manhattan. He can talk about dishes, customs, and restaurants nearly as convincingly as he can discuss which recording of *La Bohème* is the best. And because Plotkin picks out all the restaurants for the New York opera trips, suffice it to say that this is *la bella vita.*

Your home for the various New York opera tours is the Helmsley Park Lane, a grand hotel overlooking Central Park, which is within walking distance of Lincoln Center, your classroom for the week.

In addition to regular study tours of New York's opera scene, Smithsonian Journeys also offers study tours to the operas of Santa Fe, Sarasota, Italy, and France.

Prices for the five-day opera tours in North America range between $2,495 (in Santa Fe) and $2,985 (New York), based on double occupancy, and include accommodations in tony hotels (such as the Ritz-Carlton in Sarasota), a few meals (check the website for details), and all the lectures, tickets, and transportation to and from the operas.

HOW TO GET IN TOUCH
Smithsonian Journeys, P.O. Box 23182, Washington, DC 20077, 877-338-8687, www.smithsonianjourneys.org.

excavate stone tools & other ancient artifacts

CORTEZ, COLORADO

Sometimes we find a potshard that still bears the fingerprint of the individual who made it hundreds of years ago. It gives me a feeling of connection and communication with that ancient potter.
—Sharon White, Crow Canyon alumna

68 Get out your trowel and whisk broom. On the campus of the Crow Canyon Archaeological Center, a 170-acre paradise outside Cortez, Colorado, students live in Navajo hogans, spend all their time outdoors, and consider themselves dressed up if they happen to be wearing a pair of clean jeans. That's because the students at this unique facility set in a canyon between the 13,000-foot peaks of the La Plata Mountains are learning about archaeology not by reading about it, but by getting down into the dirt and actually digging. This unique school dedicated to exploring the ancestral Puebloan culture of the Mesa Verde region has always had the same mission: Get people interested in an ancient culture by letting them see it for themselves, letting them experience the thrill you can only get from, for example, uncovering a 1,400-year-old pot.

When it was started in 1983, Crow Canyon amounted to a couple of pie-in-the-sky archaeologists, living in state-surplus trailers and tepees, trying to convince whoever would listen that preserving ancient cultures is important. They were obviously pretty convincing, because their idea has morphed in a nationally recognized research center with classrooms, a lab, and student housing.

"Crow Canyon was founded to make archaeology more public—to enable nonarchaeologists to learn about and participate in archaeological research," research associate Bill Lipe explains. "The whole field has benefited. Crow Canyon has educated thousands of students and adults about what can be learned from archaeology, the difference between 'pothunting' and real archaeology, and the importance of protecting sites."

COVER-UP IN CORTEZ

There's murder. There's intrigue. And if author Tony Hillerman hears about this, he'll probably be calling. Thankfully, the massive cover-up in Cortez is only a rug—not that the world's largest Two Grey Hills rug is anything to sneeze at. Most of the Navajo weavings known as Two Grey Hills are used as wall hangings. A 5-foot-by-7-foot Two Grey Hills would be rare enough, but the one in Cortez at the Notah Dineh Trading Company is 12 feet by 18 feet. It took more than three years to weave, and the trader who commissioned Diné artist Rachel Curley to weave the unusual rug was murdered before it ever got completed.

Two Grey Hills rugs, for those of you who don't frequent Indian trading posts, are the Cadillac of Navajo rugs. They're bordered rugs that use all-natural gray and brown wools. Because the weave is fine and very intricate, it's not something just anybody can throw together. To give you some perspective, a weft count (that's the number of threads running across and woven into the warp threads) of 50 per inch is considered a high-quality rug; 80 or more qualifies the rug as a tapestry. Two Grey Hills rugs have counts of 120 or more.

Willard Leighton, known as Chis Chilly (curly hair) to the Diné or Navajo, contracted Rachel, who comes from a long line of rugmakers, to weave the one-of-a-kind rug in 1957. Before she could finish it (remember, it took three years), Leighton was murdered, so when Rachel finally finished the rug in 1960, Willard's brother Bob, who wanted the rug but couldn't afford to keep it, took it on a trading trip. In Montana, he talked a rancher into furnishing his new house with fine Navajo rugs rather than Persians and sold him the masterpiece. Bob Leighton never forgot about that rug, though, always hoping he'd see it again. Thirty years later, an art dealer contacted Leighton about a rare masterpiece rug that he'd found in Santa Barbara. Seems it was too large for the home for which it was purchased. Sure enough, it was the rug Willard Leighton had commissioned. After touring the country in an exhibit of Navajo weavings, the expensive rug is finally resting in the Leighton family's Notah Dineh Trading Post in Cortez, along with the largest collection of Navajo rugs in the Four Corners area. *Notah Dineh Trading Post, 345 West Main Street, Cortez, CO 81321, 800-444-2024, www.notahdineh.com.*

Every year, hundreds of students of all ages and nationalities work alongside archaeologists, anthropologists, and folks like Lipe to excavate thousands of artifacts, an average of 75,000 per year. They recently excavated Goodman Point Pueblo, an ancient Pueblo village that was inhabited during the late 1200s and has been protected by the federal government since 1889. The site had a large community kiva, as well as a hundred smaller kivas, plazas, towers, and a wall around it.

From March through November, Crow Canyon hosts adult research programs. In these weeklong seminars, participants get a hands-on introduction to the history of the people of the Mesa Verde region. They help on the current excavation project; learn laboratory processing, including cleaning and analyzing pottery; and take field trips to Mesa Verde National Park and Sand Canyon Pueblo, which was excavated by Crow Canyon several years ago.

"Our programs are the perfect mix of education and reflection," says Stephanie Ramsey, Crow Canyon's director of marketing. "Crow Canyon is a good place to get away; it's a hideaway. Out here, you can see every star. The night sky hits you right in the face. It's gorgeous and dramatic. In the morning, you sit on the front porch of the lodge and watch the sunrise from the canyon wall."

Adult research program tuition for members is $1,050 for a novice and $950 for alumni; nonmembers add $100. Membership fees are $50 for an adult or $85 for a family. Tuition includes all lodging, meals, and transportation to and from Cortez. Crow Canyon also offers educational trips that spotlight Pueblo cultures in Arizona, New Mexico, and Colorado and international trips that visit such sites as French caves and the Nile Delta. The educational trips, led by archaeologists and including visits to museums and ancient cliff dwellings, backcountry hikes, and excavations, range from $1,295 to $1,995.

HOW TO GET IN TOUCH
Crow Canyon Archaeological Center, 23390 Road K, Cortez, CO 81321, 800-422-8975, www.crowcanyon.org.

live off the grid

TRIPLETT, NORTH CAROLINA

*When we leave the world of the 21st century and step back to a place
where we make fire by spinning sticks, and drink from mountain springs,
and tell stories by firelight, we get a new reality.*
—T. G. Pelham, teacher at Turtle Island

69 What if you could learn to live life on your own terms? What if you didn't have to pay the electricity bill or worry about the mortgage, forget barking dogs in the neighborhood, and avoid traffic on your way to work?

You can . . . and Eustace Conway, the owner of Turtle Island Preserve, a pristine 1,000-acre stretch of North Carolina's Blue Ridge, is just the guy to teach you how. At age 17, he left his parents' suburban home in Gastonia, North Carolina, to live in a tepee. Ever since, he has lived in the woods, where he finds or makes all of his own tools, food, clothes, and shelter.

Conway offers five-day workshops in what he calls "traditional living." It's a rigorous course in living off the land. People flock to his preserve to learn such skills as how to start fires by twirling two sticks, make clothes from buckskin, and skin a rabbit with handmade stone knives. In the process, they learn biology, botany, geology, and ecology in what Conway calls the greatest classroom of all—nature itself.

"My message is to aim for a higher quality of life," Conway says. "People say, 'You can't escape reality,' but when I started living in a tepee in the woods, I realized that what I was living *was* reality. What could be more real than the natural world?"

During a five-day stay at Turtle Island's farm, you'll sleep along a sweetly gurgling stream in a primitive cabin with a roof, three walls, and an inspiring view of the stars. Not only will you learn what it's like to live without electricity, you'll learn whatever skills Conway thinks would best serve the group. That might be learning to blacksmith, cook broccoli almond soup in an outdoor kitchen, or make a blowgun.

While it's true that some folks might wonder why anyone would want to return to a primitive life where they carve their own utensils, gather their own ginseng tea

THE LAST AMERICAN MAN?

Wildlife artist Sallie Middleton told Eustace Conway on his 30th birthday, "You are the most interesting man I have ever met." Lots of people would have to agree, including Elizabeth Gilbert, who wrote a book about him called *The Last American Man*. "He represents the kind of freedom we all secretly crave," Gilbert says. "He runs his life on his own terms, and we all want that." A few of the terms under which Conway, now in his mid-40s, has lived his life:

- He lived in a tepee for 17 winters.
- At 18, he canoed 1,000 miles on the Mississippi River.
- When he was 19, he hiked the Appalachian Trail, living off the land as he went.
- He crossed the country on horseback from Georgia to San Diego in 103 days, setting a new record.
- He has eaten everything he could catch, including grubs, ant larvae, squirrel ("excellent," he notes), possum, beaver, raccoon ("very good"), and raw porcupine ("I was starving").
- He once taught a Native American tribe some of its own forgotten skills.

leaves, and bake their own bread over a campfire, Conway insists, "This way of life is easier. It's happy. What's hard is paying bills and stress."

It was in 1987 that Conway founded Turtle Island Preserve, an environmental education center and wildlife preserve near Boone, North Carolina, which has been described as a "wild monastery." All the buildings on its historically accurate farmstead are hand-carved, hand-pegged, and hand-built by Conway himself from material he harvested right there on the land. As he likes to say, "With a few sticks and bones we can wake up your world!"

A variety of courses is offered during the spring, summer, and fall. The five-day programs are generally offered every other month during these three seasons. Check the website for specific dates. Turtle Island workshops cost $180 per day for adults, $100 for kids 7 to 18; children 6 and under are free. Long-term internships of a year or longer are also available.

HOW TO GET IN TOUCH
Turtle Island Preserve, 1443 Lonnie Carlton Road, Triplett, NC 28618, 828-265-2267, www.turtleislandpreserve.com.

unlock the prehistoric past

MALTA, MONTANA

Fossil hunting is by far the most fascinating of all sports.
—George Gaylord Simpson,
paleontologist at New York's American Museum of Natural History

70 There are no school uniforms and no tests, and you'll use your muscles as much as your brain, but if you want to add to your body of knowledge, there's no school as rich as the Judith River Dinosaur Institute in Malta, Montana. Your teachers will be Leonardo, Roberta, Giffen, Ralph, Elvis, and a few other 77- to 150-million-year-old creatures that have a lot to teach not only you but all of mankind.

Nate Murphy, the khaki-clad paleontologist and curator who serves as the dinosaurs' agent and mouthpiece, organizes five-day field research trips three to four times each year. Sponsored by the Phillips County Museum and the Judith River Dinosaur Institute, which sprang up after the inventory of dinosaurs grew way beyond the walls of the county museum, these trips are hot, rugged dinosaur excavations. Basically, you'll be lifting stones, chipping at rock, and piecing together mysteries from millions of years ago. You'll learn all the stuff you could probably find in an encyclopedia, all the

TAKE A RIDE ON THE DINOSAUR TRAIL

Montana may be the only state with its own dinosaur trail. There are 13 stops on this unique trail, which has its own map and website. Joining Malta's Phillips County Museum and the Judith River Dinosaur Field Station where you can watch Murphy and his cronies prepare dinosaur fossils, the trail includes stops in the Museum of the Rockies, a Smithsonian affiliate that's headed by paleontologist Jack Horner, a consultant on *Jurassic Park;* and the Fort Peck Field Station of Paleontology, which is run by the University of Montana and serves as a state fossil repository.

facts and data that paleontologists know so far, but the most exciting part about these dinosaur digs is that you'll also likely learn things that nobody else knows yet.

One of the most exciting examples took place in 2000, when a team member on the last day of a five-day dig happened to look down and notice the exposed midsection of a *Brachylophosaurus* tail. Finding a new dinosaur specimen would have been thrilling enough, but this one had 90 percent of its skin still intact, giving paleontologists all sorts of new information about this 35-foot-long duck-billed herbivore's diet, range of movement, and methods of locomotion. Keep in mind that paleontologists normally piece together entire life histories from something as minuscule as a 2-inch tooth. Famous dinosaur researcher Robert Bakker reportedly fell to his knees when he first saw the find, tears in his eyes. "It was," he said, "like seeing the 'Pietà.'"

The new two-ton find was named Leonardo after a piece of graffiti scrawled onto a nearby rock: "Leonard Webb loves Geneva Jordan 1916." *Newsweek* ran a cover story and the body of knowledge exploded, not just for the Judith River scientists but for every paleontologist, evolutionary biologist, and, for that matter, layperson interested in prehistoric creatures.

"Paleontology is not an exact science," Murphy observes. "All we have are bones, and from there we develop theories about what the animals looked like, how they moved, and what they ate. A specimen like Leonardo will take a lot of guesswork out and really tell us if Steven Spielberg's getting it right."

The fee for Judith River's five-day expeditions vary from $895 (for the Judith River Badlands Expedition, which doesn't include lodging or food) to $1,495 (for the Little Snowy Mountains Dinosaur Project, which does include food). Your accommodations are the tent you're required to bring. Expeditions are offered in July and August to individuals 14 years and older, and the class sizes range between 12 and 20 diggers.

Murphy likes to say he's not running a "paleo dude ranch" and that the work on his expeditions is tiring and hot, but anyone who has ever taken his expeditions (including a group of regulars who call themselves the "paleochicks") claim they're loads of fun, including late night sing-alongs of such campfire classics as "Dead Skunk in the Middle of the Road."

HOW TO GET IN TOUCH

Judith River Dinosaur Institute, P.O. Box 429, Malta, MT 59538, 406-654-2323, www.montanadinosaurdigs.com.

become a polar bear expert

CHURCHILL, MANITOBA

> GUY ON A DANCE FLOOR: Er, you don't happen to know
> how much polar bears weigh?
> GIRL ON THE DANCE-FLOOR: No.
> GUY: Neither do I, but it breaks the ice.
> —From the movie *Love Life*

71 If Al Gore's *An Inconvenient Truth* put the fear of God in you, just think what it's doing to the polar bears. The Arctic sea-ice pack, which is basically the polar bears' lunch box and front yard, has shrunk 14 percent in the last 20 years. So far, Canada's 13 family groupings of polar bears (roughly 15,000 all told) are hanging in there, but, suffice it to say, this is not the vacation you want to procrastinate over.

The Churchill Northern Studies Centre (CNSC), a remote outpost on Hudson Bay, offers six trips yearly for learning about the bears that the Inuit call *nanuk*. Polar bears spend most of the year on the ice fattening up on seals, but along Hudson Bay, where the ice gets soggy by June (it used to be July), they're forced to come ashore for four months. By October, they begin congregating on the west shores waiting for the ice floes to reform. Western Hudson Bay then becomes "polar bear central."

A former rocket research center, the CNSC became a diversified research center in 1976, attracting scientists from around the world who carry out all sorts of subarctic research. To help fund their research, nearly two dozen projects at any one time, the center offers a half-dozen or so learning-adventure vacations.

On the five-day "Lords of the Arctic: Hudson Bay's Polar Bears" tour, usually held in November, you'll take tundra vehicles out to the bears' habitat, helicopters to their dens along the rugged coastline of Hudson Bay, and dogsleds to view arctic foxes, caribou, snowy owls, seals, and at least some of the area's 500 species of boreal plants and, at the right time of the year, arctic wildflowers. The trip also includes a guided walking tour and a visit to the world-renowned Eskimo Museum.

POLAR BEAR FACTS

- A male polar bear can be longer than a compact car.
- Polar bears have a clear second eyelid that protects the bear's eyes like built-in goggles.
- Some males can weigh nearly 2,000 pounds.
- Sometimes polar bears turn green. Polar bears in zoos at warmer climates are susceptible to algae that can grow in their hollow hair tubes. Although it doesn't hurt the bears (except maybe their vanity), the San Diego Zoo "cured" its polar bears in 1980 by washing them in a salt solution.
- Under their white or cream-colored fur, they have black skin that absorbs the sun's rays and keeps them warm.
- They have huge feet that work like snowshoes—even though they can weigh nearly a ton, they can walk on ice that wouldn't support a human.
- Polar bears are marine mammals and come ashore only when the ice disappears.
- Cubs weigh a mere one pound at birth.

Located about 18 miles from the town of Churchill, the CNSC has labs, classrooms, a heated observation dome, a library, a herbarium with nearly half of those 500 species of flora, and a helicopter landing pad. Accommodations are basic, with dormitory-style housing (in polar bear season, each room usually has four to six snoozers) and shared bathrooms.

The CNSC is located at the edge of the boreal forest and the low Arctic tundra and also offers programs on birding, arctic wildlife, winter survival, beluga whales (the bay is one of the most reliable spots on Earth to see belugas in the summer), wildflowers, the northern lights, and astronomy.

The polar bear trip runs about $2,000 and includes meals, train or airport shuttles, local tours, and presentations.

HOW TO GET IN TOUCH
Churchill Northern Studies Centre, P.O. Box 610, Churchill, MB R0B 0E0, Canada, 204-675-2307, www.churchillscience.ca.

tour history
in a covered wagon

BAYARD, NEBRASKA

I have never seen stars so bright or a sky so clear.
—participant on an Oregon Trail Wagon Tour

72 At last count, there were 4,739 books about the Oregon Trail on Amazon.com, so you can find out a lot about it at home. But if you *really* want to learn about the Oregon Trail, to know what those half-million hardy pioneers felt as they traversed the 2,000-mile trail up the Missouri River to the Columbia River Basin, consider a history trek in a covered wagon train near Chimney Rock, Nebraska. These four-day trips offered by Rick Baynes and his crew are about as authentic as you can get. The covered wagons are original—which means no rubber tires, no hydraulic shock absorbers, and no air-conditioning. Like the pioneers, you'll cover an average of 10 to 12 miles each day. You can either ride in the wagon (fun until the lack of shocks soaks in), ride the scout horses (like the early wagon trains, scout horses are brought along), or walk—something many of the pioneers did without shoes.

Along the trail, you'll sleep in a tent and be served meals cooked over a campfire. According to Randy Allen, who took his wife and two boys on a recent trip, it was a phenomenal, once-in-a-lifetime experience, equal to any trip he's ever taken (and that's saying a lot, because the year before, he took the family on an African safari). "My boys know more about the Oregon Trail than anybody, because they've actually lived it," Allen says.

Not only will you pass by Chimney Rock, the 325-foot spire that is hands-down the most recognizable landmark on the trail, but you'll also have mail delivered by Pony Express, be confronted by Native Americans, load the muzzles of black-powder rifles, search for Native American artifacts, learn prairie square dancing, and be regaled the entire 30-or-so-mile journey with tales about the trail's

QUICK OREGON TRAIL FACTS

Although the first Oregon Trail emigrants were Marcus and Narcissa Whitman, who made the trip in 1836, the big wave didn't begin until 1843. Over the next 25 years, more than half a million people went west in search of new land and new lives. The average trip took six months from Independence, Missouri, to the Oregon Territory. The completion of the transcontinental railroad in 1869 brought the Oregon Trail's glory days to an abrupt halt.

A common misperception is that Native Americans posed the biggest problem. Quite the contrary, most local tribes were quite friendly, even helping emigrants pull wagons out of ditches and trading with them for supplies. The real enemies were cholera, poor sanitation, drownings (in 1850 alone, 37 drowned crossing the Green River), and—somewhat surprisingly—accidental gunshots.

Other perils included heat, high winds, lethally large hailstones, dust 3 inches deep, and stampeding bison. No wonder some went insane. Elizabeth Markham, for instance, sat herself down on the bank of the Snake River and announced to her family that she was not proceeding an inch farther. Her husband was forced to take the wagons and children and leave her behind, but he later sent a son back to retrieve her. She ended up returning on her own only to inform her husband that she had clubbed their son to death with a rock. He raced back to find the boy who thankfully still clung to life. When they caught up to the wagon train again, however, he discovered that his wife had taken advantage of his absence to set fire to one of the family's wagons.

Although Chimney Rock now stands 325 feet above the plains, it was substantially higher during the great migration. Many considered it the eighth Wonder of the World. As pioneer Elisha Perkins said, "If a man does not feel like an insect when standing at its base, then I don't know when he should." According to early fur traders, Native Americans called the rock "Elk Penis." Prim and proper Anglo-Americans, though, overwhelmingly preferred the more delicate nomenclature.

A popular game for kids on the Oregon Trail was a version of Frisbee catch, except instead of plastic discs, they used bison dung. The dung was also burned for fuel.

Rufus Porter, the founder of the magazine *Scientific American,* sold more than 200 seats on an "airplane" to Oregon. In 1849, Porter advertised trips along the trail on propeller-driven balloons powered by steam engines. Unfortunately, his invention never got off the ground, and he was forced to refund all 200 tickets. Another form of transportation being advertised at that time was the "wind wagon," a cross between a wagon and a sailboat. A prototype was built and indeed it did barrel across the plains at the advertised 15 miles an hour . . . until it veered out of control and crashed.

illustrious history. "There was one old geezer telling stories who looked like he'd actually been on the Oregon Trail," Allen says.

The trip's not for everyone. Although the survival rate is considerably higher these days (one out of ten died before finishing the trek in 1843), you're still at risk for a few hazards—weather and flies, to point out just two. And you might as well leave your electric razors and blow-dryers at home, because there's no electricity out on the plains. Or even showers, for that matter. Baynes, however, is happy to point out a few horse tanks along the route that you're welcome to wash off in. Even so, he says, "Everybody ends up smelling about the same by the end of the trip."

The four-day treks are $575 for adults, $475 for kids under 12, and they include all meals (the rib-eye chuckwagon meal is to die for), a trail bag, tents, sleeping bags, soap, and towels. These treks are offered once a month in June, July, and August. Baynes's little operation along the North Platte River also offers a one-day wagon train trek ($200) most days from June into the first part of September, as well as canoe and log cabin rentals.

HOW TO GET IN TOUCH
Oregon Trail Wagon Train, Route 2, Box 502, Bayard, NE 69334, 308-586-1850, www.oregontrailwagontrain.com.

train to be an astronaut

HUNTSVILLE, ALABAMA

We came in peace for all mankind.
—Apollo 11 lunar module plaque

73 Houston, we have a vacation. If you've ever suffered from celestial wanderlust or dreamed of being an astronaut (and what self-respecting kid hasn't?), it's time to get off your duff and head to Space Camp. Don't even think about trying the "but I'm too old excuse"; John Glenn was 77 when he last ventured into space.

Every fall and winter, the U.S. Space Academy in Huntsville offers space camp for adults. You'll get to sleep in a simulated space habitat, wear a blue or orange NASA flight suit, and sample the same freeze-dried ice cream that astronauts munch in space. Of course, the main reason you're there is to take on two different space shuttle missions, one in which you'll work in mission control and another where you'll be part of the crew. Working from real-time video displays and scripts that mimic the sequence of an actual liftoff, you'll launch the shuttle, execute a space mission (perhaps deploying or retrieving a satellite), and return safely to Earth.

This is no sci-fi fantasy. You'll actually train for these simulated missions on such equipment as a zero-gravity wall, a multi-axis trainer (think how laundry feels because on this trainer you'll spin wildly in three directions while strapped to a chair), a microgravity chair (it hangs from the roof by springs and lets you hop around as if you're on the moon, weighing a sixth of what you weigh on Earth), and the MMU, the manned maneuvering unit that simulates work outside the spacecraft.

U.S. Space Camp is located at NASA's Space and Rocket Center, which grew out of the Marshall Space Flight Center. Directed by famed

---

SPACE HABITAT SPEAK

- Restrooms: waste management
- Heating and air-conditioning units: life-support systems
- The correct answer to "Are you motivated?": "Motivated! Motivated! Motivated! Sir!"

---

rocket scientist Wernher von Braun, Marshall launched the tests for man's first flights into outer space. Right after World War II, von Braun and more than a hundred other German rocket scientists were stationed at Marshall to convert their bombbuilding expertise into spaceship building.

In fact, it was von Braun himself who first concocted the notion of a space camp. He figured, there were summer camps for everything from music to tennis to karate, so why not get kids pumped up about science by giving them a glimpse into astronaut training? His scheme obviously worked. Since 1982 when it was launched, going to Huntsville to attend Space Camp has been almost as much a rite of passage as going to Orlando to shake hands with Mickey and Minnie. The adult camps were added in 1985.

Besides the three-, six-, and eight-day camps, the center offers a special three-day Aviation Challenge for fighter pilot wannabes. If you pick the latter, you'll train on a simulated fighter plane that can fly at 2,193 miles an hour, go on bombing missions, and participate in a Top Gun–style dogfight.

The three-day Adult Space Academy camps are offered over one or more weekends of August, September, and October and run $399, including accommodations, food, and visits to the Space Museum. The three-day Aviation Challenge is offered once at the end of August for the same price of $399. The six-day Adult Space Academy camps are available at the end of August and beginning of September for $899, and the eight-day camp is the last weekend of September, priced at $1,299. And unlike John Glenn, you won't have to submit to three weeks of medical testing upon your return from space.

HOW TO GET IN TOUCH
U.S. Space and Rocket Center, One Tranquility Base, Huntsville, AL 35805, 800-637-7223, www.spacecamp.com.

study at a maritime campus

ON THE SEVEN SEAS

Humankind's pursuit of knowledge has been
intricately linked to ships and the sea.
—Institute for Shipboard Education mission statement

74 Most of your shipmates will be college kids, 18- to 22-year-olds studying hard to get a semester's worth of credits in something like anthropology or women's studies. But if you're interested in traveling and learning, you'd be hard pressed to find a better vacation than the Institute for Shipboard Education's "Semester at Sea." Since 1963, this special program, first known as the University of the Seven Seas, then as World Campus Afloat, has been providing a globe-circling international education for college students who take one full semester (a hundred days) aboard a cruise ship. Nearly 40,000 students from colleges around the country have studied and traveled with the institute so far.

Every year, this floating campus opens up anywhere from 30 to 60 of its cabins to adults who want to audit the more than 70 different classes offered each semester. These "lifelong learners," as the institute calls them, participate fully in the spring, fall, or summer semester of the at-sea college, often volunteering to serve as "temporary family" to the 640 students. Although you can certainly take the classes for college credit if you want to (they're all fully accredited through the University of Virginia), you can skip all the entrance exams and simply sign up for the vicarious pleasure of taking university-level courses along with university students.

Even if you can't find the time for either of the two hundred-day round-the-world journeys fall and spring or the 65-day summer journey, you can still sign up for Seminars at Sea, abbreviated 12- to 14-day trips offered once a year during the New Year's holiday and possibly in the summer as well. These trips offer lectures, discussions, workshops, and field programs at various ports of call, usually depending on where the M/V *Explorer* needs to dock next. In 2006, for example, the Seminar at Sea took place in the Caribbean and offered Spanish-language workshops as well as lectures on whales, the colonial architecture of Antigua and Guatemala, and the history of mariachi music.

Unlike your average cruise ship, the *Explorer* has no casinos, spas, or fancy nightclub entertainment. What the 24,300-ton vessel does offer is an 8,000-volume library, nine classrooms, a computer lab, a student union, a campus bookstore, a swimming pool, a fitness center, a spa, and a health clinic. But the best perks are the interport lecturers. Over the years, students at sea have been treated to talks by Nelson Mandela, Mikhail Gorbachev, Indira Gandhi, Corazon Aquino, Mother Teresa, and Fidel Castro, who one year met with students for eight entire hours. Desmond Tutu, a frequent interport lecturer and big fan of the floating campus for global studies, even signed on to be a guest lecturer for the entire spring semester voyage of 2007.

Most of the onboard faculty are visiting professors from colleges across the country. The 70-plus classes each semester (30 in the summer) are diverse, covering subjects from engineering to theater arts. Every student is required to take global studies, an upper-level geography course that covers upclose and personal the complexity, dynamics, and interdependence of world systems.

Students are usually in class during the day, and at each port, where the ship stays for three to four days, they are given field assignments. "If you're taking an economics class, your assignment might be to meet with bankers in Hong Kong," says Kay Volkema, director of university outreach and communications. "Or if you're studying music, your might be asked to learn to play a native Vietnamese instrument. Anthropology students might visit an orphanage in Thailand or stay with a family in Panama."

The price for the hundred-day, around-the-world trip is $17,325. The 65-day summer voyage is $8,375. The Seminars at Sea range from $1,375 to $4,200.

HOW TO GET IN TOUCH
Institute for Shipboard Education, Semester at Sea Program, P.O. Box 400885, Charlottesville, VA 22904, 800-854-0195, www.semesteratsea.org.

wellness escapes

*I started wondering. Is this what we're going to do with our marriage—
reroof the house, resurface the driveway, redesign the house?*
*—Julie Madsen, a psychologist who quit her job, bought an RV, and
with her husband traveled the country looking for a new vision*

Don't you just love dictionaries? You look up a definition and end up more confused than you were when you started. Take the word wellness, for example. Here's how the dictionary describes it: "A dimension of health beyond the absence of disease or infirmity, including social, emotional, and spiritual aspects of health."

One definition of wellness would be this: the condition in which things that used to be huge and overpowering are not so big anymore. Things that you thought mattered before your vacation—say, your retirement package or that car fender your teenager accidentally ran into a telephone pole—don't count for as much.

Needless to say, this chapter includes many vacations that have traditionally been labeled "wellness," things like spas and yoga retreats and learning a brand new sport (mushing anyone?). But also included is a juicy selection of vacations you might not have considered before now, things that march against the grain. Here, "wellness vacations" are vacations that encourage you to sloooowwwww down, breathe, look at the stars, connect with your fellow travelers, view life through a whole new lens.

Not only do you come back refreshed, but you come back as a whole new you. That, my friend, is wellness.

enjoy a surfin' safari

BEACHES EVERYWHERE

If the Beach Boys can still tour, then you, my man, can still surf.
—Joe Kita, author and motivational speaker who took surfing lessons in
Vero Beach, Florida

75 Anybody who has ever tried to surf knows it's demoralizing, punishing, and psychologically damaging. So, why would anyone in their right mind take it up? Because it's still the coolest sport ever devised, that's why. Not only do you get to hang out on a beach all day with barely clad members of the opposite sex, but surfing even has its own language and music. And *if*, just *if*, you ever *do* catch a decent wave, it's a magical, intoxicating rush like no other.

The good news is that if you take a learn-to-surf camp, catching a wave—with all the mystical dividends—is a distinct possibility. In fact, if you believe the claims of a lot of surf school brochures, more than 90 percent of first-timers (they're called "flounders" in surfspeak) are able to stand up on the board within the first day. Even J. Paul Getty learned to do it.

Surfing schools are cropping up on beaches everywhere, offering beginners everything from dirt-cheap board rental to all-inclusive deals on accommodations, meals, and instruction. Surf vacations aren't just for slackers anymore. Here are a trio of schools where you can find a really sweet ride.

Hans Hedemann Surf School. Hollywood mogul Jeffrey Katzenberg is just one of the folks whom pro surfer Hans Hedemann has taught to surf. He offers five-day surf camps in Hawaii at various hotels on Oahu, including the Turtle Bay Resort on the famed North Shore. After 17 years on the pro circuit (he has a wall of awards to prove it), he decided to share the glory. Five days of group lessons are $375 (for two hours of surfing a day) or $495 for four hours; five days of private lessons are $710 (for two hours of surfing a day).

Hans Hedemann Surf School, 2586 Kalakaua Avenue, Honolulu, HI 96815, 808-924-7778, www.hhsurf.com.

Paskowitz Surf Camp. The Paskowitzes of San Clemente, California, have been called the von Trapp family of surfing. The patriarch, Doc Dorian Paskowitz, an M.D. who is now in his late 80s, started a seven-day, sleepover surf camp in 1972 at a beach just south of Richard Nixon's former residence in San Clemente. It was the first school of its kind. His nine kids, as well as his wife, Juliette, a former opera singer, joined him in offering these party-like camps, which included three meals a day, camping on the beach, and all the surfing you could handle. Son Izzy took over the business a few years ago, but the rest of the family is still involved—including Doc, who lifeguards and loves to tell stories. The Paskowitz clan now offers seven-day summer camps at San Diego's Pacific Beach ($1,250, including all meals and tent accommodations) and at Cabo San Lucas in Baja California (a more lavish version complete with hotels for $2,900). In addition, they have two-and-a-half-day clinics at Montauk, New York, on the tip of Long Island ($900).

Paskowitz Surf Camp, P.O. Box 522, San Clemente, CA 92674, 949-728-1000, www.paskowitz.com.

Surf Las Olas. Bev Sanders, the woman who revolutionized women's snowboarding (her company, Avalanche Snowboards, was one of the first to manufacture boards), started a women-only learn-to-surf school 45 minutes north of Puerto Vallarta, Mexico. The seven-day, six-night programs, best described as a cross between a slumber party and an empowerment seminar, incorporate yoga, massage, and daily surf lessons. "Women bond in a special way," Sanders says. "I especially love to see these corporate women show up. Within 24 hours they're acting like a bunch of monkeys. I always joke that I'm running a reverse finishing school, that I make girls out of women." These surf safaris range from $2,495 to $3,650 in price and include daily surf lessons, three meals a day, daily yoga sessions, a one-hour sports massage, a private one-on-one lesson, and accommodations in a beachside villa.

Las Olas Surf Safaris for Women, P.O. Box 4669, Carmel-by-the-Sea, CA 93921, 831-625-5748, www.surflasolas.com.

put your money where your heart is

NEBRASKA CITY, NEBRASKA; DORA, MISSOURI; & MEDIA, PENNSYLVANIA

> If your heart is pulling you in a direction that has
> mystery and wonder, trust it and follow it.
> —David Wilcox, singer-songwriter

76 Vacations, as we all know, cost money. And somebody benefits from the dollars you expend to "get away from it all." So here's the question: Would you rather line the pockets of the big corporations who run the major hotel chains, or would you instead like to use your buying power to support little guys who are trying to change the world? That's what most people think. So here are three amazing vacations where your dollars keep right on giving.

Lied Lodge and Conference Center. If you can't see the forest for the trees, you can thank J. Sterling Morton, the editor of Nebraska's first newspaper, who on April 10, 1872, started the tree-planting holiday we now celebrate as Arbor Day. Although it varies state to state (the holiday is also celebrated in dozens of other countries), Arbor Day is most often observed on the last Friday in April. Morton, of course, is long gone, but his 260-acre Nebraska estate is still there, along with his National Arbor Day Foundation that, like Dr. Seuss's Lorax, still "speaks for the trees."

The foundation's Lied Lodge, an environmentally friendly timber-and-stone building with 144 well-appointed rooms, offers easy access to the Kimmel Orchard, Tree House Trail, and the greenhouse where more than 300,000 trees are grown. All proceeds from the lodge are poured back into the Arbor Day Foundation's mission of environmental stewardship. Even the lodge itself is completely self-sustaining, getting all its heat and cooling from an innovative power plant fueled by wood chips. The property has lots of wooded walking trails, a fitness center, an indoor swimming pool, weekend carriage rides, and Arbor Links, an ecologically friendly golf course designed by Arnold Palmer. During the fall apple harvest, guests can pick their own apples, ride ponies and hayracks, climb trees, throw tomahawks, and taste heirloom apples. The lodge's restaurant, of course, serves its signature Arbor Day Farm homemade apple pie every day of the year.

Rooms range from $104 to $154 per night.

Arbor Day Lodge and Conference Center, P.O. Box 817, Nebraska City, NE 68410, 800-546-5433 or 402-873-8733, www.liedlodge.org.

River of Life Farm. After Myron McKee toured Guatemala in 1996 and saw the abject poverty there, he vowed that he'd go home to Missouri, sell the farm that had been in his family for three generations, and use the money to build an orphanage in Monjas, Guatemala. "It broke my heart," he remembers. "There were kids living in conditions we wouldn't let our farm animals live in." Before he signed away the deed, though, it occurred to him that once the farm was gone, not only would his own family be homeless but he'd be able to help just that one time. Instead, he hatched a plan to use his 275-acre farm fronting the North Fork River to raise money on an ongoing basis. He wouldn't build just one orphanage—he'd build a hundred.

McKee was already offering fly-fishing trips. The North Fork, after all, has been named by *Field & Stream* as one of the best trout-fishing rivers in North America. Why not bring in more tourists to his little Eden in the Ozarks? Over the next ten years, with a wing and a prayer, he managed to construct a half-dozen spacious tree-house cabins, all with rustic furniture, Jacuzzis, full kitchens, at least 590 square feet of space, and eye-popping views of the nearby springs, the Mark Twain National Forest, and the majestic river with its abundance of wild rainbow trout. Fishing enthusiasts call the River of Life's spot on the North Fork the "miracle mile." Not only do the tree-house cabins make for romantic secluded hideaways, but, for those wanting outdoor adventure, River of Life Farm can also arrange guided fly-fishing trips, canoeing, hiking, kayaking, and hunting.

You know that orphanage in Guatemala? It is being joined by a second in Kenya and soon a third in Nepal. Your next vacation might just help McKee realize that dream of a hundred new orphanages.

Tree Houses at River of Life Farm start at $175 per night.

River of Life Farm, Route 1, Box 4535, Dora, MO 65637, 417-261-7777, www.riveroflifefarm.com.

Untours. Since 1975, Hal and Norma Taussig have operated one of the most unusual travel companies in the world. If you like guided bus trips, this is definitely a company to avoid. Untours instead gives its clients a chance to experience a new country the way the locals do. On these get-acquainted sojourns (the minimum stay is two weeks), you stay in an apartment, farmhouse, or cottage in an out-of-the-way neighborhood far from the haunts of most camera-toting tourists. For example, one Untour to Italy includes a ground-floor apartment on a farm near Assisi, with a private swimming pool and "healing garden," a Ping-Pong table, a bocce court, a ceramic studio, and bicycles you can use to ride into the quaint village of Cannara. The owner even offers occasional olive oil tastings. Because your home-like lodgings come with a kitchen and utensils and because you're shopping at the local butcher shop, bakery, and grocer's, picking up your mail at the local post office, and in every other way enjoying a residential experience, you end up not with a run-of-the-mill tour but with an "untour." As Hal Taussig sees it, "When people have contact with a way of life different from their own, they are much less willing to make war on other cultures."

The most interesting thing about Untours is that all profits are plowed into the Untours Foundation, which gives low-interest start-up loans to people who normally couldn't get loans. Since the foundation began in 1992, it has given hundreds of loans to such organizations as Greensgrow, a hydroponic vegetable supplier in Philadelphia run by single moms; a vegetarian restaurant in Saigon that supports street children; and a water-bottling company that addresses clean-water issues in developing countries. The Taussigs, who don't take salaries from their company, believe in living simply and sharing the profits of their business to create a better world. The company's altruism hasn't gone unnoticed. In 1999, Untours received the "Most Generous Company in America" award from Paul Newman and *George* magazine.

Prices for a two-week Untour start at less than $1,000 (without airfare). The Italian Untour described above ranges from $2,219 to $2,649 (based on double occupancy), depending on the season, and includes airfare from New York, a ride from the airport, and two weeks' accommodations.

Untours Foundation, P.O. Box 405, Media, PA 19063, 888-868-6871 or 610-565-5242, www.untours.com.

walk on the wild side

KALALAU BEACH ON NA PALI COAST, KAUAI, HAWAII

Utility is when you have one telephone,
luxury is when you have two, opulence is when you have three—
and paradise is when you have none.
—Doug Larson, middle-distance runner who won gold medals
at the 1924 Paris Olympic Games

77 You've probably seen pictures of Kauai's Na Pali Coast. The crenellated, rainbow-adorned, ocean-plunging cliffs had starring roles in *Jurassic Park, Thorn Birds, South Pacific,* and one of the King Kong movies. Many folks who visit Kauai take an afternoon catamaran or helicopter tour to see this rugged 22-mile strip of undeveloped coastline, widely regarded as one of the prettiest in the world.

That's all fine and good, and in fact everyone should get a glimpse of paradise. But what we're recommending here is a trek along Na Pali's Kalalau Trail to Kalalau Beach, a remote postcard-perfect beach with a spectacular waterfall and guava, mango, and papaya trees for munching. It's devilishly difficult to get to—the 11-mile one-way hike (which takes most hikers a day) is steep, often muddy, and shared by mountain goats—but Kalalau Beach is like no place else on Earth.

Jackie Yellin, who has traveled around the globe, says a ten-day camping trip she recently took to Kalalau Beach was the most unusual vacation she's ever been on. "We showered every morning in the waterfall, slept unencumbered on the beach, and met the most interesting people," she recalls.

The narrow coastal trail that leads to Kalalau Beach was built through the dense jungle by native Hawaiians, hundreds of whom once lived in the remote coastal valleys, fishing or raising taro on terraced plots. Extensive stone walls, house platforms, and temple structures can still be found on the valley floors. The treacherous trail dips in and out of rain forest, through five valleys, and past dozens of waterfalls and 4,000-foot cliffs. At several turns, it spills out onto white sandy beaches.

The trailhead is located at the end of Hawaii 56 in Haena State Park, near a piece of land once owned by Elizabeth Taylor's brother Howard. After being denied a building permit, he let a bunch of hippie friends build tree houses there, and the place became known as "Taylor's Camp."

The first few miles of the Kalalau Trail are widely used. The majority of hikers stop at Hanakapiai Beach, 2 miles in, and a few go the next 4 miles to Hanakoa Falls, a stunning 100-foot falls and pool. Only the hardy continue on to Kalalau Beach.

To camp or even hike the Kalalau Trail, you have to get a state permit. It's advisable to secure one as early as possible, because two-thirds of all camping permits to Kalalau for the summer are issued a full year in advance. You're also required to sign a statement promising that you'll use "good judgment"—not a bad vow to make, considering that the trail is only inches wide in some places with sheer 800-foot drops to the sea. Signs along the way will remind you of your promise, saying, for example, "Tidal Wave Marker" or "This lifesaving equipment was donated by family and friends of Dr. Ulf Tahleson, a strong swimmer, who drowned here in March 1979." Each permit is marked in bright red letters "Swimming Not Recommended."

Camping permits can be obtained for ten dollars a day.

HOW TO GET IN TOUCH

Hawaii Division of State Parks, 3060 Eiwa Street, Lihu'e, HI 96766, 808-274-3444; www.kalalautrail.com.

stargaze at an upscale ranch

COLORADO

Stars are the streetlights of eternity.
—Anonymous

78 Rachel Carson, an incredible writer, biologist, and environmental guru, used to bemoan the fact that because stars are so available, offering us their beauty on a near-nightly basis, we tend to take them for granted. Because we can see this daunting spectacle almost any night, she says, perhaps we never will.

How long has it been since you've seen the stars? Not the faded versions that are barely discernible in a city's night sky, but the swarm of stars thick enough to stir that you can only experience when you're at least an hour or more from the bright urban lights.

That's what this entry is about—taking the opportunity to really look at the stars and ask yourself, "What if I had never seen this before? What if I knew I would never see it again?" Far from city lights, these three Colorado ranches, which offer a diversity of activities, including wrangling, cross-country skiing, and spa-going, also promise unhindered night-sky views, not to mention thousands of mountain acres and serenity that just aren't available in town.

C Lazy U. The C Lazy U and its 5,000 glorious acres have been a lot of things—a stagecoach stop in the early 1900s, a place to hunt bears and snag trout after that. Since 1946, when it was renamed C Lazy U (the Willow Creek bends and turns and clearly spells out a *C* and a *U* right there on the property), it has been known as an elegant place to be a cowpoke.

Unlike some dude ranches that put you on a horse and lead you around on a string, C Lazy U teaches its guests to really ride. If the Lone Ranger were to come galloping over the nearby hills looking for a posse to nab the varmints that done robbed the stagecoach, you'd be versed enough in horsemanship by the end of the week to join in. Of course, you might not want to, since it would mean you'd probably miss dinner at the lodge—a tragic misstep if you happen to like such things as lamb chops encrusted with pecans and gourmet mustard or perhaps a garlic brie tenderloin. Even the raspberry pancakes the next morning could put a dent in the Masked Man's recruiting ability.

In addition to its horseback-riding program, C Lazy U has lots of winter activities, including cross-country skiing, sleigh rides, and broomball ice hockey. Rates for a summer week at C Lazy U range from $2,300 to $2,975, including all meals and activities; winter rates start at $245 per night, again including meals.

C Lazy U, 3640 State Highway 125, P.O. Box 379, Granby, CO, 80446, 970-887-3344, www.clazyu.com.

Devil's Thumb Ranch. Located in a beautiful meadow with stunning views of the mountains at the Continental Divide, this ranch, too, was on the stagecoach route before the transcontinental railroad opened in 1869. The current owners of this "4,000 acres of raw Colorado," as they call it, are winning lots of eco-awards, including one from the Environmental Protection Agency, for their commitment to keeping this amazing ranch in Fraser Valley as natural and pristine as possible. Not only did Suzanne and Bob Fanch import the Broad Axe Barn (which serves as the spa and the activities center) from a farm in Indiana, thereby eliminating the need to cut down additional trees, but the new lodge and the 16 luxury log cabins are geothermally heated, using the Earth's own natural heat. The Ranch House Restaurant, a converted 1937 homestead cabin, uses organic, free-range meats and, whenever possible, locally grown produce for its unique artisan menu. You'll feast on such specialties as antelope satay or beef tenderloin with chanterelle mushroom sauce and drink rare wines from the barrel-doored wine cellar.

The ranch itself provides the quintessential outdoor mountain playground, with 60 miles of cross-country ski trails, 13 miles of snowshoe trails, a unique horsemanship and horseback-riding program, fly-fishing lessons, mountain biking, ice-skating, and even "skijoring," an up-and-coming sport where Rover pulls you on your skis. The new lodge, modeled after Mount Hood's famous Timberline Lodge, has a theater and old-fashioned bowling alley.

Long recognized as one of the country's premier Nordic resorts, Devil's Thumb offers a Thanksgiving Nordic Ski Camp every year that covers everything from technique, training, and racing to video analysis and waxing clinics. It's led by the University of Denver's Nordic coach Wolf Wallendorf and Subaru Factory team skier Eric Meyer.

Ranch Creek Spa, an elegant spa that recently opened, offers such treatments as Rocky Mountain rain therapy, body scrubs, aqua-latte baths, soaks, and hot stone massages. Prices vary for all spa treatments, beginning at $45 for a Swedish massage, to $290 for a spa package. Lodging prices begin at $145, depending upon season.

Devil's Thumb Ranch, 3530 County Road 83, Tabernash, CO 80478, 800-933-4339, www.devilsthumbranch.com.

Dunton Hot Springs. In the 1890s, the town of Dunton had a population of 500, most of whom worked the nearby mines. By 1918, the mine had shut down and Dunton, like many Colorado towns, became a ghost town. Although it had a short reincarnation in the 1970s as a hangout for hippies, bikers, and nude volleyball types who traded beers for dips in the hot springs, its bordello, saloon, and cabins basically sat boarded up for 75 years.

Then in 1994, Christoph Henkel and Bernt Kuhlman, a German and Austrian who were skiing in nearby Telluride, heard that the entire town was for sale at about the same price as a condo in Aspen. Fifteen minutes after finding the place (it's a good 45 minutes from the nearest non-ghost town), the European friends decided to snatch it up, battered facade be damned.

After funneling three million dollars into the 187-acre place (each of the 12 cabins is decorated by a Munich art dealer with a monstrous budget and extremely good taste), they found that they'd fallen so madly in love with their "vild vest" ghost town that, rather than sell lots, as they had originally intended, they'd rent them out. Before long, they opened their ghost-town spa to individual guests such as Darryl Hannah, Tom Cruise, and Ralph Lauren. The yoga room is a former Pony Express stop, the bathhouse still has bullet holes in it, the library is an old barn furnished with distressed-leather armchairs and bearskin rugs, and the dining hall is the town's old saloon with a long wooden bar scratched with names of people who have tipped the bottle there. Butch Cassidy, who allegedly stayed in Dunton after robbing his first bank in Telluride, provided one of the autographs.

Each of the 12 restored cabins, although imperfect on the outside, is tremendously luxurious on the inside, with African textiles, baronial antiques, broadband Internet, radiant floor heating, and hundreds of thousands of dollars' worth of art. Rates for an overnight stay, including all meals, start at $300 per person. A five-night spa package with all amenities is $2,200, while a three-night equestrian adventure package is $1,300. Dunton Hot Springs is reached via a 22-mile dirt road.

Dunton Hot Springs, P.O. Box 818, Dolores, CO 81323, 970-882-4800, www.duntonhotsprings.com.

never say "mush"

ELY, MINNESOTA

Give me winter, give me dogs, and you can keep the rest.
—Knut Rasmussen, the Dane
who explored Greenland in the early 20th century

79 | Originally used by Inuit to get from snowy point A to snowy point B, dogsledding is now being offered as an afternoon diversion at such tony resorts as Aspen's Little Nell and Jackson Hole's Amangani, which takes guests out for a 20-mile loop with a picnic lunch and a swim at a natural hot spring.

White Wilderness Sled Dog Adventures puts together vacations to Minnesota's Boundary Waters during which you do a whole lot more than just sitting on the back of a dogsled looking exotic in your $3,000 Spyder ski jacket. On these four-night outdoor excursions, you'll learn everything from how to care for and bond with your canine crew to how to traverse a skinny path between a fir and a pine tree and how to manage a tangle of harnesses and sled brakes.

Boundary Waters is a remote region of wilderness lakes, rivers, and forests that straddles the Minnesota-Canada border. For the same reason this area appeals to canoeists in summer, it appeals to mushers in winter: more than 1,000,000 acres of pristine lakes, the densest concentration in America, all off-limits to motorized vehicles. Mushers also like it because it's not as cold as Alaska and often gets more snow.

Peter McClelland, who owns White Wilderness Sled Dog Adventures with his wife, Chris Hegenbarth, calls himself "a naturalist by training, a musher by choice." As cofounder of the Ely Area Mushing Association, he began the company in 1994 to introduce wannabes to the Frozen North and the magic of dogsledding. He and Chris don't just sell you a dogsled trip—they adopt you for a few days, making sure you're properly dressed, filling you with exquisite, high-fat, high-protein foods (a must with temperatures from -20°F to -60°F), and tucking you away in your cozy canvas yurt at night, while the dogs nestle comfortably in the snow.

MUSH ADO ABOUT LOTS OF THINGS

If, like Jack London, you feel the "call of the wild," here are some pointers for dealing with your own Buck:

- Never yell "Mush!" Mush, a bastardization of the French *marche* (walk), is frowned upon by seasoned guides. The favored command is "Hike," which means "Go."
- "Gee" means turn right and "Haw" means go left.
- "Get up" means pull harder.
- Don't act like a drill sergeant. Screaming at your dogs only frustrates them. Treat them firmly, but don't overdo it. These puppies live to run.
- Before you go, read *Winterdance* by Gary Paulsen and *My Lead Dog Was a Lesbian* by Brian Patrick O'Donoghue.

You can choose between the "winter camping adventure," on which you overnight in a yurt, or choose more comfortable accommodations on their lodge-based trips, where you return to the comforts of a North Woods lodge each evening. White Wilderness also offers ice-fishing trips, a full-moon trip that includes a nighttime run with the dogs (offered only three times a year), and the Beargrease Special. This latter trip, held the last weekend in January, takes participants to the start and finish of the 400-mile John Beargrease Sled Dog Marathon, which runs along the north shore of Lake Superior.

Whichever vacation you choose, you won't go hungry. Hegenbarth, who designs all the menus, is famous for her fresh-baked cookies. You'll nosh on such delicacies as steaming bowls of homemade soup, pork schnitzel with chipotle apple brandy sauce, bratwurst roasted over the fire, pecan-stuffed pancakes, and her specialty: desserts such as cranberry bread pudding, fudge pecan cake, and Danish cremes.

A four-night, three-day premier yurt trip (with each person driving his or her own sled) is $1,395 per person (double occupancy) and includes all meals, lodging, guides, dogs, and sleds. The five-night Beargrease Special is $1,545. Before you go, you'll be sent a detailed clothing list for keeping warm.

HOW TO GET IN TOUCH

White Wilderness Sled Dog Adventures, P.O. Box 727, Ely, MN 55731, 800-701-6238 or 218-365-6363, www.whitewilderness.com.

acquire a piece of the rock

HUMBER VALLEY, NEWFOUNDLAND

It's as if Alaska married Ireland and had a child.
—*Brenda Walsh, Newfoundlander describing her home*

80 Name an outdoor activity. Bet you can't come up with even one that this mythic rocky island on the easternmost edge of North America "discovered" by Vikings more than a thousand years ago doesn't offer. Newfoundland has sea kayaking, hiking, biking, camping, fishing, rafting, skiing, caving, rock climbing, whale-watching, and—well, just about everything. Furthermore, the scenery amid which one partakes of these outdoor diversions is raw, unspoiled, and dramatic. A full 94 percent of the island's billion-year-old mountains, fjords, and glacial lakes is public land. There are very few traditional tourist attractions, thank goodness. Rather, people come to be stunned by miles of white-sand beaches, fjords surrounded by dense evergreen forests, and the sea that has sculpted a coastline of jagged volcanic cliffs.

A good headquarters for this remote outdoor trip is the Humber Valley Resort, an upscale vacation community on the province's west coast. Nestled on the northern bank of the Humber River and Deer Lake, the resort's 2,600 acres are within easy driving distance of Gros Morne, a national park with significant geological features.

Although the Humber Valley Resort calls its accommodations "chalets," just know that they're being uncommonly modest. Some of their chalets have as many as six bedrooms and even the three-bedroom variety has 2,000 square feet of floor space, vaulted ceilings, huge stone fireplaces, decks, hot tubs, full modern kitchens, and luxurious furnishings. The resort runs a full-time activity center, which can set up any number of the outdoor activities mentioned above. Some of the more exotic offerings are swimming with salmon, kite surfing, rappelling, canyoning down waterfalls, and cat skiing. The resort also offers weekly activities for guests such as kayak races, bonfires on the beach, guided nature walks, and "being screeched in"—a formal ritual that involves Newfoundland's special brand of screech rum, kissing a codfish, and becoming an honorary Newfoundlander.

MORE SURPRISES

- The *Titanic* sank 375 miles southeast of St. John's, Newfoundland, where it still lies 12,900 feet below sea level. Robert Ballard discovered her remains in 1985.
- There are more moose than people in Newfoundland.
- Geologists from around the world come to study the unusual formations in Gros Morne National Park. Millions of years of tectonic plate movement have created an otherworldly landscape that includes the bizarre and barren Table-lands. The park also has exotic rare orchids.
- Besides its capital St. John's, established on the island's east coast in 1583, Newfoundland is made up of tiny far-flung fishing villages. Two of the interestingly named ones are Heart's Desire and Heart's Content.
- Newfies like to host "kitchen parties." And the quintessential *scoff* (that's Newfie for meal) is a Jigg's Dinner. Whether the name comes from the lively dance or the method used to catch the local cod (i.e., to "jigg" by jerking up quickly on a line), the feast involves salted beef that has been soaked overnight, yellow split peas in a muslin bag, potatoes, turnips, and carrots, all cooked in a big pot.
- The Vikings named Newfoundland "Vinland" because they observed it was covered with "little grapes." It turns out the "grapes" were actually berries—blueberries, cranberries, partridgeberries, bakeapples, currants, dewberries, and brambleberries usually ripen to perfection here in August.

Even though the resort offers plush accommodations, the people at the Humber Valley Resort, like most Newfies, as they call themselves, are friendly and down-to-earth, not to mention fiercely independent and proud. The Newfoundlanders were the last to join Canada (in 1949), have their own time zone (1.5 hours ahead of Eastern Standard Time), and even have their own dialectical dictionary with 5,000 entries, mostly related to fishing, scenery, and weather. And they're charmingly insistent about the correct pronunciation of their beloved homeland. "Newfoundland rhymes with understand," they're quick to point out.

Rates at the Humber Valley Resort start at $175 per person ($206 Canadian) off-season, with four-person occupancy in a three-bedroom chalet per night; and go up to $875 ($1,010 Canadian) for the six-bedroom version.

HOW TO GET IN TOUCH
Humber Valley Resort, Box 370, Humber Valley, NF A0L 1K0, 866-686-8100, www.humbervalley.com.

visit a historic spa

QUAINT TOWNS & HISTORIC CITIES ACROSS AMERICA

Something about sitting there buck naked in a spa
opens me up to really examining those issues that sometimes
stay buried under to-do lists at home.
—Chelsea O'Shea, self-described spa fanatic

81 To an actress, turning 50 is almost a death sentence. To the grand old dames in this entry, 50 is merely the starting gate. We're talking about the National Register of Historic Places and, more specifically, the National Trust's Historic Hotels of America, a listing of 209 time-honored hotels and resorts that have faithfully maintained their historic integrity, architecture, and ambience. Needless to say, many of these have spas, some as fabled as the hotel itself. Here are six of note:

The American Club. Built in 1918 to house single immigrants who came to work at the Kohler Company, a renowned maker of bathroom fixtures, the brick Tudor dormitory was transformed into a luxury hotel in 1981. Walter Kohler, president of the company and governor of Wisconsin from 1929 to 1931, believed his immigrant workers deserved "not only wages, but roses, as well." His resident workers enjoyed wholesome meals, a billiard-and-tap room, and summer concerts on the front lawn. American flags were hung everywhere—Kohler's not-so-subtle hint that his immigrant workers might want to consider applying for U.S. citizenship. By 1930, Kohler had convinced nearly 700 immigrant workers to take the annual paid day off and free transportation to the county courthouse to take their oath of citizenship.

Nowadays, The American Club is a five-diamond lhotel with four garden courtyards, nine restaurants, and uncommonly opulent bathrooms. The Kohler Waters Spa, in the Carriage House of The American Club, has treatment rooms with waterfalls, a glass-enclosed rooftop deck, fireplaces, and spa treatments. Rates range from $140 to $185 for a standard room in the winter to $1,230 for the presidential suite in the summer.

The American Club, 444 Highland Drive, Kohler, WI 53044, 800-344-2838, www.destinationkohler.com.

French Lick Springs Hotel. If the walls of this elegant hotel could talk … The venerable, 443-room resort is where tomato juice was invented. It's where Franklin D. Roosevelt secured his presidential nomination in 1931 and where such guests as Clark Gable, Al Capone, and Bing Crosby sipped brandy. The French Lick Springs Hotel sits on 1,600 acres in Indiana's Hoosier National Forest and offers two golf courses, croquet, archery, horseback riding, surrey rides, two swimming pools, a bowling alley, tennis courts, and the spa—which has been updated since the mid-1800s when rich Chicagoans would take the Monon Railroad straight from the Windy City to the resort's front entrance. The new 27,000-square-foot spa still offers Pluto Mineral Springs baths, as well as head-to-toe treatments. Prices range from $139 to $1,250 per person.

French Lick Resort and Casino, 8670 W. State Road 56, French Lick, IN 47432, 812-936-9300, www.frenchlick.com.

The Greenbrier. Since 1778, people have been coming to this mountain retreat in West Virginia to "take the waters." Finally in 1830, when a stagecoach route was hacked out through the forbidding mountains, the resort became a fashionable meeting spot for wealthy Southerners. Known by various names through the years, The Greenbrier, as it's now called, has hosted dignitaries and celebrities including all U.S. presidents from Eisenhower through Clinton, Prince Rainier and Princess Grace of Monaco, Patsy Cline, and Bob Hope. Recreational activities include croquet, horseback riding, and falconry. The spa's holistic treatments are based on the healing powers of the naturally sulfurous water and mineral springs. The Greenbrier accommodations range from standard rooms priced at $307 to $408 to estate houses for $685 to $771.

The Greenbrier, 300 W. Main Street, White Sulphur Springs, WV 24986, 800-453-4858, www.greenbrier.com.

The Homestead. Twenty-two U.S. Presidents have signed the guest register at this classic Virginia mountain resort, including Thomas Jefferson who enjoyed The Homestead's mineral springs (they're now called the Jefferson Pools) when he stayed for three weeks in 1818. The Homestead was developed as a spa resort in 1766, and the octagonal wooden building where Jefferson soaked three times daily is considered America's oldest spa structure. Snuggled in the rustic beauty of the Allegheny Mountains, The Homestead's more than 3,000 acres contains three golf courses and outdoor activities including fly-fishing, falconry, trap shooting, and skiing. The spa, still fed by the historic hot springs, offers mineral baths, massages, a steam room, and saunas. Room rates—including breakfast, afternoon tea, and dinner, historical programs, nightly movies, and use of the spring-fed pools—range in peak season from $269 to $909.

The Homestead, 1766 Homestead Drive, P.O. Box 2000, Hot Springs, VA 24445, 800-838-1766 or 540-8391766, www.thehomestead.com.

Mohonk Mountain House. Built on a cliff overlooking blue Lake Mohonk, this Victorian castle is still run by the same Quaker family who started it in 1869. Twin brothers Alfred and Albert Smiley, on a picnic to the Adirondacks, fell in love with the area and decided to buy a ten-room inn and tavern and turn it into the 266-room castle and historic landmark it is today. Not only does it still have a 107-year-old Scottish links golf course, a Victorian maze, and 19th-century English gardens, but it has also added 85 miles of hiking trails, tennis, golf, boating, ice-skating, cross-country skiing, snowshoeing, and, of course, the brand new spa. The 30,000-square-foot spa has 16 treatment rooms, a solarium, an outdoor heated mineral pool, and a whole slate of yoga, Pilates, *qi gong,* and water aerobics classes. Other than horseback riding, carriage rides, spa treatments, and weekend golf (during the week, it's free), everything else (three daily meals, afternoon tea and cookies, and all other recreational activities) is included in the room rates of between $415 and $775.

Mohonk Mountain House, 1000 Mountain Rest Road, New Paltz, NY 12561, 800-772-6646, www.mohonk.com.

Ojai Valley Inn and Spa. Clark Gable, Judy Garland, and Paul Newman are just a few of the guests who have frequented this historic Spanish-style resort in southern California's Ojai Valley. Originally built in 1922 as a country club for Edward Drummond Libbey, a wealthy glass manufacturer from Ohio, the resort has 308 spacious rooms and suites with fireplaces, terraces, and spectacular mountain views. In addition to the classic 1923 golf course, the 800-acre ranch has stables and horseback riding, a tennis center, two swimming pools, and a spa that regularly makes Top 10 lists. The Kuyam mud or healing clay treatment is the spa's signature, but it also offers seasonal scrubs such as spring's pixie tangerine body scrub. Room rates range from $400 to $650, suites from $600 to $3,000.

Ojai Valley Inn and Spa, 805 Country Club Road, Ojai, CA 93023, 888-697-8780 or 805-646-1111, www.ojairesort.com.

practice an age-old healing art

EXOTIC BEACHES AROUND THE WORLD

It opened my life to things I never knew existed.
—Sue Rapp, teacher who recently attended
a Tai Chi in Paradise vacation

82 In 2008 for the very first time, the ancient martial art of tai chi will be an official Olympic event, and a trio of lucky competitors will win the gold, silver, and bronze medals. But anyone who practices this gentle, slow-moving martial art could be declared a winner. According to a recent study in the *Archives of Internal Medicine,* the age-old Chinese practice lowers stress and anxiety, improves balance, and reduces the effects of arthritis, heart problems, and depression.

In practice, tai chi (or *tai ji quan,* as it's more properly known) is a complex sequence of flowing postures with names like "White Snake Puts Out Tongue" and "Carry Tiger to the Mountain." Its series of movements requires concentration, coordination, and balance. It's practiced by everyone from 80-year-old heart patients to business executives wanting to learn strategies for dealing with conflict to *Kung Fu* star David Carradine, who made a how-to tai chi video.

Chris Luth, a *tai ji sifu* (that's Chinese for "a teacher" and "father figure") from California, leads five- to nine-day tai chi vacations. He calls these vacations Tai Chi in Paradise because he hosts them in such lush Edens as Hawaii, Bali, Costa Rica, and the Canary Islands. They're usually held on the beach at secluded resorts, near rain forests, waterfalls, and wildlife preserves.

"I made it a policy 20 years or so ago that I was only going to work in places I wanted to be," Luth says. "Basically I pick my 'paradises,' places where I can surf and snowboard and do things I want to do."

On a recent Hawaii trip, for example, participants stayed at a jungle lodge within earshot of the ocean on the Big Island. In a virtually untouched setting, they swam with spinner dolphins, snorkeled, dove, surfed, soaked in rare oceanside "warm springs,"

WITHOUT WORKING UP A SWEAT

Translated, *tai ji quan* means "supreme ultimate boxing." Even though its slow, ballet-like movements are gentle and unassuming, tai chi burns more calories than surfing and nearly as many as downhill skiing. It also has been shown to reduce ADHD and boost the immune system.

Most of all, says Luth, the head of Tai Chi in Paradise, "It creates space within yourself." He's so convinced it will benefit anyone, anyplace, anytime, that he offers a money-back guarantee. If you go on a Tai Chi in Paradise retreat and aren't totally blown away, he'll refund your money. In 20 years, no one has taken him up on that offer.

tried a hula lesson—accompanied by several hours of tai chi, *qi gong* (another ancient Chinese healing art), and yoga each day.

Luth, who founded the Pacific School of Tai Chi and Qi Gong in 1979, is a two-time tai chi national champion as well as an advanced snowboarder, surfer, and semiprofessional ice hockey player. Corporations such as Bayer, Marriott, and the National Credit Union Association hire him to give seminars on business communication, negotiation skills, and conflict management, all centered around tai chi principles. Luth started Tai Chi in Paradise in 1986 to give students a chance to expand their tai chi practice. He calls these vacations "a journey of discovery, not just of these ancient healing arts but of yourself and your relationships to life." His students call them life transforming.

"I've discovered that when my students are away from their having-to-pick-up-the-kids-in-an-hour mode, they're able to go much deeper, they can really absorb the tai chi, qi gong, and meditation," Luth reports.

The retreats are limited to 15 participants, and they offer a nice mix of class time, light-hearted playtime, and relaxation. Prices for the all-inclusive retreats vary, but an example would be the Hawaii trip mentioned above at $1,475, including accommodations, meals, and tai chi, qi gong, and yoga instruction.

HOW TO GET IN TOUCH
Tai Chi in Paradise, P.O. Box 962, Solana Beach, CA 92075, 800-266-5803, www.taichiinparadise.com.

get a pedal perspective

BIKE TRAILS & BIKER-FRIENDLY ROADS NEAR & FAR

You don't find a place on a map,
you find it in the hearts of the people that live there.
—Linda Forward, rider on Global Exchange Bike-Aid trips

83 There are hundreds, maybe thousands, of companies that offer bike trips. If you're just looking for a bike tour, you can Google "cycling vacations" and quickly get a list of many options.

But this entry focuses on some bike trips with a different twist—ones where you get all the usual benefits (fresh air, exercise, beautiful landscapes), but, more than that, you get the chance to make a difference in the world. Global Exchange, an innovative nonprofit in San Francisco that works for peace and justice, offers Bike-Aid trips, where you ride bikes for a cause. Along the route, some that crisscross the entire country, you'll meet with grassroots organizations, put in some elbow grease helping these community groups build a food shelter or restore topsoil, and share your own views on how we can build better communities.

"It becomes this exciting, grassroots, educational exchange," says Allison Happel, a participant on a recent Global Exchange bike trip. "Not only do we learn from them [the grassroots organizations], but we spread information we've gotten from other places and organizations."

Some Bike-Aid trips have a particular mission—say, to promote sustainability, to promote immigrants' rights, or to fight global warming. On the two-week Bike-Aid trip from San Francisco to the Mexican border, for example, bikers meet with such groups as the Central Coast Citizenship Project (CCCP), a Salinas organization that helps immigrants earn citizenship. Not only do the participants meet the immigrants, even getting up at 3 a.m. to join them in the fields, but they brainstorm with CCCP staffers on new ways to help the immigrant community. On

Bike-Aid Hawaii, cyclists meet with native Hawaiian activists working to preserve their islands and perhaps help them plant taro or harvest pineapple.

"Our trips have three important components," says Debbie Edrozo, Global Exchange's Bike-Aid coordinator. "There's the physical aspect, the educational component, and the community service."

Bike-Aid was started in 1984 by a couple of Stanford students and was administered by two other groups before landing with Global Exchange, which already offered a full roster of overseas "Reality Tours" that give, as they say, "the opportunity to understand issues beyond what is communicated by the mass media." The ten-week cross-country Bike-Aid ride is still the heart of the program—a great way, according to Edrozo, to witness the spirit of America that is still very creative, very grassroots, very eager to fight for justice.

Accommodations on the Bike-Aid trips vary depending on what the communities can offer. Sometimes that means camping in somebody's backyard; other times, it's sleeping in a church basement. Each rider must fill out an application and is required to raise a minimum of $1,350 for the California route, $1,200 for the Hawaii route, or $4,000 for the cross-country routes. You will also be responsible for some of your own food.

HOW TO GET IN TOUCH
Bike-Aid at Global Exchange, 2017 Mission Street, #303, San Francisco, CA 94110, 415-255-7296, www.globalexchange.org

stop to smell the roses on a walking vacation

HIKING TRAILS ACROSS THE COUNTRY & BEYOND

For every walk is a sort of crusade, preached by some Peter the Hermit
in us, to go forth and reconquer this Holy Land.
—Henry David Thoreau

84 Thoreau is most remembered for his books *Walden,* about simple living amid nature, and *Civil Disobedience,* on resistance to government. But among his published works is a small treatise on walking, about which he once wrote, "I regard this as a sort of introduction to all that I may write hereafter." In "Walking," first published in the *Atlantic Monthly* after his death is 1862, he extolled the virtues of traveling by foot, saying we should walk "in the spirit of undying adventure, never to return."

While we don't recommend never returning, a walking vacation can be great because it offers an intimacy with a place that you don't get when you're zooming through in a car. And for those of you who are thinking, "But I won't get to see much," consider this. If you drive by a field of purple flowers, you see a swatch of

ARE YOUR BOOTS MADE FOR WALKING?

"After a day's walk, everything has twice its usual value."
—George Macauley Trevelyan, British author

According to Mark Fenton, a member of the U.S. National Racewalking Team, walking shoes should have good arch support, fairly low but well-cushioned heels, and good flexibility at the ball of the foot. A few other tips:
- Try on shoes in the afternoon, when your feet are largest.
- Try them on with the socks you'll be wearing.
- Replace your shoes every six months or after 500 miles, whichever comes first.

purple, but if you walk by the same field, you get to examine the petals, notice the bee flitting in and out, maybe even figure out what type of flower it is. It's a matter of what you want to see. Lapping a bunch of time zones doesn't mean you've seen more.

By moving more slowly, you get to meet locals, stop in tiny cafés, hear about the cow that got loose last night from Farmer John's field, and breathe the fresh air. It's the only way to fully immerse yourself in the cultural and natural history of a place. And do we really need to point out the health benefits? Everyone from fitness guru Kathy Smith to your doctor will tell you that walking burns calories, boosts energy, lowers blood pressure, and reduces your risk of diabetes and perhaps even osteoporosis.

The following are two companies that offer amazing walking vacations complete with self-indulgent lodging (after all that time on your feet, don't you deserve it?), gourmet dining, and fascinating itineraries:

Classic Journeys. This company out of La Jolla, California, offers what it calls "cultural walking adventures" throughout the United States and to dozens of countries around the world. In its view, walking is the best way to travel because that way "the world can't slide past you faster than you can absorb it." Classic Journeys hires locals to lead the tours, guides who, as the brochure says, will "be the kind of person who knows the man whose wife's brother owns the olive press . . . the opening day of truffle season (and the truffle hunter who'll let you tag along) . . . and which local specialties don't appear on the menu." If you need help with anything from haggling for a rug to buying guidebooks, their guides have an "in." Typically, you'll walk for three to four hours a day. Some of their North American itineraries include Washington's San Juan Islands, Napa Valley, Utah's national parks, Nova Scotia's coasts, and Alaska's Kenai Peninsula. Prices range from $2,395 for a six-day trip to Nova Scotia to $3,895 for a ten-day tour of Vietnam. Both of these trips include accommodations, transportation within the region, and most meals.

Classic Journeys, 7855 Ivanhoe Avenue, Suite 220, La Jolla, CA 92037, 800-200-3887, www.classicjourneys.com.

Country Walkers. Leading guided walking tours at an easy (4 to 6 miles a day) to challenging (up to 14 miles a day over rugged terrain) pace, Country Walkers offers more than 80 itineraries in the United States and all over the world from New Zealand to Bhutan. According to spokesperson Bari Rosenow, "Country

Walkers is all about slowing down, enjoying the pleasures of camaraderie, and immersing yourself in authentic experiences and stunning scenery."

Following breakfast, where you'll be versed on the day's route, you'll walk for several miles, taking lunch in a village or on a trailside picnic. Each day's route is chosen to showcase a region's best attributes, including stops to taste wines at local vineyards, say, or at the home of a woman who shares homemade bread, cheese, and dried figs.

Country Walkers has been around for 28 years and is the only American company that specializes only in walking tours (many other companies such as Backroads or Boundless Journeys offer walking tours in addition to biking and multisport tours). Country Walkers must be doing something right, because repeat customers are a huge part of their business. It even has an Encore Loyalty program, à la frequent flyer programs, where you get special bonuses after so many trips. After 12 trips, for example, you can take a companion for half price on your next trip; after 15, you get a trip for free. Encore members also get first dibs on what the company calls "prototype trips"—trips that haven't been officially offered on the website, because perhaps the kinks are still being worked out. Some of Country Walkers' North American itineraries include a six-day walking trip to Quebec City and the Charlevoix, where you'll explore evergreen forests, rolling meadows, and little villages along the St. Lawrence River, and an Arizona all-women's adventure that explores the high desert landscape.

The typical price for a 6-day North American trip is $2,198. Prices overall range from $1,948 for a 4-day trip in Tuscany to $5,298 for an 11-day trip to Chile or South Africa. A 6-day North American trip ranges in price from $2,198 to $2,598.

Country Walkers, P.O. Box 180, Waterbury, VT 05676, 800-464-9255, www. countrywalkers.com.

rev your engine

LAKEVILLE, CONNECTICUT

Racing is a matter of spirit, not strength.
—Janet Guthrie, first woman to race in the Indy 500, in 1977

85 There's a reason American Express, Citibank, Pepsi, and hundreds of other corporations have sent their employees to Skip Barber Racing School. And it's not because they want faster drivers.

"It develops confidence," says Rick Roso, the company's marketing manager and an occasional instructor. "When you do something that you thought you couldn't do, something that seemed impossible, it carries over into other parts of your life."

But what's so impossible about racing a car?

"When you watch it on TV, it looks easy," Roso says. "But that's only because you don't feel the g-forces, the braking forces. When you're in a race car, it's ten times more difficult than it looks. You'd be surprised how many people don't want to come back after the first day."

That's where the confidence-building comes in. Skip Barber instructors, all competitive drivers, are masters at pushing through those psychological barriers, those fears that inevitably taunt you when you realize you're going to be hurtling around a racetrack at 130 miles an hour in a flimsy, 1,100-pound car.

That's why Roso has often heard the Three-Day Racing School—the company's bread and butter—referred to as the "Outward Bound of motor sport." According to him, it will do a lot more than teach you how to downshift, brake, corner, and pass other drivers. It will make you a better person. "When you do something this radical, it changes you," he says.

The Three-Day Racing School is held at some of the best tracks in the United States and Canada, the same tracks that pros race on—Laguna Seca, Daytona, Sebring, Lime Rock Park, to name a few. In fact, if you look at the roster of pros, you'll find that a good percentage of them have trained with Skip Barber.

Graduates of the Three-Day Racing School automatically qualify to race in the Skip Barber Race Series, North America's largest open-wheel amateur

A ROLLING CLASSROOM

Your "classroom" at the Skip Barber Racing School is a Formula Dodge, a 2.0-liter four-cylinder with 130 horsepower, high-performance street tires, and a four-speed racing gearbox. It weighs just 1,100 pounds and can brake and turn better than even the most extreme sports car. You sit inches off the ground in a semi-reclining position. The steering wheel is only about 8 inches in diameter. You'll be able to hear every gear shift, every squeal of the brake. "Racing car driving is not designed to be quiet," says the school's marketing director. "It's a very visceral experience."

championship. Drivers with career aspirations have long used the Race Series as their entrée into the sport, but most of the drivers in the series are everyday folks. On these race weekends, which culminate in four regional championships, Skip Barber brings the cars, the pit crews, and the fireproof jumpsuits. All you do is show up. And fork over the $2,695 Race Weekend fee, plus $1,195 for the 80 miles of Friday practice—mandatory if it's your first time, and two advanced on-track programs that cost an extra $2,190 to $3,195.

Skip Barber, a retired racecar driver himself, started his school in 1975 with four students and a pair of borrowed race cars. By the end of the first year, he was $10,000 in debt. But the same mentality that propelled his success as a professional driver wouldn't let him give up. Today, the company (Barber sold it in 2002 to concentrate on the famous Lime Rock Park racetrack that he was able to buy after the racing school took off) owns 200 high-performance race cars.

The fee for the Three-Day Racing School is $3,995 and includes instruction in the classroom and on the track. It's offered at its locations in Florida, Wisconsin, California, and Connecticut hundreds of times a year.

HOW TO GET IN TOUCH
Skip Barber Racing School, P.O. Box 1629, Lakeville, CT 06039, 800-221-1131, www.skipbarber.com.

ESALEN INSTITUTE & OMEGA INSTITUTE FOR HOLISTIC STUDIES

follow your bliss at a personal growth workshop

CALIFORNIA & NEW YORK

I felt like I'd stumbled into my hippie-dippie past. And part of it was confirmation that idealism can be respected and that people who care really can make a difference in our world.
—Janet Fullwood, Esalen attendee

86 By the time we're 35, most of us have accumulated so many commitments and responsibilities that we're barely hanging on. We keep telling ourselves, "I can keep this up until the kids graduate" or "until my next vacation." But the cost of being so busy and overwhelmed eventually catches up with us. Our health begins to suffer, our happiness dwindles, our spirits sag.

What this vacation offers is an opportunity to empty your proverbial cup, to get a fresh perspective. There's no better place to ponder the questions that tug at you in the middle of the night than at a holistic retreat center. All the authors of the books you've pored over—from Maya Angelou to Dr. Andrew Weil—give workshops at these healing centers. You can choose between weeklong and weekend workshops on such topics as "Afro-Cuban Drum and Dance," "The Mind beyond the Brain," "Practicing Peace in Times of War," and "Spontaneous Inventions," a class Bobby "Don't Worry, Be Happy" McFerrin offers on deepening your artistic expression. Even Goldie Hawn has been known to give workshops.

Although these days you can find a yoga studio and a Gestalt center on every corner, the two retreat centers listed below are the veritable godfathers of the human potential movement. They both have incredibly beautiful campuses, workshop leaders that are a veritable who's who, and a long list of enlightening workshops.

Esalen Institute. Perched on a rocky ledge overlooking the Pacific Ocean, this 140-acre institute in Big Sur is where Gestalt therapy guru Frederick "Fritz" Perls coached Rita Hayworth and where Ida Rolf pioneered Rolfing. Joseph Campbell, Buckminster Fuller, and Linus Pauling have all given workshops here.

The weathered redwood buildings and geodesic domes sprinkled about the grounds go back to the early 1960s, when Stanford graduate students Michael Murphy and Richard Price gave life to their vision of a sanctuary where thinkers of all stripes—philosophers, psychologists, artists, academics, spiritual leaders—could come together to pursue the "exploration of unrealized human capacities." Over the years, more than 300,000 people have taken them up on the offer, flocking to the legendary "clothing optional" mineral baths to soak and rub elbows with such folks as Joan Baez, Lily Tomlin, Hunter Thompson, Jack Kerouac, and John Lennon.

Esalen still offers more than 400 workshops every year, including weekend, five-day, and seven-day seminars. Rates range from $370 to $1,715 per person.

Esalen Institute, 55000 Highway 1, Big Sur, CA 93920, 831-667-3000, www.esalen.org.

Omega Institute for Holistic Studies. Tucked into the hills above the Hudson River an hour north of New York, Omega was founded in 1977 to help people bring more meaning and vitality to their life. "Omega is an oasis for people in a crazy society," explains Stephan Rechtschaffen, a medical doctor and cofounder of the Omega Institute. "We live in a world that is chaotic and spinning out of control, and many people come here because they feel at least for a period of time that they're able to slow down, they're able to feel a type of peace in themselves in such a way that they are able to start to bring it back into their lives. Hopefully, it can help them create more balance."

Since those early days when Rechtschaffen and his colleagues rented out boarding schools and Bennington College to hold their workshops, Omega has grown into the nation's largest holistic learning center. Every year more than 20,000 people attend workshops, retreats, and conferences on its 195-acre campus in the countryside of Rhinebeck, New York, and at sister sites, including three weeks at Maho Bay, U.S. Virgin Islands.

In addition to the workshops offered by such well-known personalities as Al Gore, Jane Goodall, and Arianna Huffington, Omega has daily yoga, tai chi, mediation, and movements classes. There's also a wellness center for saunas and massages, or you can canoe or swim in Omega's lake or hike its many wooded trails.

Cabins and tents are spread around the gardens, fields, and woodlands. Prices range from $130 for two nights of camping to $1,379 for a week in a single-room cabin.

Omega Institute for Holistic Studies, 150 Lake Drive, Rhinebeck, NY 12572, 800-944-1001, www.eomega.org.

pump your heart
at an adventure spa

THROUGHOUT THE UNITED STATES

Fitness—If it came in a bottle, everybody would have a great body.
—Cher

87 Thirty years ago, the only ones who went to spas were people like Marilyn Monroe and Joan Crawford, the famous and rich who needed to drop pounds or rejuvenate their complexions before their moviegoing public spotted them in, well, public. And the only exercise these exclusive spas offered was moving the robe-swaddled bodies of the wealthy from one treatment table to the next.

Now, of course, you can find spas everywhere that dole out manicures and massages, and exercise, as much as some of us hate to admit it, is accepted as being vital to the whole spa equation. Instead of working up a sweat in a spinning or kickboxing class in a stuffy gym that, if you're lucky, is playing an old Jimmy Stewart movie, why not fulfill the "exercise" component of your spa stay by hiking or snorkeling or horseback riding—something outdoors, preferably where the scenery contributes to making your heart pump faster? In the spa industry, these resorts are called "adventure spas." Here are a few of the best:

Miraval Life in Balance. Tucked into a valley north of Tucson, just west of the Santa Catalina Mountains, this 445-acre Sonoran Desert resort has always been known for its challenge sessions where guests push themselves to try new things, all the while being mindful of what it brings up. Perhaps best known is the resort's Equine Experience, where guests are taken to a horse ranch, given a demo on how to groom a horse, and then charged with doing it themselves. As Wyatt Webb, the psychotherapist who serves as Miraval's equine experience manager, says, "It's not about the horse." Rather, you find out all sorts of patterns of learned behaviors—how you solve problems,

SPA EVOLUTION

Spas might currently be experiencing a revolution in upscale resorts around the world, but they are by no means a new thing. Homer and other Classical writers extolled the virtues of taking to springs, baths, and spas for therapeutic and healing purposes. The Babylonians, Egyptians, and Minoans all took the waters. Spas were built across the Roman Empire, from Africa to England, expanding into entertainment complexes complete with exercise rooms, restaurants, and a menu of different types of hot and cold baths. The first Japanese *onsen* (hot spring) opened in 737 A.D. near Izumo, with the first *ryokan* (inn), offering food, accommodations, gardens, outdoor baths, and indoor soaking tubs, emerging on the spa scene centuries later. Saunas originated in Finland as early as 1000 A.D., including a healthy dose of beer and vodka. And the Ottoman were famous for their gorgeously mosaiced *hammam,* comprising steam rooms, massage platforms, and plenty of socializing. In Western Europe, natural hot springs drew the elite and wealthy as far back as the Middle Ages—Charlemagne's Aachen and Bonaventura's Poretta are prime examples, with such still famous sites as Spa, Belgium; Baden-Baden, Germany; and Bath, England, originating during the Renaissance.

Spas first took root in the United States in the 1850s, at New York's Saratoga Springs, a fashionable resort that drew Edgar Allan Poe, Franklin Roosevelt, and other elites. Elizabeth Arden opened the first day spa, Manhattan's Red Door Salon, in 1910, purveying manicures and facials; it also served as a finishing school. California's Golden Door spa opened in 1958, focusing on weight loss and fitness—only the beginning in the innovation of treatments and popularity of pampering that continues to bloom.

how willing you are to ask for help, and so on. Of course, Miraval also offers the requisite spa treatments, golf and tennis facilities, a famous doctor (Andrew Weil, who serves as the resort's director of integrative health and healing), and 106 nicely appointed casitas. The Ultimate Package, with rooms, three gourmets a day, a spa service a day (or one round of golf), round-trip transportation from Tucson airport, and use of all the facilities, start at $445 per day for double occupancy, or $595 October through December.

Miraval Life in Balance, 5000 E. Via Estancia Miraval, Catalina, AZ 85739, 800-232-3969, www.miravalresort.com.

Mountain Trek Fitness Retreat and Health Spa. The fact that the website for this spa near Nelson, British Columbia, is www.hiking.com should be your first clue that you're not going to be doing a lot of sitting around. The scenery at the spa resembles Switzerland, with big lakes and big mountains. In fact, the only thing small about this spa is the number of guests it accepts each week: 14 is the max. The Mountain Hiking program with three- and four-night options includes all meals, regular massages (in fact, nobody gets out of this resort without at least one massage), and guided hikes through the gorgeous Canadian Rockies. Prices start at $3,120 ($3,670 Canadian) for a seven-day, all-inclusive program.

Mountain Trek Fitness Retreat and Health Spa, Box 1352, Ainsworth Hot Springs, B.C., V0G 1A0, Canada, 800-661-5161 or 250-229-5636, www.hiking.com.

Red Mountain Spa. Set on 55 acres of towering cliffs and red rock formations near St. George, Utah, this godfather of adventure spas has 41 adventure guides (there's even an adventure concierge) who will take you rock climbing, geocaching (that's a treasure-hunting hike using GPS equipment), mountain biking, or hiking into nearby Bryce and Zion National Parks. The resort's three-story geodesic Sagestone Spa & Salon offers 60 types of spa treatments, and there is a full array of classes on anything physical, mental, or spiritual, from "Chi Ball Stretch" to "Navajo Storytelling." A four-night adventure package with daily guided hikes, three healthy gourmet meals, unlimited classes, a spa treatment (or health and fitness service), and a trip to Zion is $1,210.

Red Mountain Spa, 1275 E. Red Mountain Circle, Ivins, UT 84738 (mailing address: P.O. Box 2149 St. George , UT 84771), 800-407-3002, www. redmountainspa.com.

Wilderness Adventure Spa at Spring Creek Ranch. Did somebody say outdoors? At this spa in the mountains near Jackson Hole, Wyoming, not only will you participate in such adrenaline-provoking adventures as dogsledding and white-water rafting, but your treatments themselves are even performed outdoors, in an open-air tent on a butte overlooking the Teton Range. There's a mountainside meadow (they call it the Great Lawn) for outdoor yoga, an open fire beside which meditation classes are held, and *reiki* on horseback, where equine energy frees yours. Instead of saunas, you'll steam in a Native American sweat lodge. Rooms at the rustic luxurious pine-pole lodge range from $150 to $310 and include breakfast; hour-long treatments start at $120.

Wilderness Adventure Spa at Spring Creek Ranch, 1800 Spirit Dance Road, Jackson, WY 83001, 800-443-6139 (main ranch number) or 307-732-8165 (spa reservations), www.springcreekranch.com.

hike to a "club mud" through an ancient forest

PACIFIC NORTHWEST

Insert tree-hugger joke here if you must, but I swear on
my dog's dish that I felt a bolt of energy shoot up from the ground
and somehow connect me to that tree. At that moment,
I could have been the first woman, or the last, on Earth.
—Vanessa McGrady, hiker to Oregon's Terwilliger Hot Springs

88 It used to be that if you wanted to soak in a natural hot springs, you either had to stumble onto one (not an impossibility, since there are 1,661 in the United States alone), figure out how to decipher geographical survey maps, or fight the crowds at the springs that had been commercially developed. Now, thanks to the Internet and a spate of books overflowing with lists and directions to these little-known hot springs, it's quite doable to plan a whole hiking vacation around remote hot springs. And if you're going to hike and soak, you might as well do it with a stand of the Pacific Northwest's old-growth trees cheering you on.

Not only do you get an invigorating hike, but you can shed the boots, the pack, and maybe even the clothes and settle into an oh-so-relaxing gift straight from Mother Nature herself. No kids playing "Marco Polo," no teenyboppers comparing tan lines, no concession stands trying to sell you an all-beef patty. Hit it right and you'll have the primitive springs, ancient trees, and views all to yourself.

These natural, outdoor, noncommercial soaking pools are improvised, often kept "in working order" by volunteers. The springs are often creatively rigged to collect the flow of water and to maintain a proper temperature.

The bible for hot springs hiking trips in Oregon, Idaho, Washington, and British Columbia is Evie Litton's *Hiking Hot Springs in the Pacific Northwest*, which lists 140 undeveloped sites. Litton, who broke free from her job as a technical illustrator in 1983, traveled around in a camperized van to research this book.

In Washington, there are hot springs on the Olympic Peninsula, in the Cascade

Range, and near the Columbia Gorge. Idaho has dozens and dozens of them. And in southeast Oregon on the Owyhee River is the most spectacular of all, a hundred-yard chasm in the desert spilling hot water into a stream and falling down into the Owyhee. Here are just a couple of hike–hot spring combos to get you started:

Bagby Hot Springs. You'll follow a creek most of the way on this 1.5-mile hike through old-growth Douglas-fir and cedar, located in the Mount Hood National Forest, 70 miles southeast of Portland. The remote springs, although clearly marked on most maps of the Mount Hood National Forest, has been improved by a volunteer group that calls itself the Friends of Bagby Hot Springs. There's an open-air "bathhouse" with a round 6-foot cedar tub and three log tubs made from hollowed-out cedar trees, as well as an enclosed private row with five "bathhouses," each with its own hollowed-out tree tub. All you do is remove the wooden plug and the tubs quickly fill. You can regulate the temperature by adding buckets of cool water. Although Native Americans used this springs for centuries, it was first "discovered" by Robert Bagby, a miner from Amity, Oregon, in 1881. To find the trailhead, take Ore. 224 south from Estacada. You'll see a sign for Bagby, where you turn onto Forest Service Road 63. Take that road to Forest Road 70 and drive 6 miles to the trailhead parking lot. The hike getting to the springs, although relatively easy except in the springtime when the trail can get slippery and muddy, is one of the prettiest in northern Oregon, passing through rain forests, past waterfalls, and next to lots of moss-covered logs. Although the Friends of Bagby accepts donations

POWER TO THE PEOPLE

Since there are no corporations advertising these remote hot springs, we'll just pass on some comments from their fans:

- "[Soaking in a natural hot springs] is heaven, or as close to it as you can get on Earth. I've been to every hot springs from Mexico to Canada. They help your electrolytes. It sort of recharges your batteries." —"Rainy Day" James Ahola, a street musician and artist
- "The water is really good for your skin because of the high mineral content. It's really cleansing, and it feels really refreshing. It takes a lot of weight off your spine and joints." —Molly Richardson, a frequent soaker at Doe Bay Hot Springs on Washington's Orcas Island

in a collection box at the entrance, the springs are totally free. There are several Forest Service campgrounds nearby.

Bagby Hot Springs, c/o Clackamas River Ranger District, 503-630-6861.

Olympic Hot Springs. High above the Elwha River Valley in Olympic National Park, this remote cluster of steaming springs and pools is sandwiched between a forest of fir and hemlock and the rushing rapids of Boulder Creek. There are seven places to soak, including one that's next to a small waterfall. Although the Northwest Native Americans had a legend about the springs being bitter hot tears of some battling schools of fish, it's actually geothermal water that bubbles up at around 105°F, perfect for soaking. The hike is about 2.5 miles, a beautiful, winding trek through a river canyon and bordered with breathtaking mountains and forests. In the early 1900s, Olympic Hot Springs was a resort, and it even had a swimming pool and little cabins. But weather and neglect and washouts closed the roads, and eventually it disappeared from maps and park rangers quit promoting it. There's nothing left of the old resort, but the springs continue to bubble out of the rocks. To get to the trailhead, take U.S. 101 from Port Angeles about 10 miles to Elwha River Road. Turn left and follow the road for 9 miles until you can't drive any farther.

Olympic National Park, 600 E. Park Avenue, Port Angeles, WA 98362, 360-565-3000, www.nps.gov/olym.

Stanley Hot Springs. East of Lewiston, Idaho, in the Selway-Bitterroot Wilderness, this springs, a chain of hot pools, requires an 11-mile round-trip hike. Although the trail through islands of Douglas fir, pine, and cedar is well maintained, there is one point where you need to ford a river. You'll know you've reached the hot springs when 120-degree water steams out of a canyon bank, getting cooler as it flows into descending pools. Each pool is lined with logs, and the temperature can be fine-tuned by shifting rocks to admit more or less cold water to the mix. There are spacious campsites tucked into the nearby woods. One word of caution: The moose also find the springs inviting, and they get first choice of pools. The trailhead for the springs is the Wilderness Gateway Campground off U.S. 12 (milepost 122). Go past Loops A and B to the Trail 211 parking area.

Bitterroot National Forest, 1801 N. First Street, Hamilton, MT 59840, 406-363-7100, www.fs.fed.us/r1/bitterroot.

make yourself over

RESORTS ACROSS THE COUNTRY

Never eat more than you can lift.
—Miss Piggy

89 Actor Jeff Garlin lost 50 pounds on his last vacation. Okay, so that's an exaggeration. But the Golden Globe–winning actor who played Larry David's bumbling agent on the TV series *Curb Your Enthusiasm*, did lose 50 pounds, and he did it compliments of a Florida weight-loss spa that taught him how to stick with an exercise and eating plan. A self-proclaimed "lifetime member of the Hostess family," Garlin, who is diabetic and had a stroke when he was only 37, cranked up the treadmill, filled his plate with low-fat, high-fiber food, attended lectures, and submitted to twice-weekly physical exams during his week at the Pritikin Longevity Center and Spa.

"This Pritikin experience came right out and punched me in the face," Garlin says. "I thought I knew everything about food and fat, but, boy oh boy, was I wrong." By the third day, Garlin was off his diabetic medicine.

Garlin is one of thousands of Americans who are opting to spend their vacation at a weight-loss spa. Instead of a tan, they're coming home with healthier, thinner bodies. Instead of tacky trinkets, they're bringing back lists of healthy foods and exercise routines.

If terms like "fat farm," "deprivation," and "torture" come to mind, you might as well put those antiquated notions out on the curb with your old Jane Fonda tapes. Today's weight-loss spas are luxurious (Pritikin, for example, is located at a yacht club on a Florida island), fun (Garlin, after his 90-minute daily bout with the treadmill, got in 18 holes at the center's championship waterfront golf course), and relaxing.

Below are three weight-loss spas that are medically based, lavishly appointed, and guaranteed to inspire lifestyle changes that will last long after the vacation pictures have been filed away in the family photo album.

Green Mountain at Fox Run. Even though this spa in the woods of Vermont's Green Mountains doesn't have volcanic mud wraps or sea-salt scrubs, it was recently chosen by *SpaFinder* magazine as one of the world's best small spas. The reason? For more than 30 years, it has helped women adopt healthy lifestyles without dieting. In fact, a retreat at Green Mountain is designed to mirror real life. If you don't have a $50,000 treadmill at home, you're probably not going to keep up your newfound fitness regime if that's what you used at a spa. Accepting only 35 to 40 women at a time, Green Mountain offers lots of hands-on, personalized attention. The minimum stay is one week. You'll live in a cozy mountain lodge and eat meals communally. A one-week visit, including room, all meals, seminars, speakers, fitness evaluations, workshop materials, and individual nutrition and fitness consults, starts at $2,915.

Green Mountain at Fox Run, P.O. Box 164, Fox Lane, Ludlow, VT 05149, 800-448-8106 or 802-228-8885, www.fitwoman.com.

Hilton Head Health Institute. The goal of this exquisite seaside resort set amid palmettos and oaks dripping with Spanish moss is weight loss by transforming old habits. In fact, this 30-year-old resort claims that it doesn't believe in diets or gimmicky trends of any kind. Rather, it focuses on lifestyle changes that can be incorporated on a long-term basis. Started by Peter Miller, a clinical psychologist, the resort has grown exponentially and branched out beyond weight loss. Although that's still the bread and butter (or, in this case, the salmon spread and rice cakes), the institute also offers highly structured programs in smoking cessation and stress management. Choices include the Total Fitness package, where guests can choose from more than 30 fitness classes (such as Pilates, beach walking, and yoga) and the Weight Control package. Prices start at $3,550 and include healthy meals, a lifestyle assessment, a customized exercise program, and all demonstrations, lectures, and classes.

Hilton Head Health Institute, 14 Valencia Road, Hilton Head Island, SC 29928, 800-292-2440, www.hhhealth.com.

Pritikin Longevity Center and Spa. This health resort in Aventura, Florida, was founded on the best-selling books by Nathan Pritikin, the engineer who 50 years ago reversed his own heart disease and was thrust into the national spotlight when, on *60 Minutes*, he and Dr. David Lehr proposed the radical

TAKE TEN BREATHS AND CALL ME IN THE MORNING

"He lives at a little distance from his body."
—James Joyce

Most dieters wage all-out war on their bodies, despising them because they refuse to stay thin. Consequently, there's no harmony, no union—just this angry, never-ending tug-of-war. We look in the mirror and feel sick, desperately wanting to trade our bodies in for a different model. We become cut off from our bodies. It's us against them. No wonder we can't lose weight.

Maybe it's time to call a truce. Perhaps it's time to do something radical, like giving your body a little credit. Instead of constantly fighting it, how about actually sitting down and inviting it in for coffee? At least consider the possibility that it might, just *might*, know what it's doing.

The best way to be introduced to your body is to breathe—ten deep breaths into your abdomen every time you think of it. As you learn to breathe more fully, you can't help but start to listen to your body's great wisdom.

—Adapted from *Jumpstart Your Metabolism*

notion that nutrition and exercise played a starring role in many diseases. Now, of course, the link between the two is common knowledge.

Although the spa is science based and you'll be expected to meet regularly with a team of doctors, dieticians, and exercise physiologists, the setting is stunning. All 75 rooms and suites have balconies overlooking the ocean, huge whirlpool tubs, plush robes, and fresh orchids that are left on your pillow each night. As for the food, it's almost hard to believe it's good for you. Five to six times a day, you'll feast on such delights as panzanella herb salad, tuna carpaccio, stone crabs, sockeye salmon served on morel risotto, and chocolate mousse.

Besides Garlin, Pritikin has played host to such notables as Carl Reiner, Roger Ebert, Mel Brooks, and John T. Gannon, the founder of Outback Steakhouse.

Rates for a seven-day stay that includes a room, use of all the facilities, customized fitness classes, daily chair massage, a hundred-plus page cookbook, a comprehensive medical evaluation and fitness assessment, and six meals a day start at $3,600 for double occupancy.

Pritikin Longevity Center and Spa, 19735 Turnberry Way, Aventura, FL 33180, 800-327-4914 or 305-935-7131, www.pritikin.com.

get pampered on the slopes like a star

UTAH

It is better to go skiing and think of God,
than go to church and think of sport.
—Fridtjof Nansen, Nobel Prize winner

90 Greta Garbo dunked her head in icy water every morning. Why? you're undoubtedly asking. According to the reclusive movie star, cold constricts blood flow and tightens the skin—which means that Greta and you and everybody else look more beautiful in the winter mountains. So what better place to spa than at a ski resort?

If you ski Utah, site of the 2002 Olympic Winter Games, you can also score some side benefits. Like getting pampered, Hollywood style. This is the place that, every February, kowtows to all the big Tinseltown players at the uber-famous Sundance Film Festival. The rest of the year is yours.

Not only are Utah's ski resorts easy to get to (there are eight Olympic-caliber ones less than an hour from the Salt Lake City airport), but they don't need to make snow. The Wasatch Range gets nailed every winter by huge snowstorms blowing across the high desert. Five hundred inches of snow is just an average winter here. Thanks to the Great Salt Lake, which adds salt, and the nearby desert conditions, Utah's snow has only half the moisture of most other ski resorts, making the snow that much fluffier and lighter.

But we were talking about pampering. Here are just two Utah spots where you can get some high-altitude Hollywood-style pampering:

Stein Ericksen Lodge. Call it Sundance Central. Nestled mid-mountain at Silver Lake Village in Deer Valley Resort, this resort with 145 fireplaces is where the stars stay during Sundance. Ski butlers carry your skis and greet you with hot chocolate when you return from the slopes; maids tidy up your room twice a day; and the Dutch-born pastry chef makes handcrafted Belgian and French chocolates in the lodge's own atelier. Guests are treated to head-to-toe pampering at the Spa at Stein Ericksen, an intimate Norwegian sanctuary with stone floors, rich area rugs, and all sorts of unique features such as a calming rain bar and luxurious chairs and daybeds. The signature treatments are the Nordic Princess and the Norseman Vichy. Rates start at $175 per night, $340 for a grand suite.

Stein Ericksen Lodge, 7700 Stein Way, P.O. Box 3177, Park City, UT 84060, 435-669-3700, www.steinlodge.com.

Sundance Resort. Robert Redford's rustic-chic getaway sits on 6,000 protected acres of pristine wilderness. As he said when he first bought the property in 1969, "We'll ... develop very little and preserve a great deal." Although it's certainly a ski resort, it feels more like an artist colony. In fact, it's so imbued with creative energy that you might just feel tempted to pen a poem or knock out a song. And at the on-site Art Shack, you can get some help doing just that. Visiting artists offer two-hour workshops in glassblowing, jewelry making, photography, creative writing, and pottery.

The Spa at Sundance was inspired by the Sioux concept of *Hocoka*—a sacred environment for the restoration and healing of the body and spirit. In the natural wood, softly lit treatment rooms, you'll get such treatments as a cornmeal body blanket where you'll be exfoliated and detoxified with ground cornmeal and organic honey from the Sundance farm before being wrapped in a warm Sioux story blanket. Overriding all that Sundance has to offer is an ecologically sensitive philosophy. Everything is built to blend with nature. The water glasses at the Foundry Grill restaurant are recycled wine bottles. The Tree Room, the upscale "earth to table" gourmet restaurant, is wrapped around an old-growth pine tree. The soaps in the rooms are all-organic products of the Sundance Farms, as are most of the herbs, spices, and foods used in the restaurants.

Rooms during the winter season start at $246. A four-bedroom home during the holiday season is $1,656.

Sundance Resort, RR3 Box A-1, Sundance, UT 84604, 800-892-1600 (reservations) or 801-225-4107, www.sundanceresort.com.

balance mind
& body with ayurveda

MARARISHI VEDIC CITY, IOWA

I always come back from the Raj with that feeling
that you have when you're six or seven, that feeling
that there is nothing wrong with the world.
—Scott Fuller, a businessman from Wisconsin
who visits the Raj twice a year

91 Bianca Jagger, Alan Arkin, and Beach Boy Mike Love are just a few fans of a unique spa in the middle of an Iowa cornfield that offers mind and body "balancing" treatments based on the 5,000-year-old Indian principles of Ayurveda. Ayurveda has gotten a lot of buzz lately thanks to Dr. Deepak Chopra, who has written several best-selling books on the ancient medicine that was once the sole purview of Indian royalty. The Raj Maharishi Ayurveda Health Center, known to everyone simply as "the Raj," opened in April 1993 and at the time was the only Ayurveda facility outside of India specifically built to offer the unique rejuvenation treatments that restore imbalances that build up from stress and a harried lifestyle.

"People are drawn to Ayurveda because it goes beyond a one-size-fits-all prescription for good health," says Chris Clark, M.D., the Yale-trained medical director who helped develop the Raj's program. "It gives them a deep insight and understanding of their own bodies." Some folks go twice a year as a kind of spring cleaning.

Whether you opt for a three-, five-, seven-day stay or longer, you'll get a customized treatment program designed by a specialist in the Maharishi Vedic approach to health. To determine your unique thumbprint (everyone is different), you'll start with an hour-long consultation during which you'll be quizzed on your diet, daily routines, and sleep habits and given a pulse diagnosis to pinpoint your exact *dosha* (energy) profile. The goal is to achieve equilibrium among the three kinds of doshas found in the body: vata, pitta, and kapha (see sidebar).

Once your profile is completed, a tailor-made plan is prescribed for your stay—what to eat, what kind of herbal supplements to take, what kind of exercise, and which of the many purifying spa treatments would best serve your body. The purifying spa treatments, called *Panchakarma*, are aimed at prying toxins from your tissues. You'll get two to three hours a day of oil being dripped on your forehead, mud being slathered on your body, and other treatments that remove excess gunk that has accumulated over the years.

With that kind of royal treatment, it's not surprising that the ratio of staff to clientele is something like three to one. The lush spa that *Town & Country* voted one of the top five for the new millennium has 80 employees taking care of just a few dozen customers at a time.

The center certainly has some compelling success stories, including a barely walking multiple sclerosis patient who left doing pirouettes and a study by Blue Cross/Blue Shield of Iowa that found that adherents of

"I AM LIVING IN HEAVEN ON EARTH"

That is the goal of Ayurveda practitioners. *Ayurveda* is a Sanskrit word that translates as "science of life." All of its healing rituals come from ancient Sanskrit textbooks. Here are some terms that are helpful to know:

- *Abhyanga:* A head-to-toe massage with sesame oil performed by two technicians. The goal is to entice the ama to attach to the sesame oil so it can be excreted from your fat tissues, where it tends to hang out.
- *Ama:* The toxic impurities you're there to get rid of. Ama is a sticky residue that builds up in cells, impairs cellular function, and accelerates aging. It may even be why DNA makes mistakes that cause cancer.
- *Kapha:* One of the three *doshas,* or energy, it represents the elements of earth and water and governs the formation and structure of tissues, muscles, bones, and sinews.
- *Nadivigyan:* The pulse diagnosis (given by three fingers on the wrist) that determines your dosha profile.
- *Pitta:* Also a dosha, it represents the element of fire and governs metabolism and biochemical processes.
- *Vata:* The final dosha represents the element of air and controls movement, including digestion, blood circulation, and synapses in the nervous system.

Ayurveda reduced their medical costs by 92 percent. Sue Mandel was taking 12 to 14 medications a day for her chronic asthma, digestive disorders, sinus problems, malfunctioning thyroid, migraines, and back pain when she first came to the Raj. Now, she says she's down to two medications, suffers no asthma attacks, and has shed 35 pounds. Layne Longfellow, a writer and lecturer from Boulder, Colorado, says his cholesterol level dropped from 245 to 191 after an eight-day stay at the Raj.

Every evening, guest lecturers offer tips on topics such as Ayurvedic beauty techniques or how to avoid chronic disorders, and that is followed by hot milk toddies before the official bedtime of 10 p.m.

Accommodations in the lush French-style château, family-style gourmet vegetarian meals, and all services are included in the cost of your stay, which ranges from $1,900 for three days to $4,408 for seven days. Ayurveda astrological readings can be had for an extra charge.

HOW TO GET IN TOUCH

Raj Maharishi Ayurveda Health Center, 1734 Jasmine Avenue, Maharishi Vedic City, IA 52556, 800-248-9050, www.theraj.com.

explore the arctic national wildlife refuge

ALASKA

It's the crown jewel in America's natural treasure chest.
We don't want to see it scarred with oil wells, roads, and pipelines.
—Jamie Rappaport Clark,
former director of the U.S. Fish and Wildlife Service

92

The Arctic National Wildlife Refuge (ANWR) is a veritable celebrity. It pops up in the news nearly as often as Angelina Jolie. The oil industry, screaming talk show hosts, and quite a few of our politicians tell us that drilling in this pristine 19-million-acre preserve is vital for eliminating our dependence on foreign oil. The environmentalists claim it won't provide enough oil to last six months, and besides, they add, the same reasons it was protected by Dwight Eisenhower in 1960 are still there—thundering herds of caribou, wolves, polar bears, and migratory bird species from four continents.

Although listed here in the wellness chapter for its thousands of hiking, kayaking, rafting, and other outdoor activities, this vacation could also qualify for two of the other chapters. It's an intellectual retreat, because you'll finally learn what all the fuss is about, why this giant wilderness is constantly making the news, and a volunteer retreat, because once you see the magnificence of these unbroken Arctic and subarctic ecosystems in a place where you can hike for days without encountering a single artifact of civilization, you'll go home fired up to save it, too.

In 1963, Wallace Stegner wrote that it's not necessary to travel to a wilderness to know that it's worth saving. He said just knowing that such a wild sanctuary exists is enough to create a "geography of hope." But once you witness it for yourself, stand on this ground that the Inupiat and the Athabaskan have called home

WANNA SAVE THE ANWR?

It might be different if there were enough oil in the Arctic National Wildlife Refuge to drill ourselves to self-sufficiency. But there's not. At best, we might win a few years more of petroleum dependency. Here are seven things you can do that, if enough of us followed suit, would save more oil in one year than the ANWR could produce in 50.

- Skip one car ride a week. The average American drives more than 250 miles each week. Replace a weekly 20-mile car trip with telecommuting, biking, or combining errands and you'll reduce your annual emissions of the greenhouse gas carbon dioxide by nearly a thousand pounds.
- Carpool. Thirty-three million gallons of gas would be saved (not to mention reducing air pollution) if we would all simply commit to having a party every morning on the way to work. After all, it's not a party until you have at least two.
- Bike or walk if your trip is less than 2 miles.
- Take public transportation.
- Leave your car in the garage for the weekend.
- Consider trading in your SUV for a gas/electric hybrid. Think they're not cool? Cameron Diaz drives one.
- Push the government to impose higher CAFE (corporate average fuel economy) standards that require new cars to achieve designated gas mileage goals. Under President Jimmy Carter, we went from 20 to 26 miles per gallon, with a goal of 40 by 2001. When President George H. W. Bush left office 12 years later, however, we were still at 26. Had we gone ahead as planned, we could have eliminated 100 percent of all oil imports into the United States by now.

for thousands of years, it will be all you can do to stop yourself from marching on Washington.

Because there are no roads in the ANWR—just a gravel road passing next to the western tip—it's best to go with an outfitter who can arrange a flight in on a small bush plane. Wade Willis, a retired biologist, knows better than perhaps anyone where to go in the ANWR. He has spent the past 15 years exploring the best camping spots, the best places to spot wildlife, and the best places to kayak, raft, and hike. As the owner of Vision Quest Adventures, he arranges weeklong trips to show off the what he's found.

Whether you want to hike, kayak, or raft, or do all three, Vision Quest will meet you in Fairbanks or Anchorage or Juneau and take care of all the arrangements.

The staff will bring the tents, the food, and the knowledge—particularly useful are the secrets to avoiding bears. All trips are led by biologists.

The sea-kayaking trip to the ANWR is perhaps the most adventurous way to see it. But if you aren't already an experienced sea kayaker, it's probably best to choose one of Vision Quest's other kayaking itineraries in, for example, Prince William Sound, Kenai Fjords National Park, or Wrangell–St. Elias National Park. For the ANWR trip, you'll probably fly by bush plane into Demarcation Bay, a protected spot that was favored by Native hunters as well as turn-of-the-20th-century whalers. The rafting trips are usually launched on some of the less explored rivers along the North Slope, including the Canning, the Hulahula, and the Ivishak. There are also rafting trips along the famous Kongakut River, where herds of Porcupine caribou congregate during migration. Suffice it to say, seeing 130,000 caribou thunder across rushing rivers and tend to their young in greening tundra is one of the world's great wildlife spectacles.

Trips that provide all tents, sleeping bags, and outdoor accessories, including Goretex jackets and folding kayaks, start at $899 per person for 3 days up to $3,999 for the 12-day ANWR tour.

HOW TO GET IN TOUCH
Vision Quest Adventures, P.O. Box 100965, Anchorage, AK 99510, 866-529-2525 or 907-258-7238, http://alaskavisionquest.com.

take a gourmet raft trip down the rio grande

BIG BEND NATIONAL PARK, TEXAS

All you need is the ability to drink and eat.
—Francois Maeder, owner of Crumpets Restaurant

93 Big Bend National Park is one of the largest swaths of wilderness in the United States. It has its own mountain range, colorful badlands, Chihuahuan Desert scenery, and a river that has carved out three canyons more than 1,000 feet deep. Because it's located in a remote part of a gigantic state that's way down south, however, it's one of the country's least visited parks. You're more likely to run into a cactus or a javelina or a border patrolman than a restaurant, let alone a restaurant with decent food.

Yet, six to eight times a year, on the banks of the Rio Grande, you can feast from a gourmet restaurant that *Esquire* magazine once picked as one of the country's 100 best. The restaurant that made the list was Crumpets Restaurant and Bakery in San Antonio, and periodically its owner, Swiss-born chef Francois Maeder, packs up his rosemary-scented rack of lamb, his ducks, his beef Wellington, and more and heads for the river.

Since 1988, Far Flung Outdoor Center has teamed with Maeder to offer a gourmet raft trip that winds its way through the Rio Grande's Santa Elena Canyon, a twisting channel with ancient American Indian pictographs painted into the sheer 1,500-foot limestone walls. After careening through Rockslide Rapids—Class II to Class IV white water, depending on the time of year—you'll be treated to seven special meals on this three-night rafting trip. Chef Maeder, with the help of his trusty rafting guides, sets up tables with white tablecloths, fancy china, crystal wine goblets, and candles in the middle of the wilderness. A typical five-course meal might include mushroom-stuffed wild quail, smoked salmon, pâté, roasted asparagus, New Zealand rack of lamb, and prickly pear-strawberry trifle, all topped off with cognac and port. There's even live music to complete the ambience.

UPPING THE STAKES—ER, STEAKS

Francois Maeder isn't the only chef to encourage foodies to see the Milky Way. In fact, many rafting companies now offer gourmet trips. Here are a couple more of the best:

Bill Dvorak's Kayak and Rafting Expeditions. Besides gourmet food and wine, Dvorak's offers an eight-day Classical Music River Journey that floats down Utah's Green River. After you're finished rafting, you cozy up to the campfire while chamber music is performed by a Santa Fe Symphony flutist and a string quartet from the Los Angeles Philharmonic. This three-day trip takes place in July and runs $1,975. *Bill Dvorak's Kayaking and Rafting Expeditions, 17921 U.S. Highway 285, Nathrop, CO 81236, 800-824-3795, www.dvorakexpeditions.com.*

OARS (Outdoor Adventure River Specialists). This company, one of the first and biggest in the country, offers Wine on the River Adventures. These trips pair white-water rafting with sommeliers and five-star cooking. Its wine series offers trips to California's Tuolumne, Idaho's Lower Salmon, Oregon's Rogue, and British Columbia's Chilko Rivers. OARS also offers what it calls Wilderness Gourmet Trips down the Rogue and Main Salmon. Most trips are three to six days in length and range from $1,041 to $1,955. *OARS, P.O. Box 67, Angels Camp, CA 95222, 800-346-6277 or 209-736-4677, www.oars.com.*

Of course, rafting the Rio Grande is available pretty much year-round, something rafting outfitters in, say, Colorado or Idaho can't claim. Granted, the Rio Grande is not the fastest or scariest river in the United States, but the views are stupendous. Your adrenaline will get pumped up, not from a long string of Class V rapids that will churn you around like a washing machine but from floating along a wilderness waterway that passes through towering cliffs, sculpted stone spires, and a unique, inspiring desert landscape. As it says in Big Bend's official National Park Service handbook, "The land is so vast and so wild that you can feel your human smallness and frailty." That's a valuable lesson to remember. Far Flung Outdoor Center offers a whole lineup of rafting trips in Big Bend, from one-day to multiday trips through Mariscal Canyon, Temple Canyon, and Boquillas Canyon. Maeder began offering the gourmet rafting trips ten years after he moved from Switzerland to Texas. He missed the mountains ("I didn't know Texas had mountains until I visited Big Bend") and being outdoors. In fact, he bemoans the fact that some people have never left the city nor seen the Milky Way.

The three days of bacchanalian revelry start at the historic Lajitas River Crossing and meander 21 miles along the Rio Grande. "Everybody knows food tastes better outdoors . . . even if it falls in the sand," says Greg Henington, owner of the Far Flung Outdoor Center. The three-day rafting trips (Henington and his crew jokingly call them "float and bloat") are staged in February, March, April, and October; cost $775; and include seven gourmet meals, tents, rafts, and everything else you could possibly need.

HOW TO GET IN TOUCH

Far Flung Outdoor Center, P.O. Box 377, Terlingua, TX 79852, 800-359-4138, www.farflungoutdoorcenter.com, and **Crumpets Restaurant,** 3920 Harry Wurzbach Road, San Antonio, TX 78209-2410, 210-821-5600, www.crumpetsa.com.

relax in a home away from home

THE UNITED STATES & ABROAD

The global affliction of the hurry virus
has afflicted every corner of the planet.
—Carl Honoré, author of *In Praise of Slowness:
How a Worldwide Movement is Challenging the Cult of Speed*

94 It's bad enough that we work so hard at work—an average 9.5 hours a day for the typical American employee—but woe is us for letting it seep into our vacations. We attempt to cram in as much fun, visit as many guidebook sites, and eat at as many four-star restaurants as we possibly can. Even a relaxing spa vacation can quickly turn into a frantic nightmare of jumping from the Stairmaster to the yoga class to the mountain berry facials to the—well, you get the picture.

The problem with this work-like approach to a vacation is we don't take time to decompress, to reflect, to enjoy what we're doing.

So why not join the new slow travel movement? Instead of playing tourist, play house. Instead of visiting every site the guidebook insists is must-see, take a long, leisurely afternoon nap. Instead of bouncing from one hotel to the next B&B, refuse to travel farther than a few miles from your home away from home.

The term "slow travel" was coined by Pauline Kenny, a Santa Fe technical writer who started a website (www.slowtrav.com) to share information with others who, like she and her husband, Steve Cohen, enjoy renting vacation homes and digging in their heels. At first, the website was a hobby, just a way to find out where the best Italian villas were or which shopkeeper made the best bread in Umbria, but eventually it has turned into her full-time occupation. The idea behind Kenny's slow travel is to "quit zooming." Rent a house and stay there for at least a week. "You stay in one place, pretend you live there, and do the things the locals do," Kenny says. "It deepens the whole experience. The idea is to do things as well as possible, not as fast as possible."

Among the many possibilities in the United States, you can stay in a house on Lake Ruben, Georgia, or at a ski lodge in the Colorado Rockies. In Mexico, spend a week in an apartment in Mexico City's La Condesa, an area described by the *New*

York Times as much like the East Village. On a recent trip to England, Kenny and Cohen rented a cottage in Wiltshire. Wherever you go, you can stay true to the slow travel credo by staying within 30 minutes of home, get to know the locals at nearby bars, restaurants, and cafés, and walk to interesting sights, perhaps a local garden, museum, or market. Sure, you'll see only one small corner of the world, but you'll see it *in depth*—as visiting residents rather than fly-by-night tourists.

To find your own "slow vacation," check out Kenny's website, a community of some 6,000 travelers who are all sold on the stay-at-least-a-week approach. Members review vacation rental villas, apartments, farms, and cottages that make this kind of travel possible. They post trip reports, interactive maps, webcams, and lots of ideas for renting a vacation home.

HOW TO GET IN TOUCH
Slow Travel, 223 N. Guadalupe Street, #260, Santa Fe, NM 87501, www.slowtrav .com.

SILENT RETREATS

spend a weekend listening to silence

SPIRITUAL CENTERS NATIONWIDE

To hear the human heart, you need silence.
—Fr. Edward Farrell, director of the Sacred Heart Seminary of Detroit

95 One of the main characters in *The Hitchhiker's Guide to the Galaxy* is an alien named Ford Prefect. Although he acts like most Earthlings, even posing as an out-of-work actor, he is completely bamboozled by the fact that Earthlings seem to talk all the time—even if only to repeat the obvious. He concocts a number of theories for this odd behavior, including: "If human beings don't keep exercising their lips, their brains start working." And not only does all the lip exercising begin to sound like Charlie Brown's unintelligible, monotone teacher, but it's compounded by all the honking horns, ringing phones, buzzing computers, and nonstop humming of technology as well. No wonder we all want to scream: "Just shut up!"

If you long to turn down the noise, to turn inward for a change, consider signing on for a silent retreat. A silent retreat is as simple as it sounds—a day, a weekend, or even longer spent in complete silence. Although monks have been doing it for centuries, the secular community is now catching on to the immense power of silence. The fact that going without words moves people so profoundly (just talk to anyone who has tried it) demonstrates how unusual silence has become in ordinary life.

Some folks take silent retreats as a religious exercise or because they're contemplating a major life change. Others do it simply to strip themselves of nonessentials, to find that oasis within themselves. Since there's no talking, you don't need your past, your opinions, your fashion strategies, or your best jokes.

Many places offer programs built around silence, from Buddhist, Hindu, and Christian monasteries to nonsectarian retreat centers. No two silent retreats are designed the same. Some are intensive, long-term programs, while others last just two or three days and include spiritual rituals or other temporary interruptions to the silence such as lectures, group discussions, or one-on-one spiritual instruction. Still others allow you to do it yourself. These centers are open to people of all faiths, and as one wag said, "They don't offer room service, but they might just deliver your soul."

Here are five places to get the silent treatment:

Abbey of Gethsemani. This Catholic monastery founded in 1848 is where Thomas Merton wrote his best-selling book *The Seven Storey Mountain* (1948). Retreatants are invited to join the Trappist monks in their daily program of prayer, sacraments, and silent reflection, beginning with vigils at 3:15 a.m. and ending with a rosary at 7:45 p.m. Located on 2,000 acres of heavily wooded land about 50 miles from Louisville, Kentucky, the abbey offers private rooms, each with a private bath, and three meals a day. Rates are based on a voluntary donation system, but a typical offering would be $25 to $75 a day.

Abbey of Gethsemani, 3642 Monks Road, Trappist, KY 40051, 502-549-3117 (main), 502-549-4133 (retreat information), www.monks.org.

Dayspring Retreat Center. Set on 200 acres of rolling hills and forests in the Maryland countryside, this silent retreat center was built in the 1950s by an ecumenical Christian community. It can accept up to 18 retreatants at a time, most of whom design their own schedule, but Dayspring also offers what it calls "spiritual companionship" for those who request it. Some of the scheduled weekend retreats are titled "Generous Listening" and "Opening to Divine Love." Weekend retreats are $155 and include accommodations and vegetarian meals. Nightly rates for individual retreatants are $40; this rate doesn't include food, but allows access to the fully equipped kitchen.

Dayspring Retreat Center, 11301 Neelsville Church Road, Germantown, MD, 20876, 301-428-9348, www.serve.com/dayspringretreat.

Insight Meditation Society. This Buddhist retreat center, housed in an old mansion, is 1.5 hours west of Boston. It's been hosting silent retreats since 1976, with a full schedule of more than 25 two-day to three-month courses. The average retreat lasts seven to nine days. Most retreats are silent, offer daily talks and meditation instruction, and include both walking and sitting meditation. Dorm accommodations and meals are on a sliding scale and range from a "low rate" of $160 to a "high rate" of $225 for a weekend; $375 to $575 for seven days; and $480 to $740 for nine.

Insight Meditation Society, 1230 Pleasant Street, Barre, MA 01005, 978-355-4378, www.dharma.org/ims.

ALL ACTION, NO TALK

Silence has a power all its own. Be ready for some surprises when you try it. Once you slow yourself down, you might just discover how tired your body is or how angry or confused you are. "Most people today take a dim view of the monk's desire for seclusion," writes Matthew Kelty, a Gethsemani monk, in a pamphlet for those considering the monastic calling. "They see it as flight and do not appreciate the monk for fleeing. Certainly, the monk does not escape anything. It was precisely because he was tired of running that he became a monk. Those who fear their own depths and the deep of night had better find something to occupy or divert them. People in flight should not come to monasteries."

Loyola House. This 640-acre Jesuit community in Guelph, Ontario, has been offering silent retreats since 1964. Based on the spiritual exercises of St. Ignatius, the Spanish saint who lived for ten months in a cave, this community offers everything from specialized weekends to eight-day retreats to the full-blown 40-day Spiritual Exercises Institute. You can choose between a directed retreat that has two brief daily meetings with a spiritual director or a guided retreat that includes two 85-minute lectures. The dorms where you'll stay are sparse, with a single bed, sink, small writing table, and sitting chair. Buffet-style meals are served at specific times during the day in a large dining hall. Weekend retreats, which include accommodations and meals, are priced at $180 ($205 Canadian); eight-day retreats are $540 ($615 Canadian).

    Loyola House, P.O. Box 245, Guelph, ON N1H 6J9, Canada, 519-824-1250, ext. 266, www.loyolahouse.ca.

Spirit Rock Meditation Center. An hour north of the Golden Gate Bridge, this 400-acre Buddhist center offers retreats of three nights to three months and is open to rank beginners as well as experienced practitioners of *vipassana*, a meditation that calms the mind by focusing on the breath. Except for daily dharma talks and one-on-one interviews with instructors, silence reigns. Participants begin their day at 6 a.m., spend it in alternating periods of sitting and walking meditation, then turn in around 10 p.m. A typical weekend retreat including room and vegetarian meals costs $285; seven days run $850. Scholarships are available.

    Spirit Rock Meditation Center, P.O. Box 169, Woodacre, CA 94973, 415-488-0164, www.spiritrock.org.

enjoy old-fashioned ozark hospitality

BRANSON, MISSOURI

*I'd take my staff and put them up
against any Ritz-Carlton anywhere.*
—Tom Healey, manager of the Keeter Center

96 You probably already know that Branson, Missouri (pop. 6,050), has more theater seats than Broadway or Las Vegas. It has dozens of daily shows—from elaborate magic shows to body-bending acrobats to down-home Ozark bluegrass. More than seven million people visit this little burg in southern Missouri every year. Some of them camp at Table Rock Lake or Lake Taneycomo. Others stay on the main 7-mile strip near the shows, outlet malls, and all-you-can-eat buffet restaurants. But since you want a unique Ozark vacation, a true restore-your-faith-in-humanity kind of trip, forget where everyone else stays and head straight to the Keeter Center at College of the Ozarks.

Only 4 miles south of the main strip, the huge log lodge has 15 magnificent suites, all lovingly attended to by students at the college. Whether you want to hike, fish (Lake Taneycomo is one of the finest trout-fishing reservoirs in the country, thanks to the Shepherd of the Hills Trout Hatchery, which releases 70 percent of the 1.1 million trout it raises each year into Taneycomo's clear, cold water), or simply enjoy old-fashioned Ozark hospitality, the Keeter Center and its staff of determined college kids is the perfect home base for your Ozark adventure.

The students will deliver a sumptuous breakfast to your room every morning with pastries they've whipped up at their own on-site bakery and yogurt they've made at the college dairy. At night, when you return from a full day of outdoor fun followed by a heartwarming, G-rated show at one of Branson's 50-plus live theaters, you'll find homemade cookies and milk, again straight from the very cows grazing outside your back window. College of the Ozarks students also run the on-campus Dobyn's Restaurant, a gourmet restaurant with a Sunday buffet to die for.

"For these kids who run the hotel, it's not about a paycheck, it's about a degree," says Tom Healey, general manager of the Keeter Center.

Guest Dennis M. McLaughlin couldn't agree more. On a recent evaluation form, he wrote: "I have stayed at three Ritz-Carltons and been a guest at several hotels at one time or another among the top ten in the world (the Peninsula and the Mandarin in Hong Kong, the Imperial in Tokyo, and the Shangri-La in Singapore) and they don't have anything on the Keeter Center."

There's also plenty to do and see on the College of the Ozarks campus. You can visit the Fruitcake and Jelly Kitchen, the greenhouses, the dairy, the mill where students and a 12-foot waterwheel grind whole grain meal and flour, and the weaving studio where students design and produce rugs and shawls on traditional looms.

WHILE YOU'RE NEAR BRANSON

Branson calls itself the "Live Music Show Capital of the World" and that's not wishful thinking. It has stars, glitz, neon, and even a paddlewheel showboat with dinner and a ventriloquist dog act. From about 10:00 in the morning until midnight, there are always shows going on, from hunka-hunka boy groups to gospel to, well, you can just about name it. Andy Williams has a theater there, as does Jim "I Don't Like Spiders and Snakes" Stafford. The list goes on and on. Every heartwarming show is rated G and makes you feel good about being alive.

Shoji Tabuchi, a Japanese fiddle player who opened a lavish 2,000-seat theater in 1989, won a Missouri tourism award for drawing so many fans to the state. His show, picked by *U.S. News and World Report* as "unequaled anywhere for showmanship," features Shoji playing everything from country to big band, pop, swing, jazz, and classical. He also has three styles and sizes of 25 different Japanese Taiko drums, played by a group of athletic drummers who run marathons to maintain the physical stamina required to play the giant drums. Even the theater's bathrooms are amazing. The women's powder room has chandeliers, stained and jeweled glass, and a ceiling reproduced from the 1890s Empire period. There are live-cut orchids at every granite-and-onyx sink. The men's room, meanwhile, has sinks imported from Italy, black leather chairs, a marble fireplace, and a billiard room with a hand-carved mahogany pool table. Ticket prices for Shoji's show are $22–$42 in the summer. *Shoji Tabuchi Show, 3260 Shepherd of the Hills Expressway, Branson, MO 65615, 417-334-7469, www.shoji.com.*

The 1,000-acre campus is surrounded on two sides by Lake Taneycomo. But its beautiful setting and access to all those theater seats is not what makes it one of the most unusual liberal arts colleges in the United States. It is unique among American colleges because all 1,450 students pay nary a penny for tuition. Instead, each student puts in 15 hours a week at more than 80 locations around the campus.

The student body at the College of the Ozarks runs the FM radio station, the grain mill, the fire department, the hospital, and all the other campus buildings. They're up at 5 a.m. milking the herd of a hundred dairy cows, making the 30,000 fruitcakes that are given to donors and sold in the gift shop every year, or minding the exotic orchids in the greenhouse.

The college has been around in one form or another since 1906. For many years, its hotel-and-restaurant-management program ran a small lodge next to the dorms, as well as a popular restaurant called the Friendship Inn. In 2004, the college upped the ante by putting up the Keeter Center, a reproduction of the state of Maine's entry in the 1904 World's Fair in St. Louis. The actual log building, bought by a group of St. Louis doctors and moved to Lake Taneycomo by horse and buggy, served as a hunting and fishing lodge until it was sold to the College of the Ozarks, where it was used for classes for many years. Although that original lodge burned down, the College of the Ozarks was able to construct the Keeter Center to look like that historic structure. All the rustic furniture is handcrafted, and every room is a suite, complete with a fireplace, a balcony, feather pillows, and down comforters.

Suites at the Keeter Center begin at $159 for a skyline view suite, up to $269 for the presidential suite.

HOW TO GET IN TOUCH
Keeter Center, College of the Ozarks, 1 Opportunity Avenue, Point Lookout, MO 65726, 417-239-1900, www.keetercenter.edu.

stretch away your cares

Your body has more time to open, change, purify, and cleanse in a retreat environment than in a daily practice.
—Jillian Pransky, yoga teacher

97 If you already know what "downward dog," "salutations to the sun," and "tree pose" mean, you're a prime candidate for this listing—you've probably taken a yoga class or two and have experienced the benefits of this ancient Indian practice. A yoga retreat is a powerful way to deepen and strengthen what you already know. Instead of squeezing a yoga session in before the day's first meeting or after work before you rush home to make dinner for the kids, you can take a whole week to focus on nothing but yoga. On you. At a good yoga retreat, the food and the surroundings will complement your practice. There is nothing to pull you away.

So how do you find a good yoga retreat? *Yoga Journal,* found on many newsstands, lists hundreds of yoga vacations. They range from full-blown ashrams where you'll be asked to maintain a certain rhythm and protocol to retreat centers that offer activities centered around the yoga lifestyle to resorts that combine a package of yoga with, say, snowmobiling or kayaking.

It's important to know what you're looking for. At an ashram, for example, the food tends to be vegetarian, alcohol and caffeine are prohibited, and you might start your day as early as 5 a.m. Or maybe you prefer to follow a teacher who practices a certain style. Beryl Bender Birch, for example, who teaches what she calls "power yoga," once hosted a yoga retreat at Goldeneye, the former Jamaican home of author Ian Fleming of James Bond fame. Many of the well-known teachers—Baron Baptiste, Rodney Yee, and Shiva Rea, to name a few—lead retreats at all sorts of exotic spots, from Thailand to Costa Rica. But to get started, here are four of North America's best yoga retreats:

Feathered Pipe Ranch. Located on 110 pristine acres in the heart of the Montana Rockies, this ranch has hosted yoga seminars since 1975, the same year its owners cofounded *Yoga Journal.* You'll stay in a yurt, tent, or log cabin, eat organic food

BEND IT LIKE BECKHAM

Someone once described a yoga retreat as a weeklong full-body massage. If you're ready to take it up a notch, consider a vacation to a yoga ashram or what *Condé Nast Traveler* called "zen dens." An ashram usually centers around a guru, someone willing to share a particular practice with seekers. In the case of yoga ashrams, the guru is a master yogi who has devoted his or her life to spreading the practice of yoga.

There are dozens of yoga ashrams in North America and because, like everything else, these temples of devotion and asceticism have evolved with the times, many offer public workshops, seminars, and special events. Some have mandatory daily schedules and ask visitors to practice karma yoga (selfless service) by helping with kitchen, gardening, or cleaning chores. Here are just five:

Barsana Dham. You'll attend twice-daily *satsanas* at this ashram southwest of Austin. It nestles on 200 acres and is devoted to the teachings of Jagadguru Shree Kripalu Maharaj, a Hindu guru who helped his devotees find "Divine Love." *400 Barsana Road, Austin, TX 78737, 512-288-7180, www.barsanadham.org.*
Mount Madonna Center. Inspired by the teachings of Baba Hari Dass, this ashram in Watsonville, California, offers retreats in Ashtanga and karma yoga. *445 Summit Road, Watsonville, CA 95076, 408-847-0406, www.mountmadonna.org.*
Salt Spring Centre of Yoga. Established in 1981 by the Dharmasara Satsang Society, this 70-acre center has yoga workshops as well as classes in the creative and healing arts. *355 Blackburn Road, Salt Spring Island, BC V8K 2B8, Canada, 250-537-2326, www.saltspringcentre.com.*
Satchidananda Ashram. The swami for this ashram opened Woodstock (yes, *that* Woodstock) by calling music the "celestial sound that controls the whole universe." One of his devotees, Carole King, helped him acquire the nearly 1,000 acres of woodland that make up the ashram. *Route 1, Box 1720, Buckingham, VA 23921, 800-858-9642, www.yogaville.org.*
Shoshoni Yoga Retreat. Just 30 minutes from Boulder, Colorado, this ashram has daily classes in Hatha yoga, pranayama, meditation, and chanting. *P.O. Box 410, Rollinsville, CO 80474, 303-642-0116, www.shoshoni.org.*

---

straight from its famous cookbook, and study under experienced Ashtanga, Hatha, Iyengar, and Svaroopa instructors. There's only one class going each week, so you won't be distracted by other seminar-goers who are, for example, practicing primal scream techniques. In addition to its workshops, the nonprofit Feathered Pipe Foundation offers yoga tours to India, Peru, Africa, and Europe. Prices for a week at the Feathered Pipe Ranch range from $1,399 to $1,850 and include all instruction, meals, and accommodations.

Feathered Pipe Ranch, P.O. Box 1682, Helena, MT 59624, 406-442-8196, wwwfeatheredpipe.com.

Hotel Na Balam. Just 8 miles from Cancun's bustle, Isla Mujeres offers yoga retreats at its laid-back and friendly Hotel Na Balam. Small and unassuming, this hotel on the island's north end has lush tropical gardens, comfy rooms, and a large outdoor *palapa* that's perfect for practicing yoga. More than 20 yoga teachers and groups (including the Feathered Pipe Foundation) host retreats at this little-known oasis. If you care to venture farther from the hammocks that overlook one of the prettiest beaches in the Mexican Caribbean, you can visit a turtle farm or national park or swim with dolphins.

Hotel Na Balam, Calle Zazil-Ha 118, Playa Norte, Isla Mujeres, Q. Roo, Mexico 77400, 52-998-877-0279, www.nabalam.com.

Kripalu Center for Yoga & Health. Once a Jesuit seminary, Kripalu's 150 wooded acres in the Berkshires of Massachusetts provide a perfect setting for all sorts of yoga retreats and workshops. It was once dubbed the East Coast' s "*om*-central." The most popular retreat is a "Rest and Renewal" package that combines yoga with daily workshops and lots of time to enjoy the hiking trails, saunas, and lakefront beach. Packages range from $122 to $350 a day, depending on your level of accommodations; other retreats also vary in price according to length of stay.

Kripalu Center for Yoga & Health, P.O. Box 309, Stockbridge, MA 01262, 866-200-5203, 800-741-7353 (reservations), or 413-448-3400, www.kripalu.org.

White Lotus. This 40-acre mountain oasis overlooking the Pacific Ocean is a favorite of celeb yogi Sting and Dr. Andrew Weil. Retreats are offered year-round with themes such as "Spirit Dance," "Sacred Breath," and "Deepening Your Practice." You'll have time to hike in the surrounding oak and manzanita forests, meditate in the canyon on San Jose Creek, and visit the underground Hopi-style kiva. Meals are vegetarian, accommodations are in yurts, and there are plenty of Thai masseuses running around. Personal retreats, including accommodations in the yurts and use of all the facilities, can be arranged for $85 a day.

White Lotus, 2500 San Marcos Pass, Santa Barbara, CA 93105, 805-964-1944, www.whitelotus.org.

prepare to survive in the wilderness

WILDLANDS ACROSS THE UNITED STATES

Survival is more than just a superficial insurance policy. With the practice of survival, one begins to relax into the earth, to learn its rhythms, to blend in balance and harmony with all things.
—Tom Brown, Jr., owner of Tracker School

98 You won't be put into a tribe, left on a tropical island, or given a series of immunity challenges, but you will learn how to survive in the wild without carrying food, water, or matches. You'll also learn that real "survivors" don't spend a lot of time watching the popular TV show. They're too busy tracking their next meal, finding potable water, and creating a shelter out of sticks and leaves. As Boulder Outdoor Survival School states in its literature, "Stoves, sleeping bags, and tents are nice, but not necessary for a positive wilderness experience."

So why would anyone want to learn to make a hut out of mud or debris when perfectly good tents are available for less than a hundred dollars? Because, by learning to make peace with the natural world, you find out what a strong and resourceful person you really are. As our society gets more dependent on technology and further separated from nature, we lose our ability to really "see" and comprehend natural ecosystems, the species within them, and the relationships they have with all life. Getting all your information about nature from books, the Nature Channel, or, worse yet, the media doesn't nurture the passion that's necessary to preserve it.

Although there are hundreds of survival schools out there ranging from modern disaster training (i.e., how to survive a power outage or even another Hurricane Katrina) to military-style, evasion-and-escape training (usually taught by former Navy SEALs and Army Green Beret types, these are for Rambo wannabes and closely resemble boot camp), the trio below are some of the best schools for mastering wilderness training.

Boulder Outdoor Survival School (BOSS). When the producers wanted a survival consultant for Tom Hanks's tropical island scenes in *Castaway*, they contacted this school, which is headquartered in Boulder, Colorado, and run out of Boulder, Utah. The idea for BOSS, as it's customarily called, was raised in 1968 when Larry Dean Olen, author of the book *Outdoor Survival Skills* was bemoaning the fact that our society had lost its edge. He decided to design a wilderness school that would produce more adaptable and resourceful people. BOSS's seven-day field course, its signature trip since 1968, costs $1,065 and is held May through August. You'll travel in southern Utah's mountains, mesas, and canyon with nothing but a blanket, poncho, compass, knife, and a water bottle or two. The company's motto is "Know more, carry less."

Boulder Outdoor Survival School, P.O. Box 1590, Boulder, CO 80306, 303-444-9779, www.boss-inc.com.

National Outdoor Leadership School (NOLS). NOLS's leave-no-trace philosophy and leadership training have set the standard in outdoor education since 1965.

IF YOU'RE IN A PINCH

You'll carry water in a gourd, make shelters out of mud, and pick up the scent of your evening meal. But if your stomach is growling in the meantime, here are five ideas for hors d'oeuvres:

1. *Queen Anne's lace.* The carrots you buy in the grocery store were originally cultivated from a cousin of this plant. Although you'll want to avoid the leaves, its taproot is basically a carrot.
2. *Indian cucumbers.* This plant can be found in open woods and forests of the eastern United States. Its edible roots taste like cucumbers.
3. *Cattail roots.* Native Americans used to grind the starchy lower stalk and roots into meal. The leaves, besides making great weaving material, can be thrown into salads.
4. *Violets.* The leaves on this plant can be tossed into a salad or cooked as a green and have three times more vitamin C than an orange.
5. *Day lilies.* The leaves can be eaten as a green, the flowers can either be boiled and seasoned as a vegetable or be used to thicken soup, and the roots taste a little like potatoes, only crisper and sweeter.

Its catalog has more than 50 courses, including a 30-day Wind River Wilderness Course where you trek up to 10 miles a day, set up minimum-impact camps, and learn to navigate with GPS. NOLS, before you get any ideas, is not an adventure travel tour—your instructors are not going to cook, carry your gear, or tell you what to do. However, they *will* teach you such wilderness skills as how to catch and cook your own cutthroat trout and how to bake a pizza over campfire. Tuition for these classes, many of them 30-day incarnations, costs roughly $2,500. Classes are held June to September.

National Outdoor Leadership School, 284 Lincoln Street, Lander, WY 82520, 800-710-6657 or 307-332-5300, www.nols.edu.

Tom Brown Jr.'s Tracker School. Since 1978, Tom Brown has been teaching backcountry self-sufficiency to students—including a *Survivor* cast member— at his farm in New Jersey's Pine Barrens. Everyone starts with Brown's seven-day Standard Course, which teaches such skills as foraging for edible violets, making tools from stone, navigating by starlight, and building shelters from mud and debris. "After this class," says Brown, "you'll be able to survive in any condition, track a mouse across a driveway, and no longer be an alien in your own environment." Brown, who first learned these skills from Stalking Wolf, an Apache elder whom he's known since he was seven, incorporates Native American spirituality into every lesson. The school has four full-time instructors and charges $850 for the seven-day course ($950 for courses in California and Florida).

Tom Brown Jr.'s Tracker School, P.O. Box 927, Waretown, NJ 08758, 609-242-0350, www.trackerschool.com.

travel as a nontourist

ARCATA, CALIFORNIA

Instead of being a tourist, viewing everything from the outside in,
I was welcomed into the homes and culture of the country.
—Aaron Aftergood, Servas traveler

99 Most of the listings in this chapter are about physical things—learning to surf or bike or hike. But if you really want to "be well," you have to open your heart and expand your horizons in other areas, as well. Traveling with Servas is for people who know that just because they've stayed in a high-rise hotel on a Mexican beach doesn't mean they understand how Mexicans think, feel, and view the world—but who truly want to understand. It's for travelers who want to go beyond sightseeing and get to know the people on a deeper, more personal level.

Established in 1948 by Bob Luitweiler, who had studied at a Denmark folk school, Servas is an international network of hosts and travelers building peace by providing opportunities for mutually arranged individual visits, typically for two nights, between persons of diverse cultures and backgrounds (U.S. Servas is a branch of the global coordinating body). Luitweiler had witnessed the devastation of the World Wars and knew there had to be a better way to build peace. By providing opportunities for contacts between people of different backgrounds, peaceful bonds could be created one traveler at a time.

On a Servas vacation, you are invited into the homes of locals. At last count, there were some 15,000 Servas hosts located in more than 130 countries on six continents. The United States alone has roughly 1,700 hosts, from a farmer in Iowa who invites travelers to stay and help make honey to an artist in New York who'll let you watch him paint. As a traveler, you'll sleep in their homes (perhaps in the spare guest room or on the living room floor), share their meals, run errands with them, and participate in their normal life.

Hosts are discouraged from altering their lifestyles in any way. Sure, they may have some free time to show you around, to take you to meet their barber or to

DO, RE, MI

Servas, which is formed entirely of unpaid volunteers, inspires a lot of passion in its devotees, many of whom refuse to travel any other way. There's even a Servas song that was written by longtime member Barbara Whitehead, who recently passed away:

Good friends in Servas, these are my kin,
Where the doors open, I'm glad to walk in.
All the world over, we feel the same,
Love is our method and peace is our aim.
Work, study, travel—learn as we go,
So much to help with, and so much to know!
Good friends of Servas, help me to roam,
When you come my way, I'll give you a home!

the school where they volunteer on Wednesdays, but you are there to get the flavor of "real life," not life on a scripted bus tour.

You can join Servas as either a traveler or a host; many members do both. Either way, you'll go through a fairly rigorous interview process. Once you're approved, you'll get a letter of recommendation and a passport to present to potential hosts. For a small refundable deposit, you can get a list of hosts in whatever country you plan to visit.

Servas doesn't make any arrangements. Each traveler contacts potential hosts, and many Servas travelers combine visits with several hosts on a single vacation. New Yorker Herbert Rosenzweig took a ten-month trip around the world with his wife and 11-year-old daughter, staying with Servas hosts in many countries. He's still in contact with many of the new friends he made on his round-the-world vigil for peace.

Travelers pay $85 per year for international travel, or $50 stateside. The overseas program requires a deposit of $25 per set of up to five host lists, while the U.S. travelers get just two lists for $15. If you're interested in being a host, Servas suggests a donation of $40. No money exchanges hands during the visits, but travelers are welcome to bring a bag of groceries when they show up.

HOW TO GET IN TOUCH
U.S. Servas, 1125 16th Street, Suite 201, Arcata, CA 95521, 707-825-1714, www. usservas.org.

revel in a luxury spa at sea

ABOARD THE *QUEEN MARY 2*

There is always a buzz about this ship wherever we go.
—Benjamin Lyons, second officer aboard the *Queen Mary 2*

100 Not since the *Titanic* had there been as much fanfare surrounding the launch of a new ship as when the majestic *Queen Mary 2* made its maiden voyage from Southampton, England, to Fort Lauderdale, Florida, in January 2004. Name a superlative and it was being bandied about: longest, tallest, widest, most expensive. Everyone was talking about the *QM2*'s ornate planetarium, the first at sea; its 8,000-volume library, the largest at sea; and its college, the most prestigious at sea, staffed by personnel from Oxford University. Those are all great reasons to board this larger-than-life ship. But one of the perks you might have missed amid all the hoopla is the *Queen Mary 2*'s posh spa.

Run by Canyon Ranch, the *QM2*'s lush, two-deck spa could easily stand (make that "float") on its own. Measuring in at 20,000 square feet, it has 24 treatment rooms, huge fitness and locker rooms, saunas, aromatic steam rooms, and a breathtaking Aqua Therapy Centre with a waterfall and neck-massage fountains.

A staff of more than 50, trained in the same luxurious pampering as Canyon Ranch's land-based spas, does the massage and treatment honors. You can get everything from a classic Swedish or sports massage to Thai or Ayurvedic massages, as well as Rasul Rituals, a Canyon Ranch signature treatment that involves mud, oils, and steam.

You can also get facials, body scrubs, complete rundowns on your fitness profile, and a personal trainer who will strongly suggest that you don't visit (at least not daily) all ten of the ship's amazing restaurants. Not to worry—the ship's main dining rooms offer a special spa cuisine for those who are watching their figures.

Other ways to watch your figure include taking part in yoga, tai chi, and exercises classes. The *QM2* also has a jogging track, a golf-driving range, a basketball court, 50 exercise machines, and five swimming pools.

QUEEN FOR A DAY OR FOR A LIFETIME

The *Queen Mary 2,* christened by no less than the Queen of England herself, has been described as larger than life. Here's why:

- She has 17 decks and cost an estimated $800 million to build.
- Her public spaces have more than $6 million worth of art.
- She has the world's only floating planetarium. Called "Illuminations," this 500-seat auditorium offers three different shows.
- She has an acting school, staffed by members of London's Royal Academy of Dramatic Arts who also often give live performances.
- She has an exclusive champagne bar with dozens of types of expensive champagnes and a martini bar with more than three dozen different martinis on offer.
- Her boutiques and stores on board rent tuxes and sell such luxury brands as Hermès, Dunhill, Chopard, H. Stern, and Harrod's.
- She has English nannies on board to care for your kids.
- Her Grand Lobby features bas-relief panels of four continents. Included in the North American panel is no less an American icon than Homer Simpson.
- Her library is staffed by two very professional English librarians.
- She has five luxury apartments, each with its own exercise room, balcony, two full marble bathrooms, and personal butler and room service.
- She has a 6,000-square-foot casino with slot machines, blackjack, roulette, craps, and poker.

Cunard Line, which owns and operates the *Queen Mary 2,* has been in the cruise-ship business since 1840, when it began offering the first timetable passenger service across the Atlantic. Over the years, its fleet contained RMS *Carpathia,* the ship that rescued the survivors of the ill-fated *Titanic,* and the *Queen Mary* and the *Queen Elizabeth,* which between them carried more than 1.5 million troops during World War II.

Prices range from $699 for a four-day cruise in a standard room to $185,905 for a round-the-world cruise in a 2,249-square-foot suite with a two-story glass wall overlooking the ocean. Spa appointments are extra and can be scheduled in advance.

HOW TO GET IN TOUCH
Cunard Line, 24303 Town Center Drive, Suite 200, Valencia, CA 91355, 800-728-6273, www.cunard.com.

index

Index | **287**

acknowledgments

Although the author gets the glory, there is not a book written that doesn't have a team of some kind behind it. My team, for this book, was Jim Dick, Tasman Grout, and all my friends who gave me a break for the four months I had to say, "Sorry, I'd love to, but I've got this crazy deadline." Thank you, one and all. Also, I'd like to say thanks to Barbara Noe, who gave me this glorious, impossible, crazy, life-changing assignment in the first place.